LEARNING
ADOBE®
PHOTOSHOP® 6

Lisa A. Bucki

Acknowledgements

As always, working with DDC Publishing on this project has been an immense pleasure. Chris Katsaropoulos initiated the project, and I thank him for seeking my involvement. I appreciate the guidance and attention to detail provided by Jennifer Frew, who works hard to make every DDC product its best. Thanks as well to reviewer Jim Reidel for his great comments and to DDC's production and sales staff members, who add the finishing touches and bring the final package to you.

Lisa A. Bucki

Managing Editor

Jennifer Frew

Technical Editor

James Reidel

Design and Layout

Shu Chen

Elsa Johannesson

Acquisitions Manager

Chris Katsaropoulos

Cover Design

Amy Capuano

DDC Publishing Inc. Printing

10 9 8 7 6 5 4 3 2 1

Contents

Contents

Contents

Introduction

Graphics programs enable you to explore your creativity. That's why it's important for any book that teaches how to use a graphics program to include hands-on exercises for practice. *Learning Adobe® Photoshop® 6* gives you the opportunity to try the new skills you've learned about at the end of each chapter. You'll create your own image files, or use files provided especially for this book.

How This Book Is Organized

This book offers 21 chapters and three appendixes organized into seven parts. Because the Photoshop program offers so many features and there are so many graphic design considerations to learn about, each part focuses on a particular set of skills, as follows:

- **Part I, Starting Out with Photoshop,** acquaints you with the Photoshop workspace and how to work with files in Photoshop.

- **Part II, Making Basic Edits,** launches you into the creative process, teaching you how to use Photoshop's tools, how to change the image view, how to select and manipulate image content, and how to work with tools for positioning image content.

- **Part III, Using Layers, Masks, and Paths,** introduces you to some of the hottest capabilities in Photoshop: dividing content onto layers for easier editing, using masks to create special effects, and using paths to make and store selections.

- **Part IV, Fine-Tuning Your Image,** helps you advance your skills by trying specialized editing tools like the Sponge tool or Burn tool, how to manipulate the image size and resolution, how to use a filter to apply a special effect, and how to print your masterpiece.

- **Part V, Using More Advanced Techniques,** enables you to work with color channels, adjust an image's color when needed, achieve special color effects, extend Photoshop's capabilities by using plug-ins, and save your own special processing techniques as actions.

- **Part VI, Prepping Images for the Web,** shows you how to convert images for Web use, how to control transparency and other image features for better Web page integration, and how to use slices to create a clickable hotspot on a Web image.

- **Part VII, Appendixes,** offers appendixes covering special topics: digital watermarking,

working with Photoshop's preferences, and finding online resources to learn more about Photoshop.

Each chapter stands alone and presents a variety of techniques. Along the way, **Notes**, **Tips**, and **Warnings** highlight information that will help you use Photoshop more effectively and avoid making common beginner mistakes. At the end of each chapter, you'll find a hands-on exercise reviewing the chapter techniques. The book concludes with a **Glossary** of essential terms for graphic design and Photoshop.

Working with Data and Solution Files

As you work through the exercises in this book, you'll be creating, opening, and saving files. You should keep the following instructions in mind:

- Many exercises instruct you to open a file from the CD-ROM that comes with this book.

- When the application exercise includes a file name and a CD icon ☺, you should open the file provided on CD.

- All the exercises instruct you to save the files created or to save the exercise files under a new name. You should verify the name of the hard disk or network folder to which files should be saved.

To Access the Data Files

Copy data files to a hard drive:

1. Open Windows Explorer. (Right-click the **Start** button 🏁 **Start** and click **Explore**.)

2. Be sure that the CD is in your CD-ROM drive. Select the CD-ROM drive letter from the Folders pane of the Explorer window.

3. Click to select the Datafiles folder in the Name pane of the Explorer window.

4. Drag the folder onto the letter of the drive to which you wish to copy the data files (usually **C:**) in the Folders pane of the Explorer window.

OR

Access data files directly from CD:

1. Be sure that the CD is in your CD-ROM drive. Select the CD-ROM drive letter from the Folders pane of the Explorer window.

2. Click to select the Datafiles folder in the Name pane of the Explorer window.

3. Double-click directly on the file to open it or open the file through Photoshop using a File, Open command.

Teacher's Manual

While this book can be used as a self-paced learning book, a comprehensive Teacher's Manual is also available (catalog number Z94TM; price $15). The Teacher's Manual contains the following:

- Chapter objectives
- Related vocabulary
- Points to emphasize
- Solution illustrations

First Chapter

▶▶

1
Touring the Work Area

Photoshop is the leading application for creating, correcting, and enhancing image files. Photoshop's wealth of features serves the technical needs of advanced users, but at its core it offers a relatively simple interface like applications you may have used before. This first chapter leads you through the basics of navigating the Photoshop work area. You'll learn how to:

❋ Start and exit Photoshop

❋ Use the toolbox

❋ Work with a palette or context menu

❋ View and hide screen elements

❋ Find help when you need it

Starting Photoshop

As with other applications, you must start Photoshop to be able to work with its tools and create a new image. Use the following steps to start Photoshop.

1. Click on the **Start** button at the left end of the Windows taskbar. The Start menu will appear.

2. Point to **Programs**. The Programs menu will appear.

    Tip: *After you click on Start, you can point to a menu choice with a right-pointing triangle beside it by moving the mouse pointer over it. Pointing will highlight that menu choice and open a submenu. When you see the name of the program you want to start, click on the program name.*

3. Point to **Adobe**. The Adobe submenu will appear.

4. Point to **Photoshop 6.0**. The Photoshop 6.0 submenu will appear.

5. Click on **Adobe Photoshop 6.0**. The Photoshop 6.0 application window will appear.

    Note: *The first time you start Photoshop after installing it, a dialog box prompts you to configure color settings for Photoshop. You can click on No to skip this step, or click on Yes to display the Color Settings dialog box. You also can choose Color Settings from the Edit menu at any later time to change color settings in Photoshop.*

Taking Charge of the Tools

The work area in Photoshop includes a menu bar like other Windows applications, as well as a few windows that organize the tools you use to do your work. While later chapters will cover the tools in greater detail, familiarize yourself now with menus and tools and how to use them.

Note: *You can't use the various Photoshop tools until you create or open a new file. Chapter 2, "Working with Image Files," explains how to create new files in Photoshop. The illustrations here include a blank file strictly as an example.*

1. Click on **a menu name**. The menu will open.

2. Click on **a command**. The result will differ, depending on the nature of the command on which you clicked:

   • If the command has no trailing element, Photoshop will execute the command immediately.

   • If the command name is followed by an ellipsis (...), a dialog box will appear.

   • If the command name has a triangle beside it, a submenu will appear. You can then click on a command in the submenu.

3. Make choices in the **dialog box** if one appears. Typical dialog box choices include the following:

   • **Drop-down list box**. Click on the down arrow or scroll arrow to open a drop-down list or scroll through a list's choices, then click on the list item you want.

   • **Text box**. Drag over a text box entry to select it, then type a new entry.

   • **Option button**. Click on an option button to choose it and deselect other option buttons in the group.

   • **Check box**. Click on a check box to select (check) or deselect (uncheck) it.

- **Slider**. Drag a slider to choose another setting.

- **Palette**. Click on a button (icon) or palette to select it.

- **Command button**. Click on a command button to choose it.

Tip: *Clicking on a command button with an ellipsis (...) displays a dialog box. Clicking on an OK or Done button closes the dialog box and applies your choices. Clicking on a Cancel button closes the dialog box without applying your choices.*

4a. Click on **Cancel**. The dialog box will close.

OR

4b. Press **Esc**. The dialog box will close.

5. Click on **a toolbox button**. The options bar at the top of Photoshop will change to show available settings for that tool.

6. Review the **options bar choices**. These choices will work just like dialog box options.

7. Click on a **palette tab**. The settings on that tab will appear.

8. Click on the **right arrow button** in the upper-right corner of the palette window. The palette menu will appear.

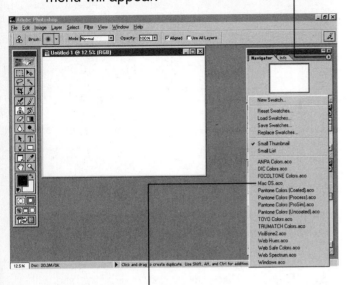

9a. Click on an **item** on the palette. The item will be selected.

OR

9b. Press **Esc**; the palette menu will close.

10. Right-click on **the image**, **a palette**, or **a toolbox tool**. The context menu (shortcut menu) with commands pertaining to the object on which you clicked will appear.

11. Click on a **context menu command**. The results will vary depending on the nature of the command:

- If the command name has a triangle beside it, a submenu will appear. You can then click on a command in the submenu.

- If the command name has an ellipsis (...) beside it, a dialog box will appear; you can then make your choices from the dialog box.

- If the command has no trailing element, Photoshop will execute the command immediately.

Hiding and Showing Screen Elements

The toolbox and the palettes consume quite a bit of the Photoshop work area. When you're not using the toolbox or a particular palette, you can close it using a command on the Window menu. If you choose the same command, Photoshop redisplays or toggles on the specified screen element. Review the applicable commands next.

1. Click on **Window**. The Window menu will appear.

2. Click on **Hide Tools**. Photoshop will hide the toolbox.

3. Click on **Window**. The Window menu will appear.

4. Click on **Show Tools**. Photoshop will redisplay the toolbox.

5. Click on **Window**. The Window menu will appear.

6. Click on **Hide Navigator**. Photoshop will close the Navigator palette, which is the top palette by default.

7. Click on **Window**. The Window menu will appear.

8. Click on **Show Navigator**. Photoshop will redisplay the Navigator palette.

9. Click on **Window**. The Window menu will appear.

10. Click on **Hide Color**. Photoshop will close the Colors palette, which is the middle palette by default.

11. Click on **Window**. The Window menu will appear.

12. Click on **Show Color**. Photoshop will redisplay the Colors palette.

> *Note: Clicking on many of the other commands on the Window menu, such as Show Swatches or Show Paths, selects a particular tab in one of the palettes.*

13. Click on **Window**. The Window menu will appear.

14. Click on **Hide Layers**. Photoshop will close the Layers palette, which is the bottom palette by default.

15. Click on **Window**. The Window menu will appear.

16. Click on **Show Layers**. Photoshop will redisplay the Layers palette.

Reviewing Help Features

When you get stuck while working in Photoshop, you can consult the product's Help system. Not only does Photoshop offer help that you can browse or search, but it also offers Internet help and news that you can consult to stay up-to-date with the latest Photoshop developments. Adobe, the publisher of Photoshop, offers extensive help and resources for Photoshop users.

Using Help Contents and Search Features

Photoshop offers a huge number of features, and using them in combination can be a little tricky. If you get stuck at any point, you can consult Help in Photoshop to learn more about the feature that's of concern. The following steps explain how to browse and search in Help.

1. Click on **Help**. The Help menu will open.

2. Click on **Contents**. The Photoshop Help system will open in the Web browser installed on your system (typically Internet Explorer).

3. Click on **a topic link** at the left side of the window. The Help topic will appear at the right side of the window, along with links to subtopics.

4a. Click and drag the scroll button down. The window contents will scroll down, so you can see additional subtopics.

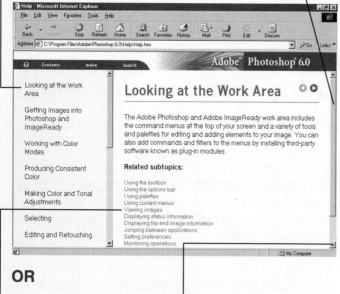

OR

4b. Click on **a scroll arrow**. The window contents will scroll down, so you can read more or see additional subtopics.

5. Click on a **subtopic** link. The subtopic information will appear at the right side of the window, so that you can read it.

6. Review **the help**. You will be able to continue to navigate in Help if the information doesn't solve any issue you're having.

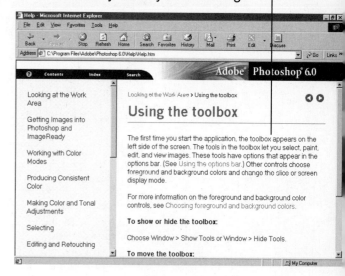

7. Click on **the Index link** at the top of the page. The index letters will appear in the pane at the left side of the screen.

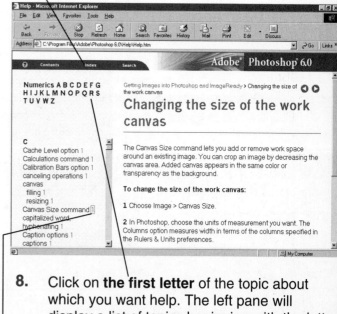

8. Click on **the first letter** of the topic about which you want help. The left pane will display a list of topics beginning with the letter you specified.

9. Click on a **topic number**. The topic information will appear at the right side of the window, so that you can read it.

10. Click on **the Search link** at the top of the page. The Find pages containing text box will appear at the left side of the screen.

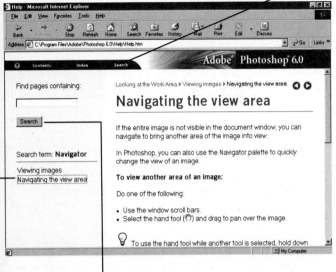

11. Type the **desired search term** in the Find pages containing text box, then click on **Search**. The left pane will display a list of help topics including the term you specified.

12. Click on a **topic**. The topic information will appear at the right side of the browser window.

13. Click on **a topic link** at the top of the page. The topic information for that earlier topic appears.

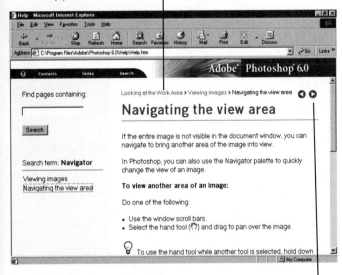

14. Click on the **back (<) button** or **forward (>) button**. The Help system navigates to another previously viewed topic.

15. Click on **File** in the Web browser. The File menu will appear.

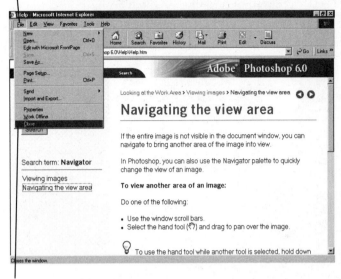

16. Click on **Close**. The Help system (and your system's Web browser) will close.

Reviewing Adobe Online

1. Click on **Help**. The Help menu will appear.

2. Click on **Adobe Online**. The Adobe Online dialog box will open.

   Tip: *Instead of Steps 1 and 2, you can click the Go To Adobe Online button at the top of the toolbox.*

3. Click on **Refresh**. If your system needs to connect to the Internet, the Dial-Up Connection dialog box will appear.

Note: *If you have an "always on" Internet connection or you have set up your system to dial automatically, skip Step 4.*

4. Click on **Connect**. Your system will dial up and log on to the Internet. Information will automatically download to your computer and associated topic links will appear in the Adobe Online dialog box.

5. Click on **OK** if the Adobe Online Status dialog box opens. The download will continue, and any needed components will be downloaded to your system.

6. Click on **a link** at the top or center of the dialog box. Photoshop will launch your system's Web browser and display the associated Web page.

7. Click on **a link** on the Web page to browse for more information. Adobe's Web site will display the proper page. You can continue browsing online to topics of interest.

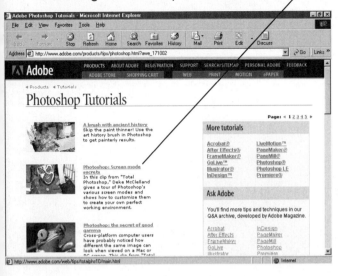

8. Click on **File** in the Web browser. The File menu will open.

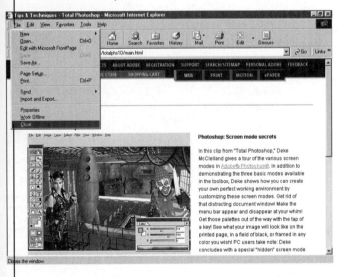

9. Click on **Close**. The Web browser window will close.

Note: *If you have an "always on" Internet connection or you have set up your system to disconnect automatically skip Step 10.*

10. Click on **Disconnect Now** in the Auto Disconnect dialog box. Your system will hang up its Internet connection.

11. Click on **Close** in the Adobe Online dialog box. The Adobe Online dialog box will close.

Note: *If the Auto Disconnect dialog box doesn't prompt you to hang up your Internet connection, you can right-click on the connection icon in the system tray area at the far right end of the Windows taskbar, then click on Disconnect.*

Exiting Photoshop

When you finish working in Photoshop or want to shut down your system altogether, you need to exit the Photoshop program. It takes just a few brief steps, as detailed here.

1. Save the currently opened file. Photoshop will preserve the latest changes to the file. The section called "Saving a File" in Chapter 2 will explain how to save a file.

2. Click on **File**. The File menu will open.

3. Click on **Exit**. The Photoshop application window will close.

Procedures

Start Photoshop

1. Click on the **Start** button 🏁Start on the Windows taskbar .... 🏢

2. Click **Programs** .... P

3. Click **Adobe**.

4. Click **Photoshop 6.0**.

5. Click **Adobe Photoshop 6.0**
    🖼 Adobe Photoshop 6.0 .

Create New File

1. Click **File**... Alt + F

2. Click **New** .... N

3. In the **Name** box type a file name....... Alt + N

4. Click **Width**... Alt + W

5. Enter the image width and select pixels, inches, cm, points, picas or columns from the drop-down list.

6. Click **Height** .... Alt + H

7. Enter the image height and select pixels, inches, cm, points, picas or columns from the drop-down list.

8. Click **Resolution**.............................. Alt + R
    and select pixels/inch or pixels/centimeter from the drop-down list.

9. Click **Mode** .... Alt + M

10. Select Bitmap, Grayscale, RGB Color, CMYK Color, or Lab Color from the drop-down list.

11. Choose the Contents option:
    - **White** .... Alt + I
    - **Background Color**...................... Alt + B
    - **Transparent** .... Alt + T

12. Click **OK** .... Enter

Hide Tools

1. Click **W**indow .... Alt + W

2. Click **Hide T**o**ols** .... O

Show Tools

1. Click **W**indow .... Alt + W

2. Click **Show T**o**ols** .... O

Select Tool

If tool is visible:

1. Click **tool button** ....*Press tool group letter*

    ✓   *For example, to choose the Paintbrush*
        tool, click the Paintbrush tool button 🖌
        or press B.

2. Create desired effect with mouse.

    ✓   *Procedures for individual tools are*
        described separately.

If tool is not visible:

1. Right-click the desired
    tool group ....*Press tool group letter*

2. Click **tool button** from tool group menu.

3. Create desired effect with mouse.

Reset Tool Default Settings

✓   *Use this procedure to reset tool default settings.*

1. Click on the **tool icon** in the tool options bar.

2. Click **Reset Tool** to restore defaults for that
    tool.

    OR

    Click **Reset All Tools** to restore default
    setting for all tools.

Add a Fill

1. Click **E**dit .... Alt + E

2. Click **Fi**l**l** L

3. Click the **Use** drop-down list and select a
    fill type.

    ✓   *If you select **Pattern** and want to choose*
        another pattern, click the Custom Pattern
        palette arrow and select a pattern. For
        further pattern options, click the Custom
        Pattern menu arrow ⊙ *and click*
        Pattern.pat or Patterns2.pat.

4. Click **Mode** and select a blending mode
    option.

5. Click **Opacity** .... Alt + O

6. Enter an opacity percentage.

7. Click **OK** .... Enter

Use Paintbrush Tool

1. Click the **Paintbrush Tool** button 🖌 .... B

2. Select the desired options from the
    Paintbrush Tool options bar:

    a. Click **Brush** and select a brush size
        and style.
        ✓   *Click the drop-down arrow again to*
            deselect the option.
        ✓   *For further brush options, click the*
            Brush menu arrow ⊙ *and click the*
            desired option.

    b. Click the **Mode** arrow and select the
        desired mode.

    c. Click in **Opacity** and enter the desired
        opacity percentage.

        OR

        Click the **Opacity** arrow and drag the
        slider to the desired opacity percentage.

    d. Click the **Wet Edges** checkbox, if
        available, to select or deselect the wet
        edges.

3. Drag in the image to paint desired effect.

Use Pencil Tool

1. Click the **Pencil Tool** button 🖉 .... B

2. Select the desired options from the Pencil Tool options bar:
    a. Click **Brush** and select a brush size and style.
        ✓ *For further brush options, click the Brush menu arrow ▶ and click the desired option.*
    b. Click the **Mode** arrow and select the desired mode.
    c. Click in **Opacity** and enter the desired opacity percentage.

        OR

        Click the **Opacity** arrow and drag the slider to the desired opacity percentage.

    d. Click the **Auto Erase** checkbox to select or deselect auto erase.

3. Drag in the image to draw desired effect.

Use Help (F1)

1. Click **Help** .... Alt + H

2. Click **Contents** .... C / F1
    a. Click the **Contents** link in Help page navigation bar.
    b. Click the desired topic in the contents pane on left.
        ✓ *The desired topic appears in the right pane.*

    OR

    a. Click the **Index** link in the Help page navigation bar.
    b. Click the desired alphabet letter.
    c. Scroll to desired topic in the index pane and click the page number link.
        ✓ *The desired topic appears in the right pane.*

    OR

    a. Click the **Search** link in the Help page navigation bar.
    b. Type a keyword(s) in the **Search** box.
    c. Click the **Search** button Search .
    d. Click the desired topic in the Search term pane.
        ✓ *The desired topic appears in the right pane.*

Close Help

•   Click the **Close** button X .

OR

1. Click **File** .... Alt + F

2. Click **Close** C

Exit Photoshop

•   Click the **Close** button X in the Photoshop window.

OR

1. Click **File** .... Alt + F

2. Click **Close** C
    ✓ *Click Yes to save the document or No to discard the document.*

Exercise 1

If you've never used Photoshop or a graphics program like it before, this exercise will give you practice from square one—starting the program. From there, this exercise reviews key features of the Photoshop program, including how to use a menu, toolbox, or palette; how to control which screen elements appear; how to get help about a feature; and how to exit the Photoshop program.

Directions

1. Start Photoshop 6.

2. Choose File|New, choose RGB Color from the mode drop-down list if needed, click on the White option button in the Contents area if needed, then click on OK to open a new image file using the current size settings.

   ✓ *You'll learn more about creating a new file in Chapter 2. We've just created a file now because few Photoshop commands and tools are available when there's no file open.*

3. Choose Edit|Fill. (That is, click on the Edit menu, then click on the Fill command.) The Fill dialog box will appear.

4. Open the Use drop-down list, then click on Pattern.

5. Open the Custom Pattern drop-down list, click on a pattern to use to fill the image, then click on the drop-down arrow again to close the list or palette.

   ✓ *If you don't see any fill patterns, click on the small button with the left arrow on the Custom Pattern drop-down list or palette, click on Load Patterns, then double-click either Patterns or Patterns 2 in the Load dialog box that appears.*

6. Click on OK to close the Fill dialog box and apply the fill.

7. Click on the Swatches tab in the Colors palette. The Swatches tab will become active.

   ✓ *If the Colors palette is not shown, click Window|Show Swatches.*

8. Click on a color in the palette. Choose a color that contrasts with the background fill you selected.

9. Click on the right-arrow button in the upper-right corner of the Navigator palette. The palette menu appears.

10. Press Esc to close the palette menu.

11. Click on the Paintbrush tool on the toolbox.

12. Right-click on the Paintbrush tool on the toolbox, then click on Pencil tool.

    ✓ *If you're not sure of a tool's name, rest your cursor on the tool and the tool's name should display.*

    ✓ *When a toolbox button has a small right-arrow in its lower-right corner, you can right-click on the tool to see additional tool choices.*

13. Right-click on the picture itself. A context menu of choices applying to the selected tool will appear.

14. Click on Normal or press Esc to close the context menu.

15. Drag with the mouse to make some diagonal lines on the image.

16. Choose Window|Hide Tools. The toolbox will disappear.

17. Choose Window|Show Tools. The toolbox will reappear.

18. Click on the Rectangular Marquee tool in the toolbox.

19. Choose Help|Contents. The initial Adobe Photoshop Help page will launch in the Web browser installed on your system.

20. Click on the Selecting link in the pane at the left.

21. Click on the Saving and Loading Selections link in the pane at the right.

22. Scroll down and read the help information.

23. Click on the Back (<) button near the upper-right corner of the right pane to back up to the list of topics.

24. Choose File|Close from the Web browser menu to close Photoshop Help.

25. Choose File|Exit in Photoshop.

26. Click on No in the message box that asks whether you want to save changes to the file you created. Photoshop will close and discard the file.

Next
Chapter

▶▶

2

Working with Image Files

When you use Photoshop to create and work with images, you store those images digitally rather than storing them as film negatives or hard copies. So, you need to learn the ins and outs of managing your Photoshop files, as well as how to transfer image files from a device into Photoshop. In this chapter, you'll learn how to do the following:

* Create a new image file

* Open a file

* Import a scanner or digital camera image

* Add file info

* Save and close a file

Creating a New File

In some cases, you may want to start the creative process with a blank canvas—a new, blank image file. Photoshop doesn't open a blank file by default when you start the program, so you must do it manually. When you create a new file in Photoshop, you can specify the file size, whether it includes a background color, and more.

1. Click on **File**. The File menu will appear.

2. Click on **New**. The New dialog box will open.

3. Type a name for your file in the Name text box.

4. Set the image settings in the Image Size box, as follows:

   - Double-click on the Width text box contents and type a new image width value. If needed, click on the down arrow for the unit list, then click on another measurement unit.

   - Double-click on the **Height** text box contents and type a new image height value. If needed, click on the down arrow for the unit list, then click on another measurement unit.

   - Double-click on the **Resolution** text box contents and type a new resolution setting value. If needed, click on the down arrow for the unit list, then click on another resolution unit.

   - Click on the down arrow for the Mode list, then click on the color mode to use.

5. Click on a Contents box option. The options work as follows:

   - **White**. Fills the image with a default white background.

   - **Background Color**. Fills the image with the background color currently selected in the Photoshop toolbox.

   - **Transparent.** Gives the image a transparent background, so that when you use the image in a document or Web page, the page background and page elements can show through the background areas of the image file.

6. Click on **OK**. The New dialog box will close, and the new image file will open onscreen.

Opening an Existing File

If you've already saved an image file, you can reopen it at any time to make changes and improvements.

1. Click on **File**. The File menu will appear.

2. Click on **Open**. The Open dialog box will open.

   Tip: *To open a file you've recently used, click on the File menu, drag the mouse pointer down to the Open Recent command, then click on the name of the file to open in the submenu that appears.*

3. Navigate to the file location. The desired file will be displayed in the file list. You may need to do one or more of the following steps to locate the file:

   - Click on the down arrow to the right of the **Look In** list, then click on the **icon** for the disk that holds the file.

- Double-click on folder icons in the list to navigate to the folder that holds the file to open.

- Click on **Up One Level** to return to a folder that's one level higher.

4. Click on the file that you want to open. A preview of the file will appear at the bottom of the Open dialog box.

   Note: *If a scroll bar appears below the list of files, click on the scroll arrow at either end of the scroll bar to scroll the list of files.*

5. Click on **Open**. The file will appear onscreen.

Using File Formats in Photoshop

Photoshop supports more than a dozen different file formats by default, so chances are you can open an image created in another program by selecting the appropriate file type from the Files of type drop-down list in the Open dialog box. Here are some of the common file formats you might use:

- **.BMP**, the Windows Bitmap format created by the Windows Paint applet.

- **.GIF**, a compact file format often used for Web graphics.

- Various forms of **.PDF** files, the Adobe Acrobat file transfer format.

- **.JPG** or **JPEG**, another file format often used for Web graphics.

- **.PCX**, an alternate to the Windows Bitmap format that was originally popularized via the PC Paintbrush program.

- **Photo CD**, a format originally developed by Kodak.

- **PICT**, a Macintosh graphics format.

- **.TIF** or **TIFF**, a common format for scanned images.

   Note: *Photoshop offers the Open As command that you can use to open and convert a file from an obscure format, such as that used by an equation editor program, to a format that Photoshop can read. After you click on File and then click on Open As, use the Look In list in the Open As dialog box to navigate to the folder holding the file to open. Select the Raw (*.RAW) file type from the Open As drop-down list, click on the file to open, then click on Open. A dialog box will prompt you to specify conversion options.*

Importing an Image

You may want to use Photoshop to improve images you generate from another source, such as a scanner or digital camera. Assuming you've installed the Windows software driver that came with the scanner or camera, Photoshop should be able to recognize the device and import images directly from it.

Grabbing a Scanner Image

Impressive scanners costing $300 or less have become widely available. You can use Photoshop to scan hard copy photos and other graphics for modifications and editing. When you're ready to scan an image, turn on the scanner and position the image on the scanner bed before continuing with the following steps. If you're not sure how to position it correctly, consult the scanner's user manual.

Note: *Be aware that copyright law generally prohibits you from using images created or photographed by others for your own commercial purposes. When in doubt, play it safe and do not use information from another source. If you need to use an image from another source for commercial purpose, you can attempt to get permission to do so in writing.*

1. Click on **File**. The File menu will appear.

2. Drag the mouse pointer down to the **Import** command. (That is, point to the command.) A submenu will appear.

3. Click on the **name of your scanner** in the submenu. The scanner software (usually TWAIN software) for your scanner will load.

Note: *From step 4 on, the steps that you use and the information that you see onscreen will differ depending on what software came with your scanner.*

4. Click on the **Preview** button or its equivalent. A preview of the image appears so you can make adjustments.

5. Size the scan area. This may involve dragging a border to define the scan area or entering width and height settings.

6. Adjust other settings. Make other scan setting changes as needed, such as choosing another scan resolution or color setting.

7. Click on **Scan** or its equivalent. Your system will scan the image and place it in Photoshop. Note that the scanning process may take a few minutes, depending on the size of the image and the speed of your system.

8. Click on **Close** or its equivalent to close the scanner software if it doesn't close on its own.

Grabbing a Digital Camera Image

Digital cameras skip the film and hard copy stage, storing images digitally directly within the camera. To work with the images, you need to install the camera software under windows, connect the camera to your system via the applicable cable, and place the camera in its playback mode. From there, you use the following procedure to copy images from the camera into Photoshop.

1. Click on **File**. The File menu will appear.

2. Drag the mouse pointer down to the **Import** command. A submenu will appear.

3. Click on the **name of your digital camera** in the submenu. The software (usually TWAIN software) for your camera will load.

Note: *From Step 4 on, the steps that you use and the information that you see onscreen will differ depending on what software came with your camera.*

4. Click on the **Folder** tab or its equivalent. The tab will appear.

5. Click on **Open Folder** or its equivalent. A dialog box will open enabling you to navigate through the files and folders stored on the camera and then select a folder to open.

6. Navigate to the file location. The desired file will be displayed in the file list. (See "Opening an Existing File" earlier in this chapter for help with the Open dialog box.)

7. Click on **Open**. Your system will display a preview of the images from the selected folder.

8a. Click on the thumbnail for the image to open.

Adding File Info

You can save special information with an image file to give it a caption, describe its origin, identify who created or shot it, and so on. The information follows professional image identification standards, but even home users may find this information useful in building a digital "photo album." Use the following process to store file info for the current file.

1. Click on **File**. The File menu will appear.

OR

8b. Click on **Select All** to select all the images.

9. Click on **Get Picture**. The selected images(s) will be copied from the camera's storage and opened in Photoshop as a new image file.

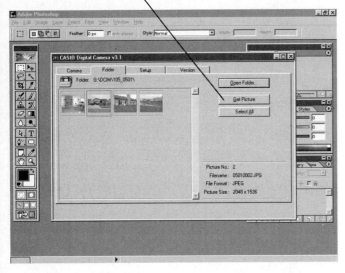

2. Click on **File Info**. The File Info dialog box will open.

3. Type entries as desired in the text boxes on the tab. Of course, you don't have to use all the entries. You can use only those that are relevant to you.

4. Click on the down arrow to the right of the **Section** list, then click on the next category to complete.

Note: If the camera software doesn't close automatically, click on the Taskbar button for the software, then click on the software window's Close button or the equivalent to close the software.

5. Repeat steps 3 and 4 to enter information for other categories of File Info.

   Note: *In some cases, you must enter text box information and click on the Add button to add the entry. Or, you can click on a button like the Today button to make the entry automatically.*

6. Click on **OK**. The File Info dialog box closes, adding the information to the file.

Saving a File

If you've just created an image file or have just imported it into Photoshop from a scanner or digital camera, you need to save the image file to name it and store it to the location of your choice on your system's hard disk. The following steps lead you through the process for saving the current file.

1. Click on **File**. The File menu will appear.

2. Click on **Save**. The Save As dialog box will open.

3. Navigate to the file location where you wish to save the file.

4. Double-click on the **File name** text box entry, then type a new name for the file.

   Tip: *To save a copy of the current file rather than the original, click on the As a Copy check box to place a check in it.*

5. Click on **Save**. The Save As dialog box will close. Photoshop saves the file and leaves it open onscreen for further work.

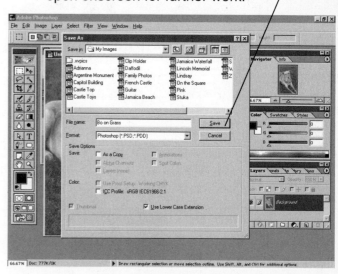

Note: *If you make changes to the file, be sure to click on File and then click on Save or press Ctrl+S to save your changes. The Save As dialog box will not appear for subsequent saves unless you click Save As rather then Save on the File menu.*

Saving to Another Format

By default, Photoshop saves new images in its Photoshop (.psd or .pdd) format. You may need to save an image in another format. For example, you may want to save the file in the Windows bitmap (.bmp) or Paint (.pcx) format to use the file in a word processor document. Photoshop enables you to save images in more than a dozen formats. Apply the following process to save the current file to another format.

1. Click on **File**. The File menu will appear.

2. Click on **Save As**. The Save As dialog box will open.

3. Navigate to the file location where you wish to save the file.

4. Double-click on the **File name** text box entry. The name will be selected.

5. Type an alternate name, if needed, for the converted file. The new name will be displayed.

6. Click on the down arrow to the right of the Format list, then click on the desired format for the converted file in the list.

7. Click on **Save**. The Save As dialog box will close.

8. Set needed options if an Options dialog box appears. An Options dialog box appears only for certain types of conversions, and the options vary depending on the conversion format.

9. Click on **OK**. Photoshop converts and saves the file, closing the original file. The converted file remains open in Photoshop for further work.

Switch Between Files

Photoshop enables you to have multiple image files open, in case you need to compare images or copy information between them. However, you can only work in one image file at a time, called the current image or active image. The following steps detail two methods you can use to select a file and make it the current or active file.

1. Click on **Window**. The Window menu will appear.

2. Click on the file name for the file to open. The file window moves to the top of other open files and becomes the active image, so you can work with the file.

3. Click on the image. It will become the active image. You can only use this method when part of the desired image's window is visible.

Closing a File

While you can have multiple images open, image files tend to consume a lot of system memory, so your system will perform better if you close images that you are not currently using. Again, the following steps identify two methods you can use to close the current image file.

1. Click on **File**. The File menu will appear.

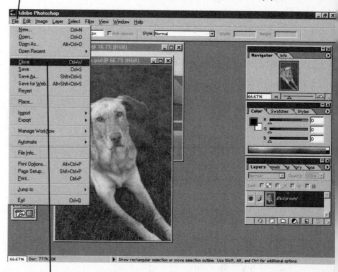

2. Click on **Close**. In some cases, a message window will open.

    Note: *If you added a new text layer, a dialog box may first prompt you to commit (finish) the layer. Click on Commit to do so.*

3. Click on **Yes** if you see the message window prompting you to save the file. Photoshop will finish saving it and the file will close.

4. Alternatively, click on **Close** for the window of the image file to close. If prompted, save your changes. Photoshop closes the image window.

Procedures

Create New File (Ctrl+N)

1. Click **File** .... `Alt`+`F`

2. Click **New** .... `N`

3. In the **Name** box type a file name .... `Alt`+`N`

4. Click **Width** .... `Alt`+`W`

5. Enter the image width and select pixels, inches, cm, points, picas, or columns from the drop-down list.

6. Click **Height** .... `Alt`+`H`

7. Enter the image height and select pixels, inches, cm, points or picas from the drop-down list.

8. Click **Resolution** .... `Alt`+`R`

9. Select pixels/inch or pixels/cm from the drop-down list.

10. Click **Mode** .... `Alt`+`M`

11. Select Bitmap, Grayscale, RGB Color, CMYK Color, or Lab Color from the drop-down list.

12. Choose the contents option:
    - **White** .... `Alt`+`I`
    - **Background Color** .... `Alt`+`B`
    - **Transparent** .... `Alt`+`T`

13. Click **OK** .... `Enter`

Open File (Ctrl+O)

1. Click **File** .... `Alt`+`F`

2. Click **Open** .... `O`

3. Select the desired folder in the **Look in** box .... `Alt`+`I`

4. Select the desired file type in the **Files of type** drop-down list .... `Alt`+`T`

5. Click the desired image file in the Open dialog box window.

6. Click **Open** .... `Enter`

Import an Image

✓ *The steps that you use and the information that you see onscreen will differ depending on what software came with your scanner.*

1. Click **File** .... `Alt`+`F`

2. Click **Import** .... `M`

3. Click on the name of your **scanner/digital camera.**

4. Click on the **Preview** button or its equivalent.

5. Size the scan area.

6. Adjust other settings.

7. Click on **Scan** or its equivalent.

Enter File Information

1. Click **File** .... `Alt`+`F`

2. Click **File Info** .... `I`

3. Select the **Section** drop-down list ...... `Alt`+`T`

4. Choose the desired section:
    - **Caption** .... `Ctrl`+`1`
    - **Keywords** .... `Ctrl`+`2`
    - **Categories** .... `Ctrl`+`3`
    - **Credits** .... `Ctrl`+`4`
    - **Origin** .... `Ctrl`+`5`
    - **Copyright & URL** .... `Ctrl`+`6`

    OR

    a. Scroll to desired section using the **Next** button .... `Alt`+`N`

    b. To scroll back, use the **Prev** button .... `Alt`+`P`

5. Enter the desired information.

6. Repeat steps 4–5 as needed.

7. Click **OK** .... `Enter`

Save a File (Ctrl+S)

1. Click **File**................................. `Alt`+`F`

2. Click **Save** .... `S`

   ✓ *If saving for the first time, Photoshop launches the Save As dialog box. See steps 3–7 of Save a File to Another Format.*

Save a File to Another Format (Shift+Ctrl+S)

1. Click **File**................................. `Alt`+`F`

2. Click **Save As**............................. `A`

3. Select the desired folder in the **Save in** drop-down list.................... `Alt`+`I`

4. Enter a file name in the **File name** box .... `Alt`+`N`

5. Select the file format in the **Format** drop-down list..................... `Alt`+`F`

6. In Save Options, select any applicable save options.

7. Click **Save** .... `Enter`

Switch Between Opened Files

• Click anywhere in the desired file window.

   ✓ *If the desired file is not in view, drag the overlying file's title bar to reveal the desired file.*

OR

1. Click **Window**........................... `Alt`+`W`

2. Click the desired file .... `1`, `2`, etc.

Close a File (Ctrl+W)

• Click the **Close** button `X` in the file window.

OR

1. Click **File** .... `Alt`+`F`

2. Click **Close**.............................. `C`

   ✓ *You may be prompted to save the file.*

Exercise 2

Each graphic image you create or use is stored in its own file, just like a word processor document or spreadsheet file. In Photoshop, you can create or open multiple image files so that you can compare files, copy part of one file for use in another, and so on. This exercise gives you additional experience with creating and using files. Next, work with choices for creating a new file; open an existing file; store descriptive information with a file; save and name a file; switch between files; save a file in a new graphic format; and close files.

Directions

1. Start Photoshop, if needed.

2. Choose File|New to display the new dialog box.

3. Specify the following image settings:
   Name   Exercise 2
   Width   4 inches
   Height   6 inches
   Resolution   150 pixels/inch
   Contents   Transparent

4. Click on OK to open the new image file using the settings you specified. The file opens in its own file window in Photoshop.

5. Use the File|Open command to open the ⊙**PS02** Photoshop file.

   ✓ *Your instructor can tell you where he or she has placed the exercise files for this book so that you can navigate to the proper disk or folder location to open the file.*

   ✓ *To open a file you've worked with recently, you also can choose File|Open Recent, and then click on the file name.*

   ✓ *In many cases, you can click on a file in the list of files in the Open dialog box to see a preview thumbnail of the image in the bottom of the dialog box.*

6. Switch to the **Exercise 2** file by clicking on its file window.

7. Switch back to the **PS02** file using the Window menu.

8. Choose File|File Info.

9. Go to the Credits section. Enter your name in the Byline text box and **Learning Photoshop 6** in the Source text box.

10. Click on OK.

    ✓ *You have to save the file to preserve the file info. If you don't need to change the file name or type, you can simply choose File|Save or press Ctrl+S.*

11. Choose File|Save As.

12. Enter **Bo** as the File Name.

13. Choose JPEG (*.JPG,*.JPE) from the Format drop-down list.

    ✓ *Consult your instructor to learn if you should save the exercise file to a particular disk or folder, and navigate to that location before clicking on Save.*

14. Click on Save.

15. Click on OK in the JPEG Options dialog box to finish the conversion.

16. Use File|Close to close the **Bo** file.

17. Click on the file window Close (X) button to close the Exercise 2 file.

    ✓ *Because you never saved the Exercise 2 file, it will not be saved on disk. Note that Photoshop did not prompt you to save the file, because you did not make any changes to it. If you had made any changes, such as adding file info, Photoshop would have reminded you to save the file before it closed.*

18. Exit Photoshop.

Part I Review Questions

1. How do you open the Photoshop program? *See "Starting Photoshop" in Chapter 1.*

2. What's the difference between a toolbox and a palette, and how do you use them? *See "Taking Charge of the Tools" in Chapter 1.*

3. Which menu holds the commands for hiding and showing the toolbox and other elements? *See "Hiding and Showing Screen Elements" in Chapter 1.*

4. What kinds of help can you get in Photoshop? *See "Reviewing Help Features" in Chapter 1.*

5. What should you do before you exit Photoshop? *See "Exiting Photoshop" in Chapter 1.*

6. How do you create a new file? *See "Creating a New File" in Chapter 2.*

7. How do you save a file? *See "Saving a File" in Chapter 2.*

8. How do get an image into Photoshop from your scanner or digital camera? *See "Importing an Image" in Chapter 2.*

9. What is File Info for and how do you add it? *See "Adding File Info" in Chapter 2.*

10. How do you convert a file to another format? *See "Saving to Another Format" in Chapter 2.*

chapter

3

Adding Content with Tools

Several of the tools in the Photoshop toolbox enable you to add content to a blank image or an image you've created or opened from another source. Painting and drawing with your computer may take some practice, but like any other skill, the results are worth the effort. In this chapter, learn how to:

❋ Choose the tool you need

❋ Set tool options and choose the colors to use

❋ Paint with the painting tools

❋ Draw with the drawing tools

❋ Add text

❋ Create a note on an image

Selecting a Tool

Photoshop uses the toolbox to organize your tools by type. Because Photoshop offers such a wealth of editing tools, the toolbox looks a bit crowded. What's more, further investigating will reveal even more tools than you initially see in the toolbox. It's great to have so many options, but it may take more than one step to find the tool you want.

You can access some Photoshop tools with one click. Others you may need to select from a tool "group" shortcut menu.

Note: *A small arrow in the lower-right corner of a toolbox button indicates that additional tools of this type are available.*

1.   Click on a tool button in the Photoshop toolbox (after you open a new or existing file, of course). The tool will become active, and available settings for the selected tool will appear on the options bar.

Note: *A tool button becomes white while the tool is active or selected, and the tool remains active until you choose another tool.*

2.   Right-click on a tool button. A shortcut menu that lists similar tools will appear.

3.   Click on the desired tool in the shortcut menu. The tool will become active, and the available settings for the selected tool will appear on the options bar. Use the active tool to create or edit your picture with that tool's effect.

Tip: *After you select a tool, the right side of the status bar displays a brief description of how to use the tool. Later chapters cover the various tools as needed, because there are so many toolbox tools and they are diverse in function.*

Setting a Tool's Options in the Options Bar

The options bar below the menu bar displays settings for the currently selected tool, such as a brush size and shape and opacity. The available settings vary widely depending on which tool you have selected. Choosing the correct settings before you draw or paint will save you time, because you won't have to go back and make changes. The following steps show an example of how to use the options bar, but keep in mind that it may display very different settings for each tool that you choose.

1. Click on the down arrow for a setting in the options bar. A list or palette will appear with the choices for the selected setting.

2. Drag the lower-right corner of a palette. The rest of the palette choices will become visible.

3. Click on the desired setting in the list palette. That setting will become active for the selected tool.

4. Click on the down arrow again if the list or palette remains open. The list or palette will close.

5. Drag the slider if a setting offers a slider rather than a list or palette. This changes the current setting for the selected tool.

6. Click on the down arrow again. The slider will close.

7. Click on a check box setting. Photoshop will either check (enable) or uncheck (disable) the setting.

Resetting Tool Defaults

When you choose the settings for a tool, they remain active until you change them. So, as you jump between the various tools, you can reset a tool to its default settings and then choose the settings that apply during your current use of the tool. The following steps show how to reset a tool.

1. Click on the tool button at the left end of the options bar. A menu will appear.

2. Click on **Reset Tool**. Photoshop resets the options bar settings to the default for the tool.

Choosing Colors

As when you choose other settings for a tool, you should choose the foreground and background colors to be used by the tool. Generally, Photoshop uses the selected foreground color when you draw lines, and the background color for gradient fills and erased areas. The Foreground Color, Background Color box near the bottom of the toolbox shows the currently selected foreground and background colors. The following steps detail the numerous methods you can use to select a new foreground or background color.

1. Click on the desired foreground color on the color bar in the Colors palette. The foreground box on the toolbox changes to show the new foreground color.

2. Press and hold the **Alt** key, then click on the desired background color on the color bar in the Colors palette. The background box on the toolbox changes to show the new background color.

3. Click on the **Swatches** tab in the Colors palette. The color swatches appear.

4. Click on the desired foreground color on the Swatches tab in the Colors palette. The foreground box on the toolbox changes to show the new foreground color.

5. Press and hold the **Alt** key, then click on the desired background color on the Swatches tab in the Colors palette. The background box on the toolbox changes to show the new background color.

6. Open the Color Picker dialog box:

   • Click on the **Foreground Color** box in the toolbox. The Color Picker dialog box will enable you to choose the foreground color.

   • Click on the **Background Color** box in the toolbox. The Color Picker dialog box will enable you to choose the background color.

   Tip: *Click on the Default Foreground Colors and Background Colors (the small button with the black and white color chips on it below and to the left of the larger color chip buttons on the toolbox) to reset the foreground and background colors to the defaults; black for the foreground and white for the background.*

7. Click on a color in the narrow band of colors near the middle of the dialog box. Photoshop will display a different range of colors in the Select Foreground Color or Select Background Color box.

8. Click on a color in the Select Foreground Color or Select Background Color box. The color you click on will become the active spot color.

9. Click on **OK**. The Color Picker dialog box will close.

10. Open the picture that has a color to use. The picture will become the active picture.

11. Click on the **Eyedropper** tool in the toolbox. The eyedropper tool will become the active tool.

12. Click on the desired foreground color. Press and hold the **Alt** key then click on a color to select the background color instead. The color you clicked on will become the active foreground color or background color. You can use those colors to paint and draw in the current image file or another file.

Working with Painting Tools

Photoshop combines features of both paint programs—which paint to change the color of pixels in the image, so that you cannot later select painted objects—and draw programs—which create objects that can be selected, edited, and rearranged later. The images you create with a paint program work much like drawing or painting on paper; to make a change, you need to erase or replace something, which can be tricky if you accidentally erase or paint over an adjoining area. A draw program works more like a collage, where you can pick up the individual collage pieces to move, resize, or reshape them. The steps in this section focus on using tools that basically color different pixels (color dots) in the picture.

Note: *Photoshop places painted information on the background layer by default. You can separate painted information by placing it on different layers in the file, which enables you to move and work with the painted information independent of other information in the image, see Chapter 8, "Working with Layers," to learn how to place content on different layers in an image.*

Painting with the Paintbrush

The Paintbrush tool enables you to use the mouse to create freehand strokes with any of a number of brush shapes. You can use this tool to create a truly "painted" effect in your image.

1. Click on the **Paintbrush** tool in the toolbox. It will become the active tool.

2. Choose the desired settings in the options bar. Your selections will become the active settings for the tool.

3. Select the foreground color to use using the method of your choice. The color you select will become active for the Paintbrush.

4. Click and drag on the picture in the work area. Keep the mouse button pressed as you drag in any desired direction. When you release the mouse button, the paint stroke will appear.

Tip: If you paint or draw on the image and make a mistake, immediately press Ctrl+Z to undo the mistake.

Drawing with the Pencil

Technically speaking, the Pencil tool functions as a drawing tool in Photoshop, recoloring pixels as you drag along with the tool. The following example illustrates how to use the Pencil tool.

1. Right-click on the **Paintbrush** tool in the toolbox. Its shortcut menu will appear.

2. Click on the **Pencil Tool**. The Pencil tool will become the active tool.

Tip: When the Pencil tool is active, you must right-click on it and then click on the Paintbrush Tool choice to return to using the Paintbrush tool.

3. Choose the desired settings in the options bar. Your selections will become the active settings for the tool.

4. Select the foreground color to use using the method of your choice. The color you select will become active for the Pencil.

5. Click and drag on the picture in the work area. Keep the mouse button pressed as you drag in any desired direction. When you release the mouse button, the finished pencil stroke will appear.

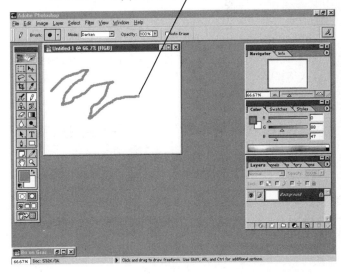

Painting with the Airbrush

The Airbrush tool can help you create a more subtle painted effect. It creates a "sprayed" effect rather than laying down solid color, and you can use it by dragging, clicking, or holding down the mouse button to apply the paint.

1. Click on the **Airbrush** tool in the toolbox. It will become the active tool.

2. Choose the desired settings in the options bar. Your selections will become the active settings for the tool.

3. Select the foreground color to use using the method of your choice. The color you select will become active for the Airbrush.

4. Click and drag on the picture in the work area. Keep the mouse button pressed as you drag in any desired direction. When you release the mouse button, the brush stroke will appear.

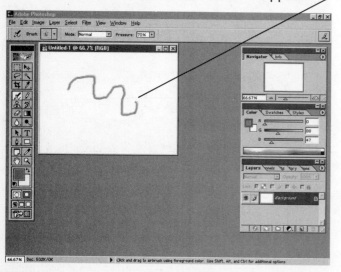

Note: *You also can click on the image while the Airbrush tool is active to "spritz" color onto selected locations. If you hold down the mouse button without moving the mouse, the airbrush tool increases the amount of paint applied, for a "thicker" application.*

Working with Drawing Tools

The drawing tools enable you to create regular shapes in an image such as a rectangle, rounded rectangle, ellipse, polygon, line, or custom shape. When you draw a shape, Photoshop by default places the shape on its own layer in the image, so refer to Chapter 8 if you have a question about working with layers.

Note: *The Pen tool is for creating paths, not drawing lines. Chapter 10, "Using Paths," explains how to work with paths.*

Drawing a Line

As one might expect, you use the Line tool to draw lines. The following steps explain how to use that tool.

1. Right-click on the **Rectangle** tool in the toolbox. Its shortcut menu will appear.

2. Click on the **Line Tool**. The Line tool will become the active tool.

3. Choose the desired settings in the options bar. Your selections will become the active settings for the tool.

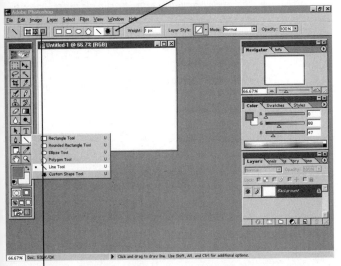

Tip: Click on the Create filled region button in the options bar if you want to place the drawing on the background layer rather than a new layer in your image. Otherwise, leave the Create new shape layer button selected. If you click on the Create new work path button instead, Photoshop will create a path and not a line. Chapter 10, "Using Paths," explains what paths are and how to use them.

4. Select the foreground color to use using the method of your choice. The color you select will become active for the Airbrush.

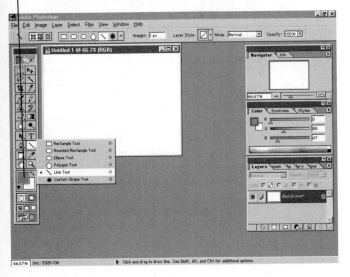

5. Click and drag on the picture in the work area. Keep the mouse button pressed as you drag in any desired direction. When you release the mouse button, the line will appear with an airbrush effect.

6. Click on the **Commit** button (✓) in the options bar. Photoshop will finalize the line.

Drawing a Rectangle, Oval, or Other Shape

As you may have noticed from the preceding set of steps, the shape tools area grouped along with the Line tool on the Photoshop toolbox. The following set of steps demonstrates how to use one of the shape tools. (They all basically work in the same way.)

1. Right-click on the **Rectangle** tool in the toolbox. Its shortcut menu will appear.

2. Click on the desired shape tool to use in the submenu. The selected tool becomes the active tool

3. Choose the desired settings in the options bar. Your selections will become the active settings for the tool.

Note: *If you choose the Custom Shape Tool, be sure to use the Shape drop-down list on the options bar to specify which kind of shape to draw. Again, leave the Create new shape layer button selected unless you want to add the shape to the current layer (whether the background layer or another layer).*

4. Select the desired foreground color using the method of your choice. The color you select will become active for the tool and will become the fill color for the drawn object.

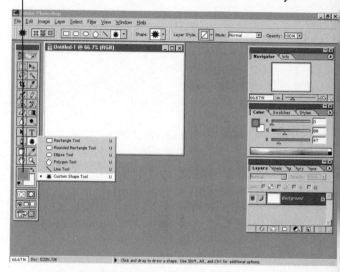

5. Click and drag diagonally on the picture in the work area. Keep the mouse button pressed as you drag in any desired direction. When you release the mouse button, the shape will appear.

6. Click on the **Commit** button (✓) in the options bar. Photoshop will finalize the shape.

Adding Type

You use the Type tool and the options bar to add text into an image. In this case, the options bar gives you a number of choices to customize the text for fun and interesting text treatments in an image.

1. Click on the **Type** tool in the toolbox. It will become the active tool.

2. Select the desired foreground color using the method of your choice. The color you select will become active for the tool and will become the fill color for the text.

3. Drag diagonally on the image in the work area. This defines the area that will hold the text.

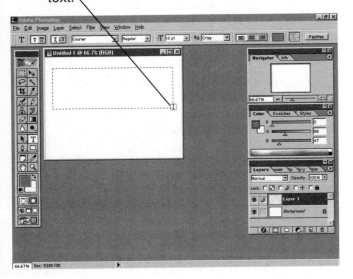

4. Choose the desired settings in the options bar. Your selections will become the active settings for the tool.

5. Type the desired text. Your text will appear in the text box.

6. Click on the **Warp Text** button on the options bar. The Warp Text dialog box will open.

7. Click on the down arrow next to the **Style** list. The available styles for warping (bending) text will appear.

8. Click on the desired warp style. The list will close, and the settings for the selected style will appear.

9. Select the desired options. The text in the image will preview your choices.

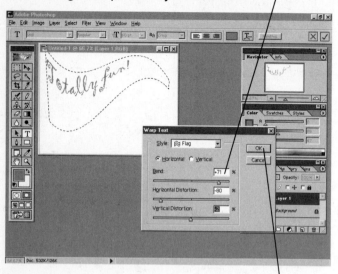

10. Click on **OK**. The Warp Text dialog box will close.

11. Click on the **Commit** button (✓) on the options bar. Photoshop will insert the text on its new layer.

Note: *To edit text, you must choose the text layer (as described in Chapter 8), choose the Text tool, click within or drag over the text on the layer, make your edits, and then click on the Commit button (✓).*

Adding a Note

If you want to add information to an image that others can read without that information printing along with the image, add a note. These steps detail the process for adding and working with notes:

1. Click on the **Notes** tool in the toolbox. It will become the active tool.

2. Click on the image in the location where you want the note to appear. A blank note box will open.

3. Type the note text. It will appear in the box.

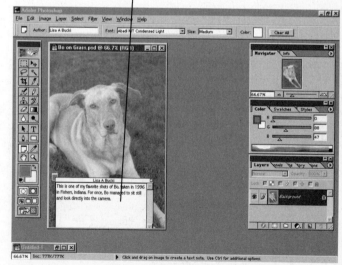

4. Click on the small **Close** box in the upper-left corner of the note. The note box will close and a note icon will appear on the image.

5. Click on the **Close** button in the note box. The note box will close.

6. Click on another tool. The Notes tool will be deselected, so you don't accidentally add another note.

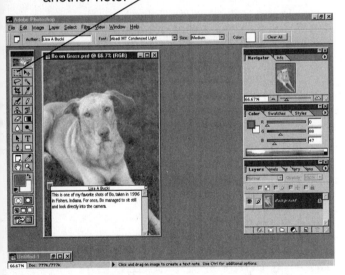

Tip: *Double-click on a note icon to open the note at any time. Click on the small close box in the upper-right corner of the note when you finish reading it. Be sure to then choose a tool other than the Notes tool before continuing. Otherwise, the Notes tool remains active.*

7. Right-click on the **note** icon. Its shortcut menu will appear.

8. Click on the **Delete Note**. A message box will open, prompting you to confirm the deletion.

9. Click on **OK**. Photoshop deletes the note from the image.

43

Procedures

Select a Tool

✓ *See the Procedures for Chapter 1.*

Reset Tool Default Settings

✓ *Use this procedure to reset tool default settings.*

1. Click on the **tool icon** in the tool options bar.

2. Click **Reset Tool** to restore defaults for that tool.

    OR

    Click **Reset All Tools** to restore default setting for all tools.

Choose a Foreground Color

1. Click the **Color** palette tab.

    ✓ *If it is not visible, click Window, Show Color.*

2. Click the **Set foreground color** button .

3. Click the desired color in the color bar.

    ✓ *If the Color Picker dialog box doesn't display, your Photoshop preferences may be set to use Windows as the Color Picker. To change this setting, click Edit, Preferences, General.*

    OR

1. Click the **Swatches** palette tab.

2. Click the desired color.

Choose a Background Color

1. Click the **Color** palette tab.

2. Click the **Set background color** button .

3. Click on the desired color in the color bar.

    OR

    Press **Alt** and click on the desired color.

OR

1. In the color palette, click the **Set background color** button .

2. Click on the **Swatches** palette tab.

3. Click the desired color.

Use the Color Picker

✓ *Use the Color Picker to customize a color choice.*

1. Double-click the desired **Set background color** or **Set foreground color** button in the Color tab or in the toolbox.

    ✓ *In addition to the Set foreground and background color buttons, Color Picker can be launched by double-clicking many other color button, such as the Set text color button.*

2. In the Color Picker dialog box, click on or drag into the desired color.

3. Click in or drag the slider control arrows to adjust the saturation and intensity of the color.

    ✓ *These settings can also be entered manually by selecting the appropriate option (H for Hue, S for Saturation, and so on) and then typing the percentage or number. Colors also have numbers, which can be entered in the # box.*

4. Click **OK** ....**Enter**

Choose Color from Image File

1. Click the desired **Set background color** or **Set foreground color** button in the Color tab or in the toolbox.

2. Click the **Eyedropper Tool** button ......

3. Click on the desired color in the Image to select it.

Use Pencil Tools

1. Click the **Pencil Tool** button .... B

2. Select the desired options from the Pencil Tool options bar:

   a. Click **Brush** and select a brush size and style.

      ✓ *For further pencil options, click the Brush menu arrow ▶ and click the desired option.*

   b. Click in the **Mode** box and select the desired style.

   c. Click the **Opacity** arrow and drag the slider to the desired pressure percentage

   d. Click the **Auto Erase** checkbox to select or deselect Auto Erase.

3. Drag in the image to draw the desired effect.

Use Paintbrush Tool

1. Click the **Paintbrush Tool** button ...... B

2. Select the desired options from the Airbrush Tool options bar:

   a. Click **Brush** and select a brush size and style.

      ✓ *For further brush options, click the Brush menu arrow ▶ and click the desired option.*

   b. Click in the **Pressure** box and enter the desired pressure percentage.

   OR

   Click the **Pressure** arrow and drag the slider to the desired pressure percentage

   c. Click the **Wet Edges** checkbox to select or deselect the wet edges.

3. Drag in the image to paint desired effect.

Draw with Shape Tools

1. Click the desired shape tool in the toolbox .... U

   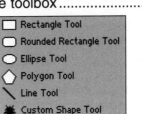

2. Select the desired options from the Shape options bar:

   ✓ *Not all options will be available with all shapes.*

   a. Click the **Create new shape layer** button.

   b. Click the **Geometry options** button ▼ and choose the desired options.

      ✓ *The Geometry options palette contains shape, sizing, and other precision shape defining options.*

   c. Click the **Mode** arrow and select the desired mode.

   d. Click in **Opacity** and enter the desired opacity percentage.

   OR

   Click the **Opacity** arrow and drag the slider to the desired opacity percentage.

   e. Click the **Anti-aliased** checkbox to select or deselect the option.

   f. For rounded rectangles, click in the **Radius** box and type the radius of the corners in pixels.

   g. For polygons, click in the **Sides** box and enter the number of sides.

   h. For lines, click in the **Weight** box and enter the line weight in pixels.

   i. For shapes, click the **Shape** box arrow and choose a shape from the Shape menu.

      ✓ *For further shape options, click the Shape menu arrow ▶ and click the desired option.*

3. Click the mouse a little to the left and above the desired position while holding down the mouse button.

4. Drag diagonally to draw the shape to the desired size and shape.

   ✓ *You can hold down the Shift key to create perfect squares with the Rectangle tool or circles with the Ellipse tool. Perfect circles and squares can also be created by choosing the Square or Circle option in the Geometry options.*

5. Release the mouse button to finalize the shape.

To create different and/or additional shapes from the Shape Options Bar:

1. Click on the desired shape button in the options bar.

2. Repeat steps 2–4.

Add Type

1. Click the **Type Tool** button ....

   ✓ *The mouse pointer becomes a box with an insertion point.*

2. Position the mouse pointer a little above and to the left of where the text should appear

3. Hold down the mouse button and drag diagonally to create the text box to the desired size.

4. Release the mouse button to finalize the text box.

5. Select the desired options from the Text Tool options bar:

   a. Click the **Create a text layer** button to create a text layer.

   b. Click the **Horizontally orient text** button to horizontally orient text.

      OR

      Click the **Vertically orient text** button to vertically orient text.

   c. Click the **Set the font family** drop-down list and select a font.

   d. Click the **Set the font style** drop-down list and select:

      • **Regular**

      • **Italic**

      • **Bold**

      • **Bold Italic**

   e. Click in the **Set the font size** box and type the desired font size.

      OR

      Click the **Set the font-size** box drop-down list arrow and select the desired font size.

   f. Click in **Set the anti-aliasing method** box and select:

      • **None**

      • **Crisp**

      • **Strong**

      • **Smooth**

   g. Select the text alignment:

      • Click the **Left align text** button to align text left.

      • Click the **Center text** button to center text.

      • Click the **Right align text** button to align text right.

   h. Double-click the **Set the text color** button and choose a text color in the Color Picker dialog box.

      ✓ *The default text color is determined by the current foreground color.*

   i. Click the **Create warped text** button and select a desired warped-text effect.

   j. Click the **Show the Paragraph & Character palettes** button to select advanced text design features.

6. Type the desired text in the text box.

7. Click the **Commit any current edits** button .

   ✓ *To cancel text, click the Cancel any current edits button* .

Add Notes

1. Click the **Notes Tool** button. .... N

   ✓ *The mouse pointer becomes a note symbol.*

2. Select any desired options from the Notes options bar:

   a. Click in the **Author** box to change the note writer's name.

   b. Click the **Font** box arrow to select a font from the drop-down list.

   c. Click the **Size** box arrow to select a font size from the drop-down list.

   d. Click the **Color** box to select a note color in the Color Picker dialog box.

   e. Click the **Clear All** button Clear All to delete a note from the Notes options bar.

3. Position the mouse pointer in the image where the note is to appear.

4. Hold down the mouse button and drag diagonally to create the note box to the desired size.

5. Type the note.

6. When finished, click the **Close notes** button.

Open a Note

● Double-click the notes icon in the image.

   OR

● Right-click the note icon and select **Open Note.**

Delete Notes

1. Right-click the note icon and select **Delete Note**.

2. Click **OK** .... Enter

Delete All Notes

● Right-click any note icon and select **Delete All Annotations**.

   OR

1. Click the **Notes Tool** button. .... N

2. Click the **Clear All** button Clear All on the Notes options bar.

Exercise 3

This exercise gives you the opportunity to practice using the toolbox tools in Photoshop 6. You use the tools to add original content into an image file, either to enhance an existing digital picture or to create your own image from the ground up. Next, try using some of the Photoshop tools to piece together a basic logo image.

Directions

1. Start Photoshop 6, if needed.

2. Create a new, blank image file using the current default size and a transparent background. (Chapter 2 covered creating a new file.)

3. Choose the Paintbrush tool from the toolbox.

4. On the options bar, choose the Spatter 28 Pixels brush style (or the similar style of your choosing).

   ✓ *Rest your cursor on the various styles to see their names.*

   ✓ *After you choose that brush style, the Brush setting actually shows a 27 for the selected style. This is a slight discrepancy in the Photoshop program.*

5. Use the method of your choice to choose a dark green foreground color to use for the brush.

6. "Scrub" up and down to paint horizontally across the center of the image, as shown in Illustration 1.

7. Choose the Type tool from the toolbox, and drag to create a text box.

8. Choose another font and font size using the options bar, and choose to center the text.

9. Use the method of your choice to choose a red color for the text.

10. Click near the center of the image, just above the green swatch you painted earlier.

11. Type **Artistic Painters**.

12. Use the Create warped text button on the options bar to apply a warp effect such as Arc Upper to the text. It should look something like Illustration 2 at this point.

13. Click on the Commit button (✓) to finish adding the text.

14. Choose the Ellipse tool from the toolbox.

   ✓ *Be sure that the Create new shape layer button* 🔲 *is selected on the options bar.*

15. Use the method of your choice to choose a bright blue foreground color.

16. Draw a circle near the center point of the image, somewhat overlapping the green swatch you painted earlier.

   ✓ *Hint: Press the Shift key while you draw to create a perfect circle.*

17. Click on the Commit button (✓) to finish creating the circle.

18. Choose the Polygon tool from the toolbox.

   ✓ *Hint: Right-click on the Ellipse tool to choose the Polygon tool.*

19. Use the options bar to choose a three-sided polygon (a triangle).

20. Use the method of your choice to choose a bright orange foreground color.

21. Draw a triangle near the center left of the image, somewhat overlapping the green swatch you painted earlier.

22. Click on the Commit button (✓) to finish creating the triangle.

23. Choose the Custom Shape tool from the toolbox.

24. Use the Shape drop-down list on the options bar to choose the shape of your choice, such as a star or a blob.

25. Use the method of your choice to choose a bright yellow foreground color.

26. Draw the shape near the center right of the image, somewhat overlapping the green swatch you painted earlier.

27. Click on the Commit button (✓) to finish creating the triangle. Your drawing should resemble Illustration 3 at this point.

28. Save the image; name it **PAINT**.

29. Close the image.

   ✓ *Your instructor may require you to print, label, and submit a copy of each image you create. If so, refer to Chapter 14 to learn more about printing Photoshop images.*

Illustration 1

Illustration 2

Illustration 3

4

Working with the Image View

As you're working with your image, you may need to zoom in to make small changes, zoom out to see how your image looks overall, and otherwise move around to ensure you're working with just the image area that you need. Photoshop offers a number of techniques that you can use to change your view of the image. In this chapter, you will master the following skills:

❋ Zoom in and out on an image

❋ View the actual pixel size or print size

❋ Zoom the image to the screen

❋ Scroll with the scroll bar

❋ Move around with the Hand tool and Navigator

Using the Zoom Tool

You may have worked with a zoom tool in another program, clicking on a file to zoom in and then clicking again to zoom back out. Photoshop's Zoom tool offers the same behavior, plus some additional features to help you quickly display an image in the view that works best. Note that zooming merely adjusts the size of the image file onscreen, so that you can work more effectively. Zooming does not adjust the dimensions of the file itself, and therefore does not affect the size at which the file prints.

Zooming In and Out

The most common zoom operations are to zoom in (get a closer view of the image) and to zoom out (get a further, more overall view of the image). The steps here illustrate these common uses for the Zoom tool.

1. Click on the **Zoom** tool in the Photoshop toolbox. The mouse pointer will change to a magnifying glass, and the options bar will show the options for the Zoom tool.

2. Click on the image, near the spot that you want to magnify. Each time you click with the default zoom pointer (a magnifying glass with a plus sign in it), Photoshop will zoom in on the image by one zoom increment.

3. Press and hold the **Alt** key, and then click on the image. Photoshop will zoom out by one zoom increment each time you **Alt+click** with the mouse pointer for zooming out (a magnifying glass with a minus sign).

Note: *The remainder of the book will use the phrase Alt+click to indicate when you should press and hold the Alt key when clicking on a screen item.*

Note: *The View menu also offers a number of zooming commands: Zoom In, Zoom Out, Fit on Screen, Actual Pixels, and Print Size.*

Zooming to Print and Pixel Size

You also can use the Zoom tool to zoom the image to one of two predetermined sizes: its pixel size (100%) or the actual print size (if you've used the Page Setup commands to change the size for the printout). Learn about these two zoom types next.

1. Click on the **Zoom** tool in the Photoshop toolbox. The mouse pointer will change to a magnifying glass, and the options bar will show the options for the Zoom tool.

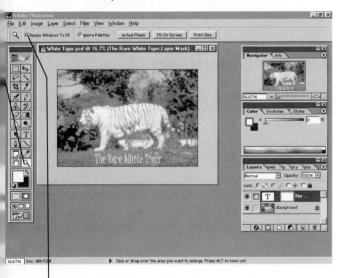

2. Click on **Resize Windows To Fit** on the options bar. Photoshop will check the check box. When checked, Resize Windows To Fit will change the window size to accommodate the zoomed image. Also check Ignore Palettes if it isn't checked by default.

3. Click on **Actual Pixels** on the options bar. Photoshop will zoom the image to 100% size (the actual pixel size).

Tip: *Double-clicking on the Zoom tool in the toolbox also zooms to 100% size.*

4. Click on **Print Size** on the options bar. Photoshop will zoom the image to the actual size it will have when printed.

Fitting the Image to the Screen

To take advantage of all the workspace available in Photoshop, you can zoom the image to the screen size using the Zoom tool, as explained here.

1. Click on the **Zoom** tool in the Photoshop toolbox. The mouse pointer will change to a magnifying glass, and the options bar will show the options for the Zoom tool.

2. Click on **Resize Windows To Fit** on the options bar. Photoshop will check the check box. When checked, Resize Windows To Fit will change the window size to accommodate the zoomed image. Also check Ignore Palettes if it isn't checked by default. Ignore Palettes turns off color palette features that may change the image's appearance as you zoom.

3. Click on **Fit On Screen**. Photoshop will zoom the image to the largest zoom setting it can fit on the screen.

Tip: *While the Zoom tool is selected, you also can right-click on the image to see a shortcut menu with commands for zooming the image.*

Changing the View Zone

If you did not opt to resize the image window as you zoomed, zooming in on the image may magnify it to such a size that the image can't fully display in the image window. When this happens, you can use a few different methods to choose which area of the image appears in the image window, thus enabling you to view and work with that portion of the image. This section explores those methods: scroll bars, the Hand tool, and the Navigator.

Using Scroll Bars

Scroll bars appear whenever you've resized the image window so that it can't display the entire image. When this happens, you use the scroll bars as described next to scroll the portion of the image that you'd like to work with into view.

1. Click on a scroll arrow on either the vertical or horizontal scroll bar. Each time you click, Photoshop will scroll the image by a small increment.

2. Drag a scroll bar box. Photoshop will scroll the image much more quickly.

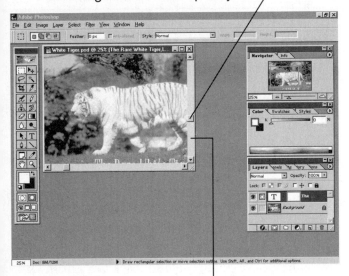

3. Click on the scroll bar itself above or below the scroll box. Depending on the scroll bar and side of the scroll box on which you click, Photoshop scrolls the image as far as possible in the designated direction.

Using the Hand Tool

You can use the Hand tool to scroll the image in multiple directions at once—much like using both scroll bars simultaneously. The following steps explain how to do so.

1. Click on the **Hand** tool on the toolbox. The mouse pointer will change to a hand pointer.

2. Drag the image with the hand pointer. Photoshop will scroll the image in the same direction that you drag.

Using the Navigator

You can use the Navigator palette for multiple purposes—to change the image zoom and to scroll the displayed portion of the image. These steps describe both uses for the palette.

1. Click on the **Navigator** tab in the Navigator palette, if needed. The Navigator tab will become active.

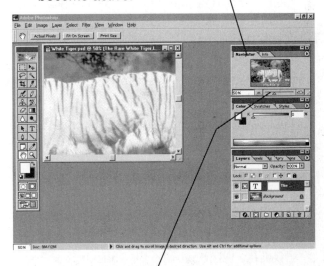

2. Drag the zoom slider in the Navigator palette. Photoshop will zoom the image to the specified size.

Note: *You also can type a zoom percentage into the text box on the Navigator palette and then press Enter, or click on one of the buttons at either end of the zoom slider in the Navigator palette to change the zoom.*

3. Drag the red box on the image thumbnail in the Navigator palette with the hand pointer. Photoshop will scroll the image to display the portion of the image bounded by the red box in the thumbnail.

Procedures

Use Zoom Tool

To zoom in (Ctrl++):

1. Click the **Zoom Tool** button [🔍] .... [Z]

2. Click the area in the image to magnify.

To zoom out (Ctrl+–):

1. Click the **Zoom Tool** button [🔍] .... [Z]

2. Press and hold [Alt].

3. Click the area in the image to reduce in magnification.

Use Zoom Tool Options

Select resize window to fit zoomed image:

*   With the Zoom Tool selected, click on the **Resize Windows To Fit** checkbox on the Zoom Tool options bar.

Zoom to actual pixel size:

*   With the Zoom Tool selected, click on the **Actual Pixels** button [Actual Pixels] on the Zoom Tool options bar.

OR

*   Double click the **Zoom Tool** button [🔍].

Fit image on screen:

*   With the Zoom Tool selected, click on the **Fit On Screen** button [Fit On Screen] on the Zoom Tool options bar.

View image print size:

*   With the Zoom Tool selected, click on the **Print Size** button [Print Size] on the Zoom Tool options bar.

✓ *The View menu also provides zoom-in and zoom-out controls and options.*

✓ *See text for a discussion of the Ignore Palettes checkbox.*

Zoom in and Out with Navigator Palette

To zoom in:

1. In the Navigator palette, click the **Zoom In** button [△] to magnify.

2. Drag the red image frame box to the desired viewing area in the Navigator palette image thumbnail.

To zoom out:

*   In the Navigator palette, click the **Zoom Out** button [△] to reduce magnification.

Change View Zone

1. Drag the horizontal and vertical scroll bars of the image window as needed.

2. Click the horizontal and vertical scroll arrows of the image window as needed.

OR

1. Click the **Hand Tool** button 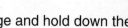 .... [H]

2. Click an area in the image and hold down the mouse button.

    ✓ *The mouse pointer becomes a "grasping" hand.*

3. Drag desired area into view.

4. If you need to scroll additionally to the desired viewing area, release the mouse button and repeat steps 2–3 as needed.

OR

In the Navigator palette, drag the red image frame box around the desired viewing area.

Exercise 4

Photoshop not only provides the tools for creating detailed image files, but also for correcting images. To ensure an image looks precisely as you'd like it to, you need to be able to view it in a variety of ways. You need to be able to zoom in close to make tiny corrections, but also to zoom back out to verify the overall image appearance. This exercise gives you the opportunity to try the various zooming methods available in Photoshop, as well as how to navigate in an image that's zoomed to a large magnification.

Directions

1. Start Photoshop, if needed.

2. Use the File|Open command to open the ☉ **PS04** Photoshop file.

3. Select the Zoom tool in the toolbox.

4. Click on the image twice, in the approximate location shown in Illustration 1. This zooms in the image view.

5. Alt+click once on the image to zoom back out slightly.

6. With the Zoom tool still active, click on Print Size on the Options bar.

7. Click on Fit On Screen in the options bar.

8. Click on Actual Pixels in the options bar.

9. Click on the Navigator tab in the Navigator palette, if needed.

10. Drag the zoom slider in the Navigator palette until the text box to the left of it shows a zoom of approximately 250%.

    ✓ *You also can type a zoom percentage into the text box beside that zoom slider and then press Enter to change the zoom.*

11. Drag the red box in the Navigator palette until it surrounds the lower-left corner of the image, as shown in Illustration 2. The image scrolls accordingly.

12. Select the Hand tool in the toolbox.

13. From the upper-right corner of the image, drag down and to the bottom center, as shown in Illustration 3.

14. Click on the left arrow of the bottom (horizontal) scroll bar three times. The image scrolls slightly to the left.

15. Drag the scroll box on the right (vertical) scroll bar to the top of the bar.

16. Click on Fit On Screen on the options bar.

17. Close the **PS04** file.

Illustration 1

Zoom tool

Illustration 2

Illustration 3

Hand tool

Next
Chapter

▶▶

5
Selecting Image Content

Precision image editing requires making precision selections. Before you can delete, move, fill, or replace part of an image, you have to select the portion of the image with which you want to work. Photoshop offers a number of selection tools that you can use to zero in on an area to edit with precision and control. This chapter teaches you how to:

※ Select rectangular or oval shapes

※ Make an irregular selection

※ Select by color

※ Add or remove part of the selection

※ Cancel the selection

Using the Marquee Tool

The Marquee tool appears in the upper-left corner of the Photoshop toolbox. Use the Marquee tool to make selections that are regular in shape—rectangles, squares, ovals, circles, or one-pixel borders (also called a row or column selection).

Note: *If the area to select appears on a particular layer, you need to select that layer in the Layers palette before using any type of tool to make the selection. See Chapter 8, "Working with Layers" to learn more about selecting layers.*

Selecting a Rectangle

The steps here show you how easy it is to make a selection that's rectangular in shape.

1. Right-click on the **Marquee** tool in the Photoshop toolbox. The menu for the Marquee tool will appear.

2. Click on **Rectangular Marquee Tool**. The Rectangular Marquee tool will become active.

3. Click on the **New selection** button on the options bar, if needed.

4. Make an entry (in pixels, up to 250) in the Feather text box on the options bar. The feathering setting will become active.

   Tip: *Feathering blurs the edges of the selection. The results of feathering become more apparent if you copy and paste the selection.*

5. Click on the down arrow next to the Style drop-down list. The list will appear.

6. Click on **Normal**. The normal selection method will become active.

   Note: *If you chose the Constrained Aspect Ratio or Fixed Size choices from the Style drop-down list, the Width and Height text boxes become active. Make an entry in one of the text boxes (for Constrained Aspect) or both text boxes to specify a selection size, then click on the image to make the selection.*

7. Click and drag on the image over the area to select. (Press and hold Shift as you drag to select a perfect square.) The selection marquee will appear on the image.

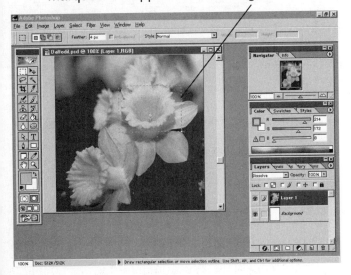

Selecting an Ellipse

If you need to make a round or elliptical selection instead, you can use the following steps to do so.

1. Right-click on the **Marquee** tool in the Photoshop toolbox. The menu for the Marquee tool will appear.

2. Click on **Elliptical Marquee Tool**. The Elliptical Marquee tool will become active.

3. Click on the **New selection** button on the options bar, if needed.

4. Make an entry (in pixels, up to 250) in the Feather text box on the options bar. Leave the Anti-aliased check box checked. The feathering setting will become active.

Tip: Anti-aliasing fixes jaggedness along the edges of a selection, which occurs when the selection marquee has curves.

5. Click on the down arrow next to the **Style** drop-down list. The drop-down list will appear.

6. Click on **Normal**. The normal selection method will become active.

Note: If you chose the Constrained Aspect Ratio or Fixed Size choices from the Style drop-down list, the Width and Height text boxes become active. Make an entry in one of the text boxes (for Constrained Aspect) or both text boxes to specify a selection size, then click on the image to make the selection.

7. Click and drag on the image over the area to select. (Press and hold Shift as you drag to select a perfect circle.) The selection marquee will appear on the image.

Note: *If you see the phrase Shift+drag in the rest of the book, it means you should press and hold the Shift key while dragging. Release the mouse button before you release the Shift key.*

Selecting a Row or Column

Use the Single Row Marquee tool or Single Column Marquee tool to select a one-pixel-wide area in the image. You can then cut or copy and paste the selection to use it as a border in another image.

1. Right-click on the **Marquee** tool in the Photoshop toolbox. The menu for the Marquee tool will appear.

2. Click on **Single Row Marquee Tool** or **Single Column Marquee Tool**. The specified marquee tool will become active.

3. Click on the **New selection** button on the options bar, if needed.

4. Click on the image over the area to select as a border. The selection marquee will appear on the image.

    Note: *Because Photoshop operates primarily as a paint program, you may find that you can't separate out an area that you'd like to select, no matter which selection technique you use. That's why you retain more editing flexibility in an image on various layers. See Chapter 8, "Working with Layers" to learn how to create and use layers.*

Using the Lasso Tool

Like the Marquee tool, the Lasso tool offers a few different techniques you can employ to make selections in an image. The Lasso tool's variations enable you to make selections that are not typical or symmetrical in shape. You can select an irregular area by dragging (Lasso tool), select a polygon by clicking to place the angles (Polygonal Lasso), or get help selecting an irregular area with the Magnetic Lasso.

Selecting an Odd Shape

You can use the Lasso tool to drag around selections that are irregular in shape, but don't necessarily have a lot of angle points. (If the shape does have a lot of angles or corners consider using the Polygonal Lasso tool, described next.)

1. Right-click on the **Lasso** tool in the Photoshop toolbox. The menu for the Lasso tool will appear.

2. Click on the **Lasso Tool**. The Lasso tool will become active.

3. Click on the **New selection** button on the options bar, if needed.

4. Make an entry (in pixels, up to 250) in the Feather text box on the options bar. Leave the Anti-aliased check box checked. The feathering setting will become active.

5. Drag around the desired area to select on the image around the area to select; drag all the way back to the starting point or release the mouse to close the selection. The selection marquee will appear on the image.

Selecting a Polygon

Use the Polygonal Lasso tool to select odd shapes that do have corners and angles, as the following steps demonstrate.

1. Right-click on the **Lasso** tool in the Photoshop toolbox. The menu for the Lasso tool will appear.

2. Click on the **Polygonal Lasso Tool**. The Polygonal Lasso tool will become active.

3. Click on the **New selection** button on the options bar, if needed.

4. Make an entry (in pixels, up to 250) in the Feather text box on the options bar, and leave the Anti-aliased check box checked. The feathering setting will become active.

5. Click around the area to select on the image to specify corners for the selection; double-click the last point to close the selection. The selection marquee will appear on the image.

Tip: *You can press the Alt key while using either the Lasso tool or Polygonal Lasso tool to switch between freehand drawing and clicking to set corner points. Press Delete while using any Lasso tool to remove the most recently drawn selection segment.*

Using the Magnetic Lasso

The Magnetic Lasso tool helps you make a selection by snapping to fastening points along the edge of a shape in an image.

1. Right-click on the **Lasso** tool in the Photoshop toolbox. The menu for the Lasso tool will appear.

2. Click on **Magnetic Lasso Tool**. The Magnetic Lasso tool will become active.

3. Click on the **New selection** button on the options bar, if needed.

4. Change other settings on the options bar as needed:

    *   Make an entry (in pixels, up to 250) in the Feather text box on the options bar, and leave the Anti-aliased check box checked. The feathering setting will become active.

    *   Change the Width text box entry (in pixels, between 1 and 40) to set the search width for the tool. The tool will look for edges within the specified zone beside the points you identify with the mouse.

- Change the Edge Contrast text box entry (in percentages between 1 and 100) to identify how much contrast the tool requires. A lower setting will enable the tool to find edges with less contrast, while a higher setting will restrict the tool to find only high-contrast edges.

- Change the Frequency text box entry (between 0 and 100) if needed. A higher setting causes the tool to set more fastening points, and vice versa.

5. Drag and click on the area to select on the image to specify the selection border. (Clicking manually places a fastening point.) The selection marquee will appear on the image.

Selecting Pixels with the Magic Wand

If all the pixels in the area that you want to select are about the same color and adjoin one another in the image, you can use the Magic Wand tool to select the area with by clicking.

1. Click on the **Magic Wand** tool in the Photoshop toolbox. The Magic Wand tool will become active.

2. Click on the **New selection** button on the options bar, if needed.

3. Change other settings on the options bar as needed:

- Change the Tolerance text box entry (between 0 and 255) to specify how much variation can occur between the colors included in the selection. A low entry will result in a smaller selection zone composed of fewer like colors, and vice versa.

- Leave the Anti-aliased check box checked. The tool will smooth the edges of the selection.

- Leave the Contiguous check box checked. The tool will select all adjoining pixels of the same (or similar) color, not just the pixel on which you click.

- Click on the Use All Layers check box to select it if desired. The tool will then select the matching colors on all layers in the picture.

4. Click on the desired image color with the **Magic Wand** tool. The selection marquee will appear on the image.

Selecting by Color Range

Selecting by color works somewhat like the Magic Wand tool, except it enables you to select all the pixels of the specified color in the image—not just adjoining or contiguous pixels.

1. Click on **Select**. The Select menu will appear.

2. Click on **Color Range**. The Color Range dialog box will open.

3. Click on the down arrow beside the Select list. The Select list will open.

4. Click on a selection type in the list. If you choose anything other than Sampled Colors from the list, Photoshop immediately previews the color selection in the dialog box, and you can skip to Step 8. If you choose Sampled Colors, continue with the next Step.

5. Drag the **Fuzziness** slider to change its setting, if needed. Increasing this value will cause Photoshop to select colors similar to the color you select for the match.

6. Click on the **Eyedropper Tool** button to select it, if needed. The Eyedropper tool will become active.

7. Click on the desired color in the picture. If you choose anything other than Sampled Colors from the list, Photoshop immediately previews the color selection in the dialog box.

8. Click on **OK**. The dialog box will close and Photoshop will display marquees around the matching selections in the picture.

Note: To add or remove colors from the selection, click on either the Add to Sample or Subtract from Sample button (next to the Eyedropper Tool button), then click a color on the image.

Adjusting a Selection

Once you've made a selection, you can change the boundaries of the selection (selected area). The following steps run through the possibilities for modifying a selection.

1. Drag from the center of the selection, with the mouse pointer that looks like an arrow plus a box. The selection will move to another location.

Tip: Pressing an arrow key "nudges" the selection by one pixel in the specified direction.

2. Click on the **Add to selection**, **Subtract from selection**, or **Intersect with selection** button on the options bar, if available for the active selection tool. The selection tool will begin to use the specified selection method.

3. Click or drag on the image as required for the active selection tool. Depending on the selection method selected in Step 2, Photoshop adds to, removes from, or crops out information included in the selected area.

Tip: You also can press Shift then use a selection tool to add a selection.

Tip: To remove the latest selection you've added, don't press Delete! Press Ctrl+Z to undo the selection, instead.

4. Click on **Select**. The Select menu will appear.

5. Click on **Inverse**. Photoshop will select the area that previously was not selected in the image, and vice versa.

Note: You also can right-click on a selection and then click on Save Selection to save a selection as a new channel in the image. See "Saving a Selection" and "Loading a Selection" in Chapter 8, as well as Chapter 15. "Understanding Colors and Channels."

Deselecting a Selection

When you need to deselect the selection, you can do so with ease.

1. Click on **Select**. The Select menu will appear.

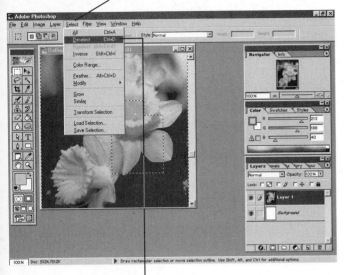

2. Click on **Deselect**. Photoshop will remove the selection immediately.

3. Click on the gray area within the image window, if it appears. Photoshop will remove the selection immediately, if you're using the Rectangular Marquee, Elliptical Marquee, or Lasso tool. (Follow Steps 1 and 2 for the other selection tools.)

4. Click on **Select**. The Select menu will appear.

5. Click on **Reselect**. Photoshop will reinstate the selection immediately.

Procedures

Select a Rectangle Marquee

1. Click the **Rectangular Marquee Tool** button ▣ .... Ⓜ

2. Select any desired options from the Rectangular Marquee Tool options bar:

   a. Click the **New selection** button ▣ to make one selection.

   OR

   Click the **Add to selection** button ▣ to make multiple selections.

   b. Click in the **Feather** box and type a pixel size from 1–250.

   c. Click the **Style** arrow and select a selection style from drop-down list.

   ✓ *The Constrained Aspect Ratio and Fixed Size options require a Height box and Width box setting.*

3. Click in the image and hold down the mouse button a little to the left and above the desired selection.

4. Drag diagonally to select the marquee.

5. Release the mouse button to finalize the marquee.

Select an Elliptical Marquee

1. Click the **Elliptical Marquee Tool** button ▣ .... Ⓜ

2. Select any desired options from the Elliptical Marquee Tool options bar:

   a. Click the **New selection** button ▣ to make one selection.

   OR

   Click the **Add to selection** button ▣ to make multiple selections.

   b. Click in the **Feather** box and type a pixel size from 1–250.

   c. Click the **Anti-aliased** checkbox to select or deselect it.

   d. Click the **Style** arrow and select a selection style from drop-down list.

   ✓ *The Constrained Aspect Ratio and Fixed Size options require a Height box and Width box setting.*

3. Click in the image and hold down the mouse button a little to the left and above the desired selection.

4. Drag diagonally to select the marquee.

5. Release the mouse button to finalize the marquee.

Select a Row or Column Marquee

1. Click the **Single Row Marquee Tool** button ▣ .... Ⓜ

   OR

   Click the **Single Column Marquee Tool** button ▣ .... Ⓜ

2. Select any desired options from the options bar:

   a. Click the **New selection** button ▣ to make one selection.

   OR

   b. Click the **Add to selection** button ▣ to make multiple selections.

   ✓ *The Feather box should be set at 0.*

3. Click in the image to select the desired row or column marquee.

Use the Lasso Tool

1. Click the **Lasso Tool** button L

2. Select any desired options from the Lasso Tool options bar:

   a. Click the **New selection** button ▣ to make one selection.

      OR

      Click the **Add to selection** button ▣ to make multiple selections.

   b. Click in the **Feather** box and type a pixel size from 1–250.

   c. Click the **Anti-aliased** checkbox to select or deselect it.

3. Click and hold down the mouse button at the starting point of the desired selection.

4. Drag the Lasso tool mouse pointer around the desired selection.

   ✓ *The free-end of the lasso "rope" in the mouse pointer—not the lasso shape itself— is the Lasso tool's stylus.*

5. Release the mouse button when the selection reaches the starting point to finalize the selection.

Use the Polygonal Lasso Tool

1. Click the **Polygonal Lasso Tool** button ▣ L

2. Select any desired options from the Polygonal Lasso Tool options bar:

   a. Click the **New selection** button ▣ to make one selection.

      OR

      Click the **Add to selection** button ▣ to make multiple selections.

   b. Click in the **Feather** box and type a pixel size from 1–250.

   c. Click the **Anti-aliased** checkbox to select or deselect it.

3. Click and hold down the mouse button at the starting point of the desired selection.

4. Drag the Polygonal Lasso tool mouse pointer and release the mouse button to select the corner of the polygon selection.

5. Repeat steps 3–4 until the desired number of sides are created leading back to the starting point.

   ✓ *The free-end of the lasso "rope" in the mouse pointer—not the lasso shape itself— is the Polygonal Lasso tool's stylus.*

6. When the mouse pointer is close enough to finalize the selection, a small "full-circle" symbol will appear to the right of the mouse pointer.

7. Release the mouse button to finalize the selection.

   ✓ *To make selections that have both freehand and polygonal sides, press Alt to switch between the Lasso and Polygonal Lasso tool mouse pointers.*

Use the Magnetic Lasso Tool

1. Click the **Lasso Tool** button L

2. Select any desired options from the Lasso Tool options bar:

   a. Click the **New selection** button ▣ to make one selection.

      OR

      Click the **Add to selection** button ▣ to make multiple selections.

   b. Click in the **Feather** box and type a pixel size from 1–250.

   c. Click the **Anti-aliased** checkbox to select or deselect it.

   d. Click in the **Width** box to add a width in pixels from 1–40.

   e. Click in the **Edge Contrast** box and type a percentage.

   f. Click in the **Frequency** box and type the number fastening points from 1–100.

3. Click and hold down the mouse button at the starting point of the desired selection.

4. Drag the Magnetic Lasso tool mouse pointer around the desired selection.

   ✓ *The free-end of the lasso "rope" in the mouse pointer—not the lasso shape itself—is the Lasso tool's stylus.*

5. Release the mouse button when the selection reaches the starting point to finalize the selection.

Use the Magic Wand Tool

1. Click the **Magic Wand Tool** button ⧉ ..... W

2. Select any desired options from the Lasso Tool options bar:

   a. Click the **New selection** button ⧉ to make one selection.

      OR

      Click the **Add to selection** button ⧉ to make multiple selections.

   b. Click in the **Tolerance** box and type the tolerance from 1–255.

   c. Click the **Anti-aliased** checkbox to select or deselect it.

   d. Click the **Contiguous** checkbox to select or deselect it.

   e. Click the **Use All Layers** checkbox to select or deselect it.

3. Click the color area in the image to make the desired selection.

Select by Color Range

1. Click **Select** .... Alt + S

2. Click **Color Range** C

3. Click the **Select** arrow and choose the desired selection type .... Alt + C , ↓ , Enter

4. Click the **Selection** option button to preview selection in selection window.

   ✓ *For sampled colors, perform steps 5–6*

5. Click in the **Fuzziness** box and enter a number from 1–200.

   OR

   Drag the Fuzziness slider to the desired setting.

6. Click the **Eyedropper Tool** button ⧉ in the Color Range dialog box.

7. Click in the image to select the desired color.

   ✓ *The other eyedropper buttons allow for adding ⧉ or subtracting ⧉ from the sampled colors in making the color range selection.*

8. Click **OK** .... Enter

Move a Marquee Selection

1. Click in the marquee selection and hold down the mouse button.

   ✓ *The mouse pointer changes to a solid black arrowhead.*

2. Drag the marquee to the desired position.

Subtract from a Marquee Selection

1. Click the desired marquee tool button ⧉⧉⧉⧉⧉ .... M / L

2. Select any desired options from the options toolbar.

   ✓ *Consult the procedure for the chosen marquee selection tool to review the option choices.*

3. To subtract (crop) from the active marquee selection, click the **Subtract from selection** tool button ⧉ on the options bar.

4. Click and drag on the selection to crop the desired area.

5. Release the mouse button to finalize the selection.

   ✓ *More than one kind of Subtract from selection tool can be used on an active selection.*

Intersect with a Marquee Selection

1. Click the desired marquee tool button
 .... M/L

2. Select any desired options from the options toolbar.

   ✓ *Consult the procedure for the chosen marquee selection tool to review the option choices.*

3. To create a selection from the intersection of one marquee selection tool with an active marquee selection, click the **Intersect with selection** tool button 🔲 on the options bar.

4. Click and drag on the selection to intersect the desired area.

5. Release the mouse button to finalize the selection.

   ✓ *More than one kind of Intersect with selection tool can be used on an active selection.*

Deselect a Marquee Selection (Ctrl+D)

- Right-click on the marquee and click **Deselect**.

OR

- If in view, click on the gray area within the image window.

OR

1. Click **Select** .... Alt + S

2. Click **Deselect** .... D

Reselect a Marquee Selection (Shift+Ctrl+D)

1. Click **Select** .... Alt + S

2. Click **Reselect** .... E

Exercise 5

Selecting part of an image is a key skill. In order to make a change to any part of an image, you have to select that image content first. Photoshop provides you a great deal of control in making selections, so that you can help get the image details right. You can select a particular shape, such as a rectangle or ellipse. You can use the Lasso or Magnetic Lasso tools to select irregular shapes in the image. Use a menu command or the Magic Wand tool to make a selection based on image color. Once you've made a selection, you can add additional selected regions to it, or remove the selection altogether to enable you to make a new selection. Practice all of those techniques in this exercise.

Directions

1. Start Photoshop, if needed.

2. Use the File|Open command to open the ⊙ PS05 Photoshop file. Zoom the image if needed.

3. Select the Rectangular Marquee tool in the toolbox, if needed.

4. Drag on the image to select the center portion of the flower, as shown in Illustration 1.

   ✓ *The blinking dashed line that appears around the selection is called the selection marquee.*

5. Select the Elliptical Marquee tool in the toolbox.

   ✓ *Right-click on the Rectangular Marquee tool to find the Elliptical Marquee tool.*

6. Drag on the image to select the center portion of the flower again.

7. Select the Lasso tool in the toolbox.

8. Use it to select the lower-right petal of the flower, as shown in Illustration 2.

9. Select the Magnetic Lasso tool in the toolbox.

   ✓ *Right-click on the Lasso tool to find the Magnetic Lasso tool.*

10. Use it to select the entire outline of the flower.

    ✓ *Press Delete to delete the last fastening point added by the Magnetic Lasso tool or that you added by clicking. Press Esc to clear the whole selection marquee (before you complete it). Drag all the way back to the first fastening point or double-click from any location to complete the selection.*

11. Select the Magic Wand tool on the toolbox.

12. Click on a portion of the upper-right petal to select a contiguous area with the color on which you clicked.

13. Choose Select|Deselect.

    ✓ *You have to remove the current selection to be able to select by color range from all of the image.*

14. Choose Select|Color Range.

15. Drag the Color Range dialog box partially out of the way, so you can see both it and the flower image.

16. Increase the Fuzziness setting to 75.

17. Click on the flower, near the edge of its central trumpet, as shown in Illustration 3.

18. Click on OK to finish the selection.

19. Select the Elliptical Marquee tool on the toolbox.

20. Press and hold the Shift key, then drag to add to the selection.

    ✓ *For some selection tools, the options bar includes Add to selection, Subtract from selection, and Intersect with selection buttons. You can click one of those before making the selection to alter how the new selection works along with the prior selection that you made.*

    ✓ *You also can choose Select|Inverse to select the area of the image that's not included in the current selection. This is a convenient way to select the area around a flower after you've first selected the flower itself, for example. The Select menu includes additional commands you can use to alter the selection.*

21. Move the mouse within the selection until you see the pointer that includes small arrow and a box, then drag the selection in any direction.

22. Choose Select|Deselect to remove the selection.

23. Choose Select|Reselect to choose the selection again.

24. Choose Select|Deselect to remove the selection one last time.

25. Close the file without saving it.

Illustration 1

Rectangular Marquee tool

Selecting

Illustration 2

Illustration 3

Next
Chapter
▶▶

6
Changing a Selection

After you've selected part of the image, the fun begins. You can then start manipulating the selection to change the appearance of the image or share information between image files. This chapter introduces you to the basic changes you can make once you've selected part of the information on a layer in the image. (Chapter 8, "Working with Layers," explains how to layer information.) When you finish this chapter, you'll know how to:

❋ Delete, move, or copy what you've selected

❋ Change a selection by transforming or rotating it

❋ Fine-tune the selection marquee

❋ Save and reuse a selection

❋ Undo a change

❋ Work with the History palette

Deleting a Selection

In the last chapter, you learned that you can press the Delete key while you're creating a selection using the Lasso tool to remove the most-recently-added segment. Pressing Delete has a different effect once you've finished the selection—it clears the content within the selected area. The steps that follow describe how to clear or delete the content in a selected area.

1. Make a selection in the image using the selection tool of your choice. The selection marquee will appear.

2. Click on **Edit**. The Edit menu will appear.

3. Click on **Clear**. The selection will disappear completely from the current layer.

   Tip: *You can press the Delete key in place of Steps 2 and 3.*

Moving a Selection

Moving a selection requires a tool you haven't used earlier—the Move tool. Trying to drag while the selection tool you used is active moves the selection marquee only, not the actual image content within that selection. No matter which layer you're working on or what type of content you're dealing with, the Move tool works the same.

1. Make a selection in the image using the selection tool of your choice. The selection marquee will appear.

2. Click on the **Move** tool on the Photoshop toolbox. The Move tool will become active.

3. Click on options bar options to check them as needed. If you check Auto Select Layer, clicking on an area on the image will select its layer. If you check Show Bounding Box, the selection box may change to show handles.

   Note: *If other buttons become active on the options bar, clicking one of them aligns information within the selection marquee, such as text, relative to the borders of the selection marquee.*

Chapter 6: Changing a Selection

4. Drag the selection from within the marquee. The selection will move to a new location when you release the mouse button.

Copying a Selection

You can copy a selection to reuse it in another location, such as on another layer in the image file or in a completely new file. This comes in handy, because once you've drawn or scanned in image content, you can reuse it as often as you need to with a minimum of effort. This example illustrates how to create a new image file from content that you copy.

1. Make a selection in the image using the selection tool of your choice. The selection marquee will appear.

2. Click on **Edit**. The Edit menu will appear.

3. Click on **Copy**. Photoshop will copy the selection to the Windows Clipboard, a memory holding area.

Note: *Rather than starting a new image at this point, you could switch to another open image file, then jump to Step 8.*

4. Click on **File**. The File menu will appear.

5. Click on **New**. The New dialog box will open.

6. Change the dialog box settings as needed. The changes you make will affect the size of the new image. You may not need to change the Width and Height entries; typically, those will reflect the size of the copied selection. (See "Creating a New File" in Chapter 2 to refresh your memory about the New dialog box settings.)

7. Click on **OK**. The new image file will open.

8.   Click on **Edit**. The Edit menu will appear.

9.   Click on **Paste**. Photoshop will paste the copied selection into the new file.

Note: *Don't forget to save the new image file after you've pasted the selection into it.*

Transforming a Selection

Photoshop offers a number of transformations you can make to affect a selection in an image. The table below reviews the types of transformations you can make.

Transform	Enables you to...
Scale	Change the size of the selection while maintaining its vertical-to-horizontal proportions.
Rotate	Chang the angle positioning of the selection, such as rotating it 90 degrees in a clockwise direction.
Skew	Drag one side of the selection to "angle" the selection, such as changing a square selection to a slanted square (rhombus).
Distort	Drag the corner handle bounding the selection to "stretch" the selection in multiple directions at once.
Perspective	Simultaneously resize opposite (parallel) boundaries of the selection to achieve one-point perspective.
Flip	Flip the selection horizontally or vertically.

1.   Make a **selection** in the image using the selection tool of your choice. The selection marquee will appear.

2.   Click on **Edit**. The Edit menu will appear.

3.   Point to **Transform**. The Transform submenu will appear.

4.   Click on the desired transform command. If you choose **Rotate 180°**, **Rotate 90° CW** (clockwise), **Rotate 90° CCW** (counter-clockwise), **Flip Horizontal**, or **Flip Vertical**, the transformation will appear immediately. If you choose one of the other transforms, the options bar will become active and special transform handles will appear around the selection.

Note: *To transform text, just go to the layer that holds the text; you don't need to select the text itself. The Distort and Perspective transformations aren't available for text.*

5. Drag a handle. The transformation will occur. Alternatively, you can use the text boxes on the options bar to enter precise transformation settings.

6. Click on the **Commit** button (✓) at the right end of the options bar. Photoshop finalizes the transform.

   Note: *Whenever you see a Cancel (X) button on the options bar, you can click on that button to cancel the application of the current command or tool settings.*

   Note: *You also can choose the Free Transform command on the Edit menu and then drag handles on the selection to transform the selection.*

Modifying Part of the Selection

The Select menu gives you a number of commands for adjusting the selection marquee itself. You may use these features before you use other features for altering a selection to be sure that you're working with the proper selection.

Changing the Selection Border

You can add another selection around the current selection marquee so that the specified area within the two marquees becomes the selection. You could then remove that selection or fill it in some way to create a visual border around the selection.

1. Make a selection in the image using the selection tool of your choice. The selection marquee will appear.

2. Click on **Select**. The Select menu will appear.

3. Point to **Modify**. The Modify submenu will appear.

4. Click on **Border**. The Border dialog box will open.

5. Type a new entry (between 1 and 200 pixels) for the **Width** text box. The entry will appear in the text box.

6. Click on **OK**. The dialog box will close, and the new border selection will appear.

   Note: *Use the Fill and Stroke commands on the Edit menu to fill in the selected border.*

Smoothing the Selection

If you've selected by choosing a color (as described under "Selecting by Color Range" in Chapter 5), your selection may end up with some stray pixels that are surrounded by a selection marquee. Alternatively, if you've used a lasso tool, the selection might be a bit more jagged in shape than you now wish. To simplify the selection in such instances, you can smooth the selection.

1. Make a selection in the image using either a color selection method or a lasso tool. The selection marquee or marquees will appear.

2. Click on **Select**. The Select menu will appear.

3. Point to **Modify**. The Modify submenu will appear.

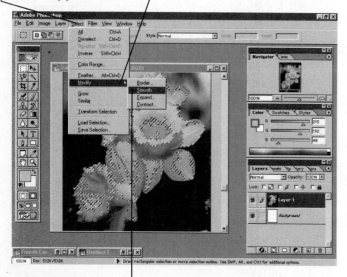

4. Click on **Smooth**. The Smooth dialog box will open.

5. Type a new entry (between 1 and 100 pixels) for the **Sample Radius** text box. The entry will appear in the text box.

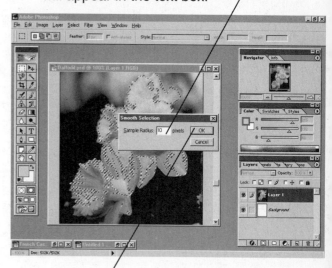

6. Click on **OK**. The dialog box will close, and Photoshop will use the radius setting you entered to add pixels to and eliminate them from the selection.

In making the comparison, Photoshop treats each pixel in the selection as the center of a circle, with a radius of the width you specified. Depending on whether most of the pixels in the circle are selected, Photoshop will add pixels to the selection (most are selected) or remove them from the selection (most aren't selected).

Note: *You also can use the Grow and Similar commands on the Select menu to expand a selection that you've made by color. The Grow command adds pixels adjoining the current selection that have similar colors to the selection, while Similar adds pixels of similar colors from the entire image to the selection.*

Expanding or Contracting the Selection

Expanding or contracting the selection really moves the selection marquee rather than affecting the selection itself. Using this method provides more accuracy than dragging or using a color technique like smoothing to increase the size of the selection, because you specify exactly how many pixels to add or remove from the selection, in terms of height and width.

1. Make a selection in the image using the selection tool of your choice. The selection marquee will appear.

2. Click on **Select**. The Select menu will appear.

3. Point to **Modify**. The Modify submenu will appear.

4. Click on **Expand** or **Contract**. The Expand or Contract dialog box will open.

5. Type a new entry (between 1 and 100 pixels) for the **Width** text box. The entry will appear in the text box.

6. Click on **OK**. The dialog box will close, and the new border selection will appear.

    Note: *You can use the Feather command on the Select menu to feather or soften the edge of the selection; this affects the selection if you copy or paste it, or apply another effect like a filter.*

Saving a Selection

When you save a selection, you give it a name in the Photoshop file. Then, you can easily load the selection in the future. This enables you to repeatedly select exactly the same pixels—which is tough no matter which selection technique you originally used to make the selection.

1. Make a selection in the image using the selection tool of your choice. The selection marquee will appear.

2. Click on **Select**. The Select menu will appear.

3. Click on **Save Selection**. The Save Selection dialog box will open.

4. Click in the **Name** text box, then type a name for the selection. The name will appear in the text box.

5. Click on **OK**. The Save Selection dialog box will close, and the saved selection will be added to the file.

Note: *Be sure to save the file to save the named selection. Also, note that saving the selection creates a new channel from the selection. Chapter 15, "Understanding Colors and Channels," explains how to work with channels.*

Loading a Selection

When you need to apply a selection that you've previously saved—that is, to reselect a previous selection—you can load the selection.

1. Click on **Select**. The Select menu will appear.

2. Click on **Load Selection**. The Load Selection dialog box will open.

3. Click on the down arrow next to the **Channel** box. The list of saved selections will appear.

4. Click on the desired selection. It will appear as the Channel selection.

5. Click on **OK**. The Load Selection dialog box will close, and the selection marquee will appear in the file.

Undoing a Change

The Edit menu offers a number of commands that you can use to undo prior changes and actions, such as deselecting a selection.

1. Click on **Edit**. The Edit menu will appear.

2. Click on **Undo (Action Name)**. Photoshop will undo your most recent change or action.

3. Click on **Edit**. The Edit menu will appear.

4. Click on **Step Backward**. Photoshop will undo your next most recent change or action.

    Note: You can repeat Steps 3 and 4 to step further backward through your changes, then repeat Steps 5 and 6 to step further forward. To redo a single change, click on Redo (Action Name) in the Edit menu.

5. Click on **Edit**. The Edit menu will appear.

6. Click on **Step Forward**. Photoshop will redo the change or action you undid by stepping forward.

    Note: You may not always have the option of undoing a particular change. Some changes cannot be undone. In other cases, Photoshop may combine or link other changes so that they cannot be undone individually.

Using the History to Undo Changes

The History palette provides one last method for discarding (undoing) actions and changes to a selection that you've made previously. When you use the History palette, you select a change or action out of the sequence of actions you've performed during the current work session with the image file. When you remove that selected action or change, Photoshop undoes that action or change, plus all the changes below it in the History list.

1. Click on the **History** tab in the Layers palette. The History palette will appear.

    Tip: *You also can click on Window and then click on Show History to display the History palette.*

2. Click on the down scroll arrow for the scroll bar. The list of changes and actions in the History list will scroll down.

3. Right-click on the change or action to undo in the list. The shortcut menu will appear.

4. Click on **Delete**. A message box asking you to confirm the History deletion will open.

5. Click on **Yes**. Photoshop will close the dialog box and undo the specified change and changes below it in the History palette.

Procedures

Delete a Selection

1. Make a selection in the image.

    ✓ *See the Procedures in Chapter 5 for making selections.*

2. a. Click **Edit** .... Alt + E

    b. Click **Clear** .... E

    OR

    Press **Delete** .... Del

Move a Selection with the Move Tool

1. Click the **Move Tool** button ⊹ V

2. Select any desired advanced options from the Move Tool options bar:

    a. Click the **Auto Select Layer** checkbox to automatically select an area that is on an image layer.

        ✓ *If layers, such as a text layer are present, the applicable alignment and edge distribution buttons can be used to make precise adjustments.*

    b. Click in the **Show Bounding Box** checkbox to resize the moved selection with sizing handles.

        ✓ *This option activates its own options toolbar for setting exact size and position of the moved area. Click the Commit button ✓ to finalize any sizing and positioning change.*

3. Click on the selection to be moved and hold down the mouse button.

4. Drag the moved selection to the desired area in the image.

5. Release the mouse button to finalize the move.

Copy a Selection

1. Make a selection in the image.

    ✓ *See the Procedures in Chapter 5 for making selections.*

2. Click **Edit** .... Alt + E

3. Click **Copy** C

Paste a Selection in a New File

1. Create a new file.

2. Click **Edit** .... Alt + E

3. Click **Paste** .... P

Transform a Selection

1. Make a selection in the image.

2. Click **Edit** .... Alt + E

3. Click **Transform** .... A

4. Click the desired transformation from the submenu or press the keyboard shortcut:

    ✓ *Transformations that flip or rotate the selection in a predetermined way do not have option bars and do not require the following steps.*

    ✓ *Transformations that change the shape of the selection activate an options bar for making precision size and position settings.*

5. Enter any desired precision settings on the options bar.

6. If needed to finalize the transformation, drag a handle on the selection to create the desired transformation.

7. Repeat step 6 as needed.

8. Click the **Commit** button ☑ to finalize the transformation.

   ✓ *Click the Cancel button to undo the transformation.*

Change Selection Border

1. Make a selection in the image.

2. Click **Select** .... `Alt`+`S`

3. Click **Modify** .... `M`

4. Click **Border** .... `B`

5. Click in the **Width** box and type an entry in pixels from 1–64.............. `Alt`+`W`

6. Click **OK** .... `Enter`

Smooth Selection

1. Make a selection in the image.

2. Click **Select** .... `Alt`+`S`

3. Click **Modify** .... `M`

4. Click **Smooth**... `S`

5. Click in the **Sample Radius** box and type an entry in pixels from 1–16........ `Alt`+`S`

6. Click **OK** .... `Enter`

Expand or Contract a Selection

1. Make a selection in the image.

2. Click **Select** .... `Alt`+`S`

3. Click **Modify** .... `M`

4. a. Click **Expand**....................................... `E`

   b. Click in the **Expand By** box and type an entry in pixels from 1–100 .... `Alt`+`E`

   OR

   a. Click **Contract**................................... `C`

   b. Click in the **Contract By** box and type an entry in pixels from 1–100 .... `Alt`+`C`

5. Click **OK** .... `Enter`

Save a Selection

1. Make a selection in the image.

2. Click **Select** .... `Alt`+`S`

3. Click **Save Selection** .... `S`

4. Click in the **Name** box and type a name for the selection .... `Alt`+`N`

5. Click **OK** .... `Enter`

Load a Selection

1. Click **Select** .... `Alt`+`S`

2. Click **Load Selection** .... `L`

3. Click in the **Channel** box arrow and click on the desired selection .... `Alt`+`C`

4. Select an operation option for the loaded selection:

   • **New Selection**........................... `Alt`+`N`

   • **Add to Selection**...................... `Alt`+`A`

   • **Subtract from Selection**............ `Alt`+`S`

   • **Intersect with Selection**............ `Alt`+`I`

5. Click **OK** .... `Enter`

Undo Change or Command (Ctrl+Z)

Immediately after making change to undo:

1. Click **Edit**... `Alt`+`E`

2. Click **Undo (action name)** .... `U`

Redo Change or Command (Ctrl+Z)

Immediately after undoing a change:

1. Click **Edit**... `Alt`+`E`

2. Click **Redo (action name)**.

Step Backward (Undo) from One or More Changes or Commands (Alt+Ctrl+Z)

1. Click **Edit** .... `Alt`+`E`

2. Click **Step Ba̲ckward** .... `K`

3. Repeat step 2 as needed to undo more than one change or command.

Step Forward (Redo) from One or More Changes or Commands (Shift+Ctrl+Z)

1. Click **Edit** .... `Alt`+`E`

2. Click **Step For̲ward** .... `W`

3. Repeat step 2 as needed to undo more than one change or command.

Use History to Undo Specific Change

1. Click the **History** tab in the Layers palette.

2. Scroll to desired change or command to undo.

3. Right-click on the change or command to undo.

4. Click **Delete**.

5. Click **Yes** to finalize the undo action....... `Enter`

Exercise 6

You select some of the content in an image to make changes to that content. This exercise examines a few of the basic changes you may want to make to a selection. First and foremost, you'll practice how to delete, move, or copy a selection. You'll see how to transform or rotate a selection, or make changes to the selection marquee. You'll also work with various methods for undoing changes, including a simple undo, backing up, and using the History palette.

Directions

1. Start Photoshop, if needed.

2. Use the File|Open command to open the ⊙ **PS06** Photoshop file. Zoom the image if needed.

3. Use the selection tool of your choice to select the castle tower area in the picture.

4. Select the Move tool on the toolbox.

5. Drag the selection to a new location, as shown in Illustration 1.

6. Choose Edit|Clear to delete the selection.
   - ✓ *You also can press the Delete key to clear the selection.*

7. Undo the deletion.
   - ✓ *You can use the Edit|Undo (Action) command or press Ctrl+Z to undo your most recent change.*

8. Choose Edit|Step Backward. This undoes your next-most-recent action, moving the selection.

9. Choose Edit|Copy to copy the selection.

10. Use the File|New command to create a new file. Enter **CTOP** as the Name for the new file then click OK to create it without changing any other settings.

✓   *When you copy a selection and then create a new file, the New dialog box suggests a file size identical to the width and height of the area you copied. So, the new file will always be able to display all of the material that was copied.*

11.   Choose Edit|Paste to paste the copied information into the new file.

✓   *By default, Photoshop created a new layer when you pasted the copied image information. That layer will be selected by default, so you can just continue working as described here. Chapter 8 will give you more practice with using layers.*

12.   Switch to the **PS06** file and close it without saving changes.

13.   Use the Polygonal Lasso tool to select the triangular roof of the castle tower.

✓   *You right-click on the Lasso tool to find the Polygonal Lasso tool. The Polygonal Lasso tool works like the Lasso tool, except it uses straight lines only. Click at each corner point, then click on the starting point to close the selection marquee loop.*

14.   Choose Edit|Transform|Distort.

15.   Drag the top middle selection handle to make the castle roof taller, as shown in Illustration 2.

16.   Click on the Commit button (✓) at the right end of the options bar to finish the change.

17.   Use the Edit|Transform|Rotate command, drag a handle, and click on Commit to rotate the selection.

18.   Use the Select|Modify|Border command to increase the selection marquee border width to 15 pixels.

19.   Select the History tab in the Layers palette.

20.   Scroll down the list of changes on the palette, if needed, then delete the last two changes from the list.

✓   *To delete a change, right-click on it, then click on Delete. Click on Yes in the dialog box that appears to confirm the deletion. Note that if you delete a change that's not the bottom (last or most recent) in the list, all changes below it in the list will be deleted as well.*

21.   Use the Select|Save Selection command to save the selection with the name **Roof**.

✓   *You may have to reselect the roof first.*

22.   Use Select|Deselect to remove the selection.

23.   Use the Select|Load Selection command to reapply the Roof selection.

✓   *Use the Channel drop-down list in the Load Selection dialog box to find your selection.*

24.   Save the file with the name **CTOP**, then close the file.

Illustration 1

Illustration 2

Next
Chapter
▶▶

7

Using Positioning Tools

Photoshop provides more precision editing tools than perhaps any other graphics program. Now that you know how to select and move image content, you may want to try out tools that you can use to align selections perfectly. Before you start making many moves in your image files, review this chapter to learn the following skills:

✳ Displaying a grid you can use for alignment

✳ Displaying rulers you can use for alignment

✳ Snapping a selection to a guide or grid

✳ Adding custom alignment guides and locking them in place

Showing and Hiding the Grid

You can display nonprinting gridlines in the current image window and then use those gridlines to help you align selections in the image. You can show and hide the grid as needed, turning it on to position selections and turning it back off when you want to assess the image's background or overall appearance.

Note: See the "Guides & Grid" section in Appendix B to learn about setting grid preferences.

1. Click on **View**. The View menu will appear.

2. Point to **Show**. The Show submenu will appear.

3. Click on **Grid**. The gridlines will appear immediately in the current image file.

4. Make a selection and use the **Move** tool to align it. The selection will be better aligned with a gridline.

Note: If the selection "jumps around" and won't align as you think it should, the Snap To feature might be active. This feature is discussed in "Using Snap and Snap To" in this chapter.

5. Click on **View**. The View menu will appear.

6. Point to **Show**. The Show submenu will appear.

7. Click on **Grid**. The gridlines will disappear immediately from the current image file.

Showing and Hiding Rulers

The rulers come in handy when you need to position selections (such as a logo inserted on a new layer) at a precise location within the image. Turn on the rulers when you need to position selections based on measurements, and turn them back off when you no longer need them.

1. Click on **View**. The View menu will appear.

2. Click on **Show Rulers**. The rulers will appear immediately in the current image window.

   Note: The vertical ruler appears along the left side of the image window, and the horizontal ruler appears across the top of the ruler.

3. Make a selection and use the **Move** tool to align it; watch the dotted gray lines on the rulers to judge position as you drag. The selection will drop into the specified location when you finish dragging.

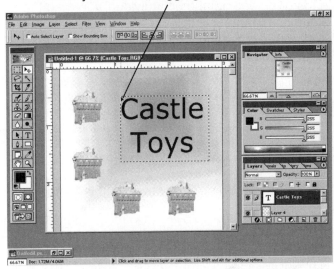

   Tip: Make your selection tight to the object, then drag by a corner for very precise positioning.

4. Click on **View**. The View menu will appear.

5. Click on **Hide Rulers**. The rulers will disappear from the image window.

Using Snap and Snap To

The snap to feature in Photoshop ensures that a selection aligns to the grid or the custom guides that you add as you drag. You can turn snapping to grids or guides off and on individually, or use the Snap command to toggle on and off all snapping. By default, snapping to both the grid and guidelines is turned on in Photoshop.

Note: *The grid must be displayed to enable the command for turning on or off snapping to the grid. In contrast, the command for turning on or off snapping to guidelines is available whether or not you've added guidelines into the image file, as described in the next section.*

1. Click on **View**. The View menu will appear.

2. Point to **Snap To**. The Snap To submenu will appear.

3. Click on **Guides** or **Grid**. The check beside the feature you clicked will be removed, and the selected snap to feature will no longer be active. The next time you move a selection, it will not snap into position.

   Note: *Turning off snapping can help when you need position selections relative to one another rather than relative to a grid.*

4. Click on **View**. The View menu will appear.

5. Point to **Snap To**. The Snap To submenu will appear.

6. Click on **Guides** or **Grid**. A check will appear beside the feature you clicked, and the selected snap to feature will become active again. The next time you move a selection, it will snap into position.

7. Click on **View**. The View menu will appear.

8. Click on **Snap**. The check beside the Snap command will be removed, and all snapping will no longer be active. The next time you move a selection, it will not snap into position.

9. Click on **View**. The View menu will appear.

10. Click on **Snap**. The check beside the Snap command will be reappear, and all snapping will become active again. The next time you move a selection, it will snap into position.

Adding Guides

Guides in a sense serve as custom gridlines. You put a guideline into position so that you can align selections to it. Ideally, you would add a guideline in a location where no gridline occurs or use guidelines rather than the grid. Also, because guidelines appear in blue, you can add a guideline to highlight an important grid location.

Tip: *You don't have to display the rulers to add guidelines; if you do, however, you can use a ruler to add a guideline more quickly—as one of the techniques the steps here demonstrates.*

1. Click on **View**. The View menu will appear.

2. Click on **New Guide**. The New Guide dialog box will open.

3. Click on an Orientation option. Photoshop will use the specified type of guide.

4. Select the **Position** text box contents, and type a new entry. Photoshop will use the specified position for the guide.

Tip: *If you include in (for inches) with the Position entry, Photoshop uses inches of measure for positioning the guideline. If you don't include a measurement abbreviation (you also can use cm for centimeters and pt for points), Photoshop by defaults assumes you're entering a measurement in pixels (px).*

5. Click on **OK**. The guideline will appear at the position you specified.

6. Drag from a Ruler. Another guideline will appear where you released the mouse button.

Tip: *Press and hold Shift as you drag to have the guideline snap to successive increments on the applicable ruler.*

7. Click on the **Move** tool in the Photoshop toolbox. The Move tool will become active.

8. Drag a guideline. The guideline moves to a new location.

9. Click on **View**. The View menu will appear.

10. Click on **Clear Guides**. Photoshop will immediately delete all the guidelines you've added.

Locking Guides

You can lock guides to prevent any accidental guideline changes. (For example, you could mistakenly move a guideline rather than the selection, especially when the selection falls very close to the guideline.) When you need to change guidelines, unlock them first.

Note: *Locking guidelines doesn't prevent you from clearing them. If you unintentionally clear guidelines, immediately undo the change.*

1. Click on **View**. The View menu will appear.

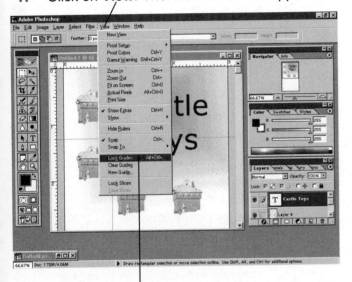

2. Click on **Lock Guides**. Photoshop will immediately lock the guides into position. A check mark will appear beside the Lock Guides command on the menu.

3. Click on **View**. The View menu will appear.

4. Click on **Lock Guides**. Photoshop will immediately unlock the guides and remove the check mark beside the Lock Guides command.

Procedures

Show Gridlines (Alt+Ctrl+')

1. Click **View**.................................... `Alt`+`V`
2. Click **Show** .... `H`
3. Click **Grid** to select the gridlines................ `G`

Hide Gridlines (Alt+Ctrl+')

1. Click **View**.................................... `Alt`+`V`
2. Click **Show** .... `H`
3. Click **Grid** to deselect the gridlines............ `G`

Show Rulers (Ctrl+R)

1. Click **View**.................................... `Alt`+`V`
2. Click **Show Rulers** .... `R`

Hide Rulers (Ctrl+R)

1. Click **View**.................................... `Alt`+`V`
2. Click **Hide Rulers** .... `R`

Use Snap To

1. Click **View**.................................... `Alt`+`V`
2. Click **Snap To**.................................... `T`
3. Click **Guides**.................................... `G`

   OR

   Click **Grid** .... `R`
   ✓ *Guides and gridlines can also be selected at one time.*

Turn On Snap (Ctrl+;)

1. Click **View**.................................... `Alt`+`V`
2. Click **Snap** to select snapping.................. `S`

Turn Off Snap (Ctrl+;)

1. Click **View**.................................... `Alt`+`V`
2. Click **Snap** to deselect snapping.............. `S`

Add Guides

1. Click **View**.................................... `Alt`+`V`
2. Click **New Guide**.................................... `E`
3. Click the **Horizontal** orientation option button.................................... `Alt`+`H`

   OR

   Click the **Vertical** orientation option button.................................... `Alt`+`V`
4. Click in the **Position** box and enter a measurement and measurement abbreviation if necessary (**in** for inches; **pt** for points; **cm** for centimeters; **px** for pixels) .... `Alt`+`P`
   ✓ *If no abbreviation is entered, the measurement is in pixels by default.*
5. Click **OK** .... `Enter`

Add Guides from Ruler

1. Click anywhere on the desired ruler and hold down the mouse button.
2. Drag the guide to the desired position.
   ✓ *Press `Shift` to have guideline snap to successive increments on the applicable ruler.*
3. Release mouse button to finalize the guide.

Move Guidelines

1. Click the **Move Tool** button `[▶⊕]` .... `V`
2. Drag the guide to a new position.

Clear Guides

1. Click **View** .... Alt + V

2. Click **Clear Guides** .... S

Lock Guides (Alt+Ctrl+;)

1. Click **View** .... Alt + V

2. Click **Lock Guides** .... K

Exercise

As noted in the last exercise, Photoshop provides many tools enabling you to have control over the smallest details in the images you create and edit. You've now practiced moving a selection to a random location in an image, but what if you need more control over the position of selections in an image? You can use a variety of Photoshop features to help you achieve precise vertical and horizontal alignment for elements in your composition. This exercise examines how you can use gridlines, rulers, and guides to identify the proper position for your selections. You also see here how to use the snap to feature to ensure precision alignment.

Directions

1. Start Photoshop, if needed.

2. Use the File|Open command to open the ⊙ **PS07** Photoshop file.

3. Save the file as **CTOY**.

4. Choose View|Show|Grid. Gridlines appear on the image.

   ✓ By default, solid gridlines appear one inch apart, with four subdivisions (a dotted gridline each quarter inch). You can choose Edit|Preferences|Guides & Grid to adjust the grid distance and appearance.

5. Select the castle graphics on the left and position them as shown in Illustration 1.

   ✓ If you're having trouble positioning the castle selections, that's because the snap to feature may be interfering. The snap to feature tries to force the edges of the selection marquee to align to a gridline. You can choose View|Snap to turn the snap to feature off (or back on) as needed.

6. Choose View|Show|Grid to turn off the gridlines.

7. Choose View|Show Rulers if they are not already displayed. A vertical ruler appears along the left edge of the ruler, and a horizontal ruler appears across the top of the image.

8. Move the pointer around the image. Notice how a dashed marker line on each ruler indicates the current mouse position.

9. Select each of the castles you didn't move previously. Move one to a position so that the peak of the roof is at 1 ¾" on the horizontal ruler and 2 ¾" on the vertical ruler. Move the other so that the peak of the roof is at 3" on the horizontal ruler and 2 ¾" on the vertical ruler. Illustration 2 shows how this should look.

   ✓ To make your positioning so precise, position the mouse on the peak of the roof as you drag the selection, and view the marker lines on the rulers as you drag.

10. Drag down from the top ruler to create a guide, and drop it into place at the 2" mark on the vertical ruler.

11. Open the View menu and make sure that the Snap command is checked. If it isn't, click on Snap to turn the snap to feature back on.

12. Select the text in the image.

13. Use the Move tool to position the text so that the base of the letters in the word "Toys" rests on the 2" guideline as shown in Illustration 3.

    ✓ *The tail of the y, which hangs below the baseline, is called a descender in type lingo.*

14. Save and close the file.

Illustration 1

Illustration 2

Illustration 3

Part II Review Questions

1. How do you select a tool? *See "Selecting a Tool" in Chapter 3.*

2. What is the difference between painting tools and drawing tools? *See "Working with Painting Tools" and "Working with Drawing Tools" in Chapter 3.*

3. What's a fast way to change the portion of the image that appears in the window? *See "Using the Hand Tool" and "Using the Navigator" in Chapter 4.*

4. What can you select with the Marquee tool? *See "Using the Marquee Tools" in Chapter 5.*

5. What different selections does the Lasso tool offer? *See "Using the Lasso Tool" in Chapter 5.*

6. How do you deselect a selection? *See "Removing a Selection" in Chapter 5.*

7. How do delete selected image content? *See "Deleting a Selection" in Chapter 6.*

8. Can you reuse a selection? *See "Saving a Selection" and "Loading a Selection" in Chapter 6.*

9. What if I need to undo a change? *See "Undoing a Change" and "Using the History to Undo Changes" in Chapter 6.*

10. Can Photoshop align selections that I move? *See "Using Snap and Snap To" in Chapter 7.*

8

Working with Layers

The ability to create content on layers has long set Photoshop apart from other programs with paint capabilities. Creating content on separate layers enables you to retain control of the placement and effects for various individual elements in an image. (If you simply created objects on one layer in Photoshop, they would "blend" together.) By using transparency on the various layers and positioning objects carefully, you can create interesting and complex compositions while keeping your options for making changes later open. In this chapter, you'll learn how to:

✳ Use various methods to create a layer

✳ Select layers

✳ Change layer settings

✳ Arrange layers

✳ Merge layers to flatten the image

Creating a Layer

Every image file by default has one special layer called the *background layer*. An image can have more layers than your computer's memory can probably handle—up to 8,000. Some actions, such as adding text, create a new layer automatically. In other instances, you may need to create a layer manually before adding elements into it. This section explains how to do this.

Note: *When you create a new image, it sometimes helps to click on the Transparent option in the New dialog box. This ensures that a white background won't hide other layers you may add.*

Making a New Layer

The simplest way to create a new layer is to simply add a new, blank layer.

1. Click on **Layer**. The Layer menu will appear.

2. Point to **New**. The New submenu will appear.

3. Click on **Layer**. The New Layer dialog box will open.

   Tip: *A layer set organizes layers, much as a folder organizes files on a hard disk. Click on Layer, point to New, then click on Layer Set to create a layer set.*

4. Type a name for the layer into the **Name** text box. The specified name will be used for the layer.

5. Click on a choice from the **Color** and **Mode** lists, if needed. Making a color choice will apply a color to the new layer's listing in the Layers palette. Making a Mode choice will apply a layer blending mode, which controls how the individual pixels on the layer blend with pixels on other layers.

   Tip: *Some blending modes enable the Fill with... check box. You can click on it to check it and apply the applicable neutral color.*

6. Type a new entry into the **Opacity** text box, if needed, or click on its arrow and then drag the slider for the setting. Photoshop will make the layer's contents more transparent.

7. Click on **OK**. Photoshop will close the New Layer dialog box and create the new layer, which will appear in the Layers palette.

Selecting a Layer

Selecting a layer makes it the current or active layer, so that the changes you make next will apply to the layer. You use the Layers palette to select a layer, as shown here.

● Click on the layer name in the Layers palette. The layer will appear selected in the Layers palette, making it the active layer.

Note: *You can hide a layer's contents by clicking on the Visibility button (eye icon) to the left of the layer name in the Layers palette. The layer's content disappears immediately. Click on the box where the Visibility button previously appeared to redisplay the layer.*

Duplicating a Layer

When a layer has content that you'd like to reuse, you can duplicate the layer in the image file. Then, you can position the layer content or add different effects independently.

1. Select the desired layer. The layer name appears selected in the Layers palette.

2. Click on **Layer**. The Layer menu will appear.

3. Click on **Duplicate Layer**. The Duplicate Layer dialog box will open.

4. Type a name for the layer into the As text box. The specified name will be used for the layer.

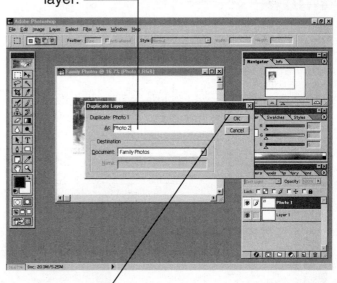

5. Click on **OK**. Photoshop will close the Duplicate Layer dialog box and create the new layer, which will appear in the Layers palette.

Note: *You can create a new image file by duplicating a layer. To do so, click on the down arrow beside the Document choice, then click on New. Type a name for the new file in the Name text box, then click on OK.*

Copying a Layer between Images

When a layer has content that you'd like to reuse, you can make a copy of the layer and paste it into another image file.

1. Open or create the image file to which you want to copy the layer. The image window appears in Photoshop.

2. Open the image file that has the layer to copy. The image window appears in Photoshop.

   Note: *Make sure you position the image windows so that you'll be able to drag and drop between them. This means that you need to be able to see at least part of the image window for the image you opened in Step 1.*

3. Click and drag the layer from the Layers palette.

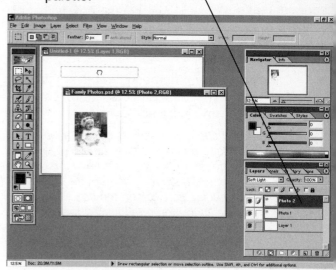

4. Drop the layer on the window for the file into which you want to copy the layer. The new layer appears immediately in the destination image.

   Note: *When the image files use different resolutions, the contents of the copied layer may appear larger or smaller. In such a case, you can select layer content and transform it to another scale or shape, as described in Chapter 6. If the layer contents simply appear in the wrong location, use the Move tool on the toolbox to move the layer.*

Adding a Fill Layer

You can add a fill layer to color the entire image background. This technique is preferred over drawing a colored box on a layer, which can leave a white edge around the image.

1. Click on **Layer**. The Layer menu will appear.

2. Point to **New Fill Layer**. The New Fill Layer submenu will appear.

3. Click on **Solid Color**. The New Layer dialog box will open.

4. Type a name for the layer into the **Name** text box. The specified name will be used for the layer.

5. Make a choice from the **Color** and **Mode** lists, if needed. Making a color choice will apply a color to the new layer's listing in the Layers palette. Making a Mode choice will

apply a layer blending mode, which controls how the individual pixels on the layer blend with pixels on other layers.

6. Type a new entry into the **Opacity** text box, if needed, or click on its arrow and then drag the slider for the setting. Photoshop will make the layer's contents more transparent.

7. Click on **OK**. Photoshop will close the New Layer dialog box and open the Color Picker dialog box.

8. Click on a color in the narrow band of colors near the middle of the dialog box. Photoshop will display a different range of colors in the Pick a solid color box.

9. Click on a color in the Pick a solid color box. The color you click on will become the active color.

10. Click on **OK**. Photoshop will close the Color Picker dialog box and create the new fill layer. Its name will appear in the Layers palette. ─────

Tip: *You can change the type of fill for a layer after you create it. To do so, first select the layer. Then click Layer|New Fill Layer and select Solid Color, Gradient, or Pattern.*

Adding a Gradient Layer

A gradient layer blends one or more colors, for another interesting background effect.

1. Click on the foreground color for the gradient on the color bar in the Color palette. The selected color will become the foreground color (first color) for the blend.

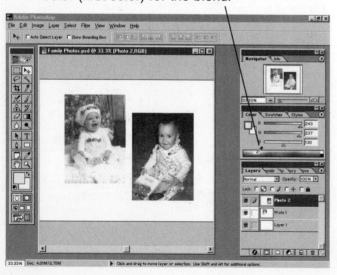

2. Click on **Layer**. The Layer menu will appear.

3. Point to **New Fill Layer**. The New Fill Layer submenu will appear. ──────

4. Click on **Gradient**. The New Layer dialog box will open.

5. Type a name for the layer into the **Name** text box. The specified name will be used for the layer. ──────

6. Make a choice from the **Color** and **Mode** lists, if needed. Making a color choice will apply a color to the new layer's listing in the Layers palette. Making a Mode choice will apply a layer blending mode, which controls how the individual pixels on the layer blend with pixels on other layers.

7.	Type a new entry into the Opacity text box, if needed, or click on its arrow and then drag the slider for the setting. Photoshop will make the layer's contents more transparent.

8.	Click on **OK**. Photoshop will close the New Layer dialog box and open the Gradient Fill dialog box.

9.	Click on the down arrow beside the **Style** box, then click on a gradient style. Photoshop will apply the selected style.

Note: *If needed, click on the down arrow beside the Gradient box, and then click on a new gradient to use. Photoshop will apply the selected gradient and its colors. If you click on the Gradient box itself, the Gradient Editor dialog box opens. You can use it to edit the gradient style, or click on the arrow button at the top right of the Presets section of the dialog box and then click on a choice at the bottom of the submenu that appears to see other gradient possibilities.*

10a.	Type a new entry into the **Angle** text box, if needed. Photoshop will adjust the gradient to the specified angle.

OR

10b.	Drag the bar in the Angle circle. Photoshop will adjust the gradient to the specified angle.

11.	Type a new entry into the **Scale** text box, if needed, or click on its arrow and then drag the slider for the setting. Photoshop will adjust the proportion of dark to light (or various colors) in the gradient.

12.	Click on **OK**. Photoshop will close the Gradient Fill dialog box and create the new fill layer. Its name will appear in the Layers palette.

Note: *If your gradient layer appears on top of the other layers in the image and covers the objects from those layers, don't panic. See the later section called "Arranging Layer Order" to learn how to fix the problem.*

Adding a Pattern Layer

You can fill a layer with a pattern, but you first must create the pattern. To do so, you make a selection from another image and load it as the pattern, as described here.

1. Open or create the image file that holds the area to use as the pattern. The image appears in its own window.

2. Select the area to use as a pattern using the selection tool of your choice. The selection marquee will appear.

3. Click on **Edit**. The Edit menu will appear.

4. Click on **Define Pattern**. The Define Pattern dialog box will appear.

5. Type a name for the pattern in the Name text box. Photoshop will use the name you specify to identify the pattern.

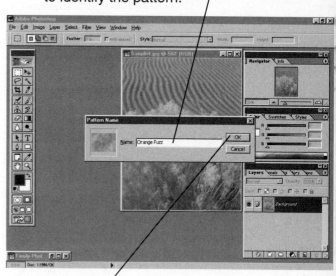

6. Click on **OK**. The Define Pattern dialog box will close.

   Note: *You can close the file from which you created the pattern at this point, if you want.*

7. Open or create the image file into which you want to add a pattern layer. The image appears in its own window.

8. Click on **Layer**. The Layer menu will appear.

9. Point to **New Fill Layer**. The New Fill Layer submenu will appear.

10. Click on **Pattern**. The New Layer dialog box will open.

11. Type a name for the layer into the **Name** text box. The specified name will be used for the layer.

12. Make a choice from the **Color** and **Mode** lists, if needed. Making a color choice will apply a color to the new layer's listing in the Layers palette. Making a Mode choice will apply a layer blending mode, which controls how the individual pixels on the layer blend with pixels on other layers.

13. Type a new entry into the **Opacity** text box, if needed, or click on its arrow and then drag the slider for the setting. Photoshop will make the layer's contents more transparent.

14. Click on **OK**. Photoshop will close the New Layer dialog box and open the Pattern Fill dialog box.

15. If needed, click on the down arrow beside the Pattern Picker box, then click on another pattern in the palette that appears; click on the down arrow again to close the palette. Photoshop will apply the selected pattern.

16. Type a new entry into the **Scale** text box. Photoshop will adjust the size of the repeated pattern section accordingly.

17. Click on **OK**. Photoshop will close the Pattern Fill dialog box and create the new fill layer. Its name will appear in the Layers palette.

117

Deleting a Layer

When you want to remove a layer from the image, it's fastest to use the Layers palette, as detailed here.

1.   Right-click on the desired layer in the Layers palette. A shortcut menu will appear.

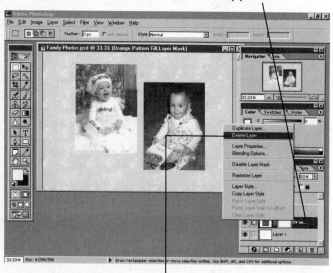

2.   Click on **Delete Layer**. A warning message box will open.

     Note: Be sure to right-click on the layer name, not the layer or mask thumbnail in the Layers palette. Otherwise, you may see a different shortcut menu.

3.   Click on **Yes**. Photoshop will complete the deletion.

Note: Be sure to right-click to the right of the layer name in the Layers palette to display the proper shortcut menu. If you select a layer in the Layers palette, you also can use the Delete Layer command on the Layer menu to delete it.

Setting Layer Properties

The layer properties include the layer's name and the color used to identify the layer in the Layers palette. You can change either of these settings as needed.

1.   Right-click on the desired layer in the Layers palette. A shortcut menu will appear.

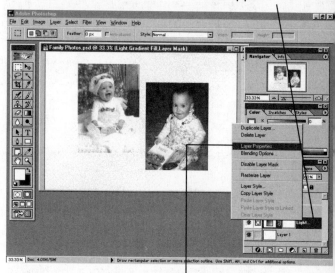

2.   Click on **Layer Properties**. The Layer Properties dialog box will open.

3. Change Name and Color settings as needed. Photoshop will display the changes.

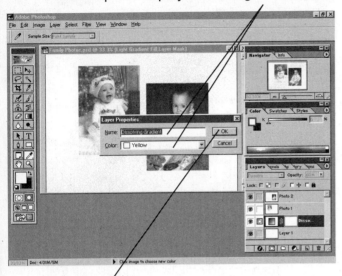

4. Click on **OK**. Photoshop will apply the changes.

Choosing a Layer Style

The layer style consists of some of the settings you made when creating the layer, such as its opacity and blend mode. The style also includes special effects you might want to add to the layer's contents.

1. Right-click on the desired layer in the Layers palette. A shortcut menu will appear.

2. Click on **Blending Options**. The Layer Style dialog box will open.

Note: You can change the style for any layer, not just fill layers. The style (effect) you choose applies to the layer contents, whether those contents include text, objects you've drawn, or scanned photos.

3. Click on a style in the Styles list.

4. Change Blending Options as needed. The Preview will change to show the impact of your changes.

5. Click on **OK**. Photoshop will close the Layer Style dialog box and apply the changes. The Layers palette will show the effects applied to the layer.

Tip: You also can click on a layer, then click on the Add a Layer Style button in the bottom-left corner of the Layers palette to add a style (effect) without changing other layer settings

Arranging Layer Order

You need to arrange layers to control how the various layer contents relate to one another and which portions of one layer might hide areas on another layer.

Note: *If the image content is on the Background layer, you can't arrange it relative to any other layers in the image (especially if there's only one other layer in the image). You can double-click on the Background layer in the Layers palette, change settings in the New Layer dialog box as desired, and then click on OK to convert the Background layer to a regular layer.*

1. Click on the desired layer in the Layers palette. Photoshop will select the layer.

2. Click on **Layer**. The Layer menu will appear.

3. Point to **Arrange**. The Arrange submenu will appear.

4. Click on an arrangement choice. For example, you might want to click on **Send to Back** to send a fill layer all the way to the back. Photoshop will apply the new layer position immediately.

Tip: *Press and hold Ctrl then click a layer in the Layers palette to select the layer contents.*

Grouping and Ungrouping Layers

You group layers by creating a layer set, then dragging the layers into and out of the set on the Layers palette.

1. Click on **Layer**. The Layer menu will appear.

2. Point to **New**. The New submenu will appear.

3. Click on **Layer Set**. The Layer Set dialog box will appear.

4. Type a name for the set into the **Name** text box. The specified name will be used for the set.

5. Make a choice from the Color and Mode lists, if needed. Making a color choice will apply a color to the new set's listing in the Layers palette. Making a Mode choice will apply a blending mode, which controls how the individual pixels on the layers in the set blend with pixels on other layers in the set.

6. Type a new entry into the Opacity text box, if needed, or click on its arrow and then drag the slider for the setting. Photoshop will make the set's contents more transparent.

7. Click on **OK**. Photoshop will close the New Layer dialog box and create the new layer, which will appear in the Layers palette.

8. Drag and drop a layer name onto the set name in the Layers palette. The layer will be added into the set.

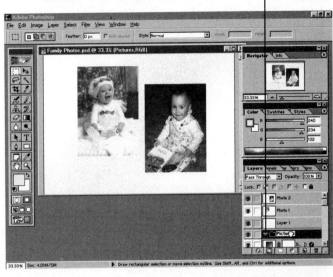

Note: *To remove a layer from the set, drag it back off the set and drop it elsewhere in the list on the Layers palette.*

Flattening the Image

Flattening the image combines all the layer contents on a single layer, which can make the file size more compact. Use this process only if you're finished editing your image, and undo the action immediately if you've done it by mistake.

1. Click on **Layer**. The Layer menu will appear.

2. Click on **Flatten Image**. Photoshop immediately combines the contents of all the layers onto a single layer.

    Note: Click on Edit, then click on Undo Flatten Image (or press Ctrl+Z) to separate the image back into layers. Alternatively, use the History palette to undo the Flatten Image command.

Procedures

Create a New Layer (Shift+Ctrl+N)

1. Click **Layer** .... Alt + L

2. Click **New** .... N

3. Click **Layer** L

4. In the **Name** box, type a name .... Alt + N

5. Select the desired layer options:
    a. Click the **Color** arrow and select a color from the drop-down list.

✓ *This color is used to identify the new layer in Layers palette. If you don't need a color to identify the new layer, chose None.*

b. Click the **Mode** arrow and select the desired mode.

c. Click in **Opacity** and enter the desired opacity percentage.

    OR

    Click the **Opacity** arrow and drag the slider to the desired opacity percentage.

6. Click **OK** .... Enter

Select a Layer

- In the Layers palette, click on the layer's name or thumbnail.

Hide a Layer's Content

- In the Layers palette, click on the **Layer visibility** button 👁 to the left of the layer's thumbnail and name to deselect it.
  - ✓ *To show a hidden layer, click the "eyeless" Layer visibility button.*

Duplicate a Layer

1. Click **Layer**..................................... Alt + L
2. Click **Duplicate Layer** .... D
3. In the **As** box, type a name for the layer .... Alt + A
4. Click **OK**..................................... Enter

Copy a Layer Between Images

1. Open or create the image to which the layer will be copied (the destination image).
2. Open the image file that contains the layer to be copied (the source image).
3. Drag the desired layer from the Layers palette of the source image to the destination image window.
   - ✓ *The mouse pointer becomes a hand with the outline of the copied layer.*
4. Release the mouse button to finish copying the layer.

Add a Fill Layer

1. Click **Layer**... Alt + L
2. Click **New Fill Layer** .... R
3. Click **Solid Color** .... O
4. In the **Name** box, type a name............ Alt + N
5. Select the desired layer options:

   a. Click the **Color** arrow and select a color from the drop-down list.
      - ✓ *This color is used to identify the new layer in Layers palette. For example, choose Green to identify a color that will be chosen in the Color Picker dialog box (step 7 below) that is mostly green.*

   b. Click the **Mode** arrow and select the desired mode.

   c. Click in **Opacity** and enter the desired opacity percentage.

      OR

      Click the **Opacity** arrow and drag the slider to the desired opacity percentage.

6. Click **OK** .... Enter

7. Select a color in the Color Picker dialog box.
   - ✓ *See Chapter 3 for the procedure to choose a color in the Color Picker dialog box.*

8. Click **OK** .... Enter

Add a Gradient Layer

1. Select a foreground color.
   - ✓ *See Chapter 3 for the procedure to choose a foreground color in the Color palette or with the Eyedropper tool.*

2. Click **Layer** .... Alt + L
3. Click **New Fill Layer**................................. R
4. Click **Gradient** .... G
5. In the **Name** box, type a name .... Alt + N
6. Select the desired layer options:

   a. Click the **Color** arrow and select a color from the drop-down list.
      - ✓ *This color is used to identify the new layer in Layers palette.*

   b. Click the **Mode** arrow and select the desired mode.

   c. Click in **Opacity** and enter the desired opacity percentage.

      OR

      Click the **Opacity** arrow and drag the slider to the desired opacity percentage.

7. Click **OK** .... `Enter`

8. Select the desired options in the Gradient Fill dialog box:

    a. Click on the **Gradient** box arrow and select a preset gradient.

        OR

        Click in the **Gradient** box, create a custom gradient in the Gradient Editor dialog box, and click **OK**.

    b. Click the **Style** box arrow and select a gradient style from the drop-down list.

    c. Click in the **Angle** box and type angle degrees .... `A`

        OR

        Drag the bar in **Angle** circle to adjust the angle.

    d. In the **Scale** box, type a percentage ..... `S`

        OR

        Click the **Scale** box arrow and drag the slider to the desired percentage.

    e. Click the **Reverse** checkbox to reverse the fill direction .... `R`

    f. Click the **Dither** checkbox to select a dithered fill .... `D`

9. Click **OK** .... `Enter`

Create a Pattern Layer

1. Open or create the image that holds the area to use as the pattern.

2. Select the area to use as a pattern.

3. Click **Edit** .... `Alt`+`E`

4. Click **Define Pattern** .... `D`

5. In the **Name** box, type a name for the pattern .... `Alt`+`N`

6. Click **OK** .... `Enter`

Add a Pattern Layer

1. Open or create the image in which to add the pattern layer.

2. Click **Layer** .... `Alt`+`L`

3. Click **New Fill Layer** .... `R`

4. Click **Pattern** .... `R`

5. In the **Name** box, type a name .... `Alt`+`N`

6. Select the desired layer options:

    a. Click the **Color** arrow and select a color from the drop-down list.

        ✓   *This color is used to identify the new layer in Layers palette.*

    b. Click the **Mode** arrow and select the desired mode.

    c. Click in **Opacity** and enter the desired opacity percentage.

        OR

        Click the **Opacity** arrow and drag the slider to the desired opacity percentage.

7. Click **OK** .... `Enter`

8. Select the desired options in the Pattern Fill dialog box:

    a. Click on the **Pattern Picker** box arrow and select a pattern.

    b. In the **Scale** box, type a percentage ..... `S`

        OR

        Click the **Scale** box arrow and drag the slider to the desired percentage.

9. Click **OK** .... `Enter`

Delete a Layer

1. Right-click on the layer to delete in the Layers palette.

    ✓   *For best results, right-click in the blue area to the right of any layer icons in the layer's selector.*

    OR

    Click the menu button ⊙ in the Layers palette.

2. Click **Delete Layer**.

3. Click **Yes** .... `Enter`

Change a Layer's Identification Properties

1. Right-click on the layer to change in the Layers palette.

    ✓ *For best results, right-click in the blue area to the right of any layer icons in the layer's selector.*

    OR

    Click the menu button ▶ in the Layers palette.

2. Click **Layer Properties**.

3. Choose the desired setting options:

    a. In the **Name** box, type a new name .... Alt + N

    b. Click the **Color** arrow to select a new color from the drop-down list.

4. Click **OK** .... Enter

Change Layer Blending Options/Style

1. Right-click on the desired layer in the Layers palette.

    ✓ *For best results, right-click in the blue area to the right of any layer icons in the layer's selector.*

    OR

    Click the menu button ▶ in the Layers palette.

2. Click **Blending Options**.

3. Under Styles, select the desired blending option.

4. Under Blending Options, choose the desired blending settings.

5. Click **OK** to finalize the new style settings .... Enter

Arrange Layer Order

1. Select the desired layer in the Layers palette.

2. Click **Layer** .... Alt + L

3. Click **Arrange** .... A

4. Click the desired arrangement:

    a. **Bring to Front (Shift+Ctrl+])** .... F

    b. **Bring Forward (Ctrl+])** .... W

    c. **Send Backward (Ctrl+[)** .... K

    d. **Send to Back (Shift+Ctrl+[)** .... B

    ✓ *Keyboard shortcuts shown in parentheses.*

Group Layer

1. Click **Layer** .... Alt + L

2. Click **New** .... W

3. Click **Layer Set** .... A

4. In the **Name** box, type a layer set name .... Alt + N

5. Select the desired layer set options:

    a. Click the **Color** arrow and select a color from the drop-down list.

    ✓ *This color is used to identify the new layer in Layers palette*

    b. Click the **Mode** arrow and select the desired mode.

    c. Click in **Opacity** and enter the desired opacity percentage.

    OR

    Click the **Opacity** arrow and drag the slider to the desired opacity percentage.

6. Click **OK** .... Enter

7. In the Layers palette drag and drop the desired layers into the layer set.

Ungroup a Layer from a Layer Set

1. In the Layer palette, select the desired layer in the layer set.

2. Drag and drop the layer in the Layers palette outside of the layer set.

Flatten an Image

1. Click **Layer** .... Alt + L

2. Click **Flatten Image** .... F

Exercise 8

Layers immensely increase Photoshop's flexibility. They enable you to separate text, background, and foreground content, preserving your ability to edit separate elements of your image composition. Through layering, you also can control how content overlaps. You learned earlier in the book that adding certain elements to an image, such as adding text, automatically creates a new layer in the image. Even so, Photoshop provides you with total control over the layers in any image, as you'll learn in this exercise. You can add, select, duplicate, copy, and delete layers. You can create special types of layers with fills, gradients, and patterns. You can change a layer's properties and style, and control the order in which layers appear in the image. You also can group layers into a layer set, or remove layers from your image altogether.

Directions

1. Start Photoshop, if needed.

2. Create a new image file with the following settings:

Name	**PHOTOS**
Width	6 inches
Height	4 inches
Resolution	72 pixels/inch
Mode	RGB Color
Contents	White

3. Choose Layer|New|Layer to start adding a new layer.

4. Click on OK in the New Layer dialog box to finish adding the new, blank layer. It appears as Layer 1 in the Layers palette.

5. Right-click on Layer 1 in the Layers palette, click on Delete Layer in the shortcut menu, then click on Yes in the dialog box that appears to confirm the deletion.

6. Open the ☺PS08-1 Photoshop file and drag the file window by its title bar so you can see the window for your blank image behind it.

7. With the **PS08-1** window still selected (active), drag Layer 1 from the Layers palette onto the center of the window for the **PHOTOS** file as shown in Illustration 1, then release the mouse.

    ✓ *If you don't drag to the center of the image, the photo from the copied layer could get cut off. It's best to try to get all the content onto the copied layer. Then, you can select the content on the layer and move it.*

8. Close the **PS08-1** file.

9. Back in the **PHOTOS** file, select the photo on Layer 1 and move it to the left side of the image.

10. Right-click Layer 1 on the Layers palette, click on Duplicate Layer in the shortcut menu, then click on OK in the Duplicate Layer dialog box. (You don't need to enter a name for the new layer in the As dialog box in this example.) The Layer 1 Copy layer will appear in the Layers palette.

11. Click on the Visibility button (eye icon) to the left of Layer 1 in the Layers palette. Layer 1 will be hidden, although that won't be obvious because the layer copy is identical.

12. Select the Layer 1 Copy layer, select the photo on it, and move it to the right side of the image.

13. Click on the Visibility button (eye icon) to the left of Layer 1 in the Layers palette. Layer 1 will reappear, so you'll be able to see the photos on the Layer 1 and Layer 1 Copy layers side by side.

14. Delete the Layer 1 Copy layer.

15. Open the **PS08-2** Photoshop file and drag its Layer 1 into the **PHOTOS** file. The new layer will appear as Layer 2.

16. Close the **PS08-2** file and move the image on Layer 2 of the **PHOTOS** file to the right side of the image. The image should now resemble Illustration 2.

17. Choose Layer|New Fill Layer|Pattern. The New Layer dialog box will appear.

18. Enter **Transparent Fill** in the Name text box, change the Opacity setting to 50%, then click on OK. The Pattern Fill dialog box will appear.

19. Open the palette of patterns by clicking on the drop-down arrow beside the current pattern. Click on the Denim pattern (or the pattern of your choice) to select it, then click on the drop-down list arrow again to close the palette.

20. Click on OK in the Pattern Fill dialog box. The dialog box will close and the new pattern layer will appear.

21. Click on the new layer in the Layers palette if it isn't selected by default.

22. Choose Layer|Arrange|Send to Back. The layer will no longer cover the photos, as shown in Illustration 3.

23. Right-click on the Transparent Fill layer in the Layers palette and choose Layer Properties.

24. Change the layer Name if desired, choose Blue as the Color, then click on OK. The Layers palette will show the new color.

25. Right-click on Layer 1 and click on Blending Options. The Layer Style dialog box will appear.

26. Click on the Inner Glow and Bevel and Emboss check boxes to check them.

27. Click on the Inner Glow style name itself (beside its checkbox). The Inner Glow options will appear to the right, in the dialog box.

28. Drag the Size slider to the right to increase the setting to 20 or 21 px (21 pixels) then click on OK. The glow style will appear around the Layer 1 photo.

29. Apply the same style (Blending Options) settings to Layer 2.

30. In the Layers palette, click on the down arrow beside the layer name for Layer 1 and Layer 2 (beside the *f* icon) to collapse the names of the effects applied to the layer.

31. Choose Layer|Flatten Image. The Layers palette immediately shows that all the layers have been combined onto the Background layer.

32. Save and close the file.

Illustration 1

Illustration 2

Illustration 3

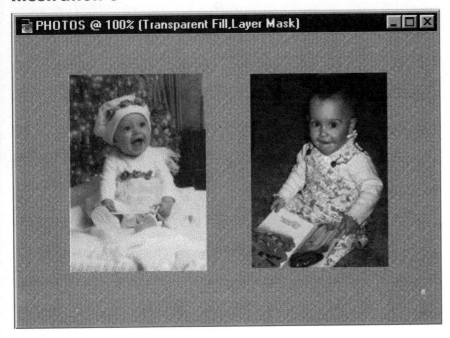

Next Chapter ▶▶

chapter

9
Adding Variety with Masks

If you've ever taped off an area while you're doing a painting project to protect that area from drips and spatters, you've created a mask. In Photoshop, you apply a mask to designate part of an image for changes, but shield (mask) the unselected areas against those changes. In this way, you can apply different effects and filters in varying portions of the image or layer. Read on to see how to:

❋ Set options for a quick mask

❋ Work in Quick Mask mode

❋ Create and use a layer mask

❋ Explore mask examples

Changing Quick Mask Options

Before you change to Quick Mask mode, you can set a few different options that affect how Quick Mask mode behaves.

1. Double-click on the **Edit in Quick Mask Mode** button on the toolbox. The Quick Mask Options dialog box will open.

2. Click on an option in the Color Indicates area. Photoshop will apply the mask color to either the **Masked Areas** or **Selected Areas** in the image, depending on your selection.

3. Click on the **Color** box. The Color Picker dialog box will open.

4. Click on a color in the narrow band of colors near the middle of the dialog box. Photoshop will display a different range of colors in the Pick a Solid Color box.

5. Click on a color in the Select Quick Mask color box. The color you click on will become the active mask color.

6. Click on **OK**. Photoshop will close the Color Picker dialog box and return to the Quick Mask Options dialog box.

7. Type a new entry into the **Opacity** text box, if needed. Photoshop will make the mask color more or less transparent, depending on your entry.

8. Click on **OK**. Photoshop will close the Quick Mask Options dialog box and apply the new settings the next time you use Quick Mask mode.

9. Click on the **Edit in Standard Mode** button on the toolbox. This turns off Quick Mask mode so that you can make a selection.

Using Quick Mask to Adjust a Selection

Quick Mask mode enables you to use a selection on the current layer as a temporary mask. Once you've masked the area, you can make the needed changes to the unmasked area, then turn off Quick Mask mode to remove the mask.

1. Make a selection on the current layer using the selection method of your choice. The selection marquee will appear.

Tip: See the earlier chapter "Selecting Image Content" to refresh your memory about the various selection methods. One trick is to select the area that you don't want to mask, and then click on Select and click on Inverse to select the image areas that previously were not selected. (The figure here shows an inverted selection.)

2. Click on the **Edit in Quick Mask Mode** button on the toolbox. The Quick Mask mode will become active, and the mask color appears over the masked area.

3. Make the desired change to the masked area, using a toolbox tool or filter. The mask boundaries will change accordingly. This example shows the mask with the Sprayed Strokes filter applied and some additional painting to extend the mask.

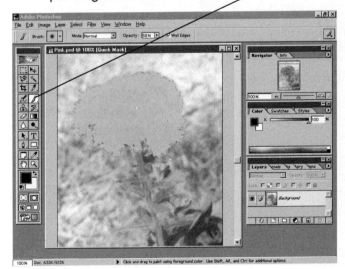

Tip: *Chapter 13, "Using a Filter," explains how to use the Photoshop filters. Applying some filters does affect the unmasked area or the entire layer, depending on the nature of the filter, so you may need to experiment a bit.*

Note: *Paint or draw on the non-masked area with a color other than white to create a semi-transparent masked area. Use white to exclude an area from the mask and black to include the area to the mask (the hidden area).*

4. Click on the **Edit in Standard Mode** button on the toolbox. Photoshop will leave Quick Mask mode and return to the altered selection. You can then apply the needed changes to the selected areas, as described later under "Putting a Mask to Work."

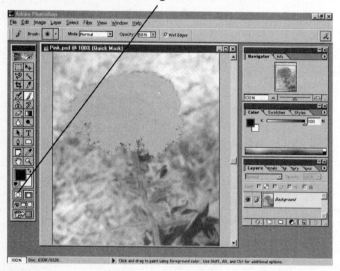

Using Layer Masks

You can add a mask to a particular layer in the image, so that you can hide part of the layer from display or even apply effects only to the area selected by the mask. By adding layer masks to various layers, you can mix and match effects as needed in the image.

Note: *You can't add a layer mask to the background layer, so you may need to add an additional layer such as an adjustment layer or duplicate the background layer and delete the original to work with a layer mask on the background layer content itself.*

Creating a Mask on a Layer

Adding a mask on a layer will have different effects, depending on the layer's contents. For text layers, it enables you select text and apply filters without *rasterizing* the text layer (that is, converting the layer to pixels rather than a vector layer). For layers with small photos, fills, and other objects, the layer mask excludes the information not contained within the mask area, so it doesn't display in the image. For adjustment layers like a Hue/Saturation layer, the mask enables you to adjust the image color only within the areas defined by the mask.

Note: *You also can create a special, color-related type of mask that's called an* alpha channel. *See "Adding an Alpha Channel" in Chapter 16 to learn more.*

1. Click on the layer to which you want to add a mask in the Layers palette. The layer will become the current or active layer.

2. Make a selection on the current layer using the selection method of your choice. The selection marquee will appear.

Note: *When you add certain types of layers, such as gradient fill layers, they automatically include a mask that includes all the layer content. It's often best to delete this mask by right-clicking on the mask thumbnail in the Layers palette, then clicking on Discard Layer Mask. See the later section called "Changing or Trashing a Mask" for more. If you try to add another mask without deleting the first one, Photoshop will add a clipping path instead.*

3. Click on the **Add a mask** button on the bottom of the Layers palette. Photoshop will create the mask immediately.

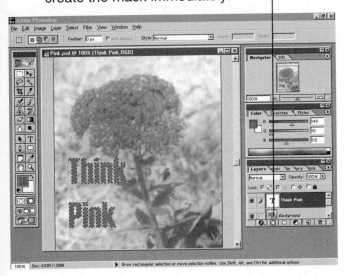

Tip: Press and hold the Alt key as you click to invert the selection in the mask.

4. Review the mask thumbnail in the Layers palette. The black area in the thumbnail will show the zone that the mask hides or excludes.

Changing or Discarding a Mask

The selection on a layer mask isn't permanent once you've made it, so you can adjust the mask at a later time by painting or drawing. You also can delete a mask from a layer altogether.

1. Click on the desired layer in the Layers palette. The layer will become the current or active layer.

2. Click on the mask thumbnail. The mask will become active.

3. Double-click on the **Set Foreground Color** box on the bottom of the toolbox. The Color Picker dialog box will open.

4. Click on the color to use for the mask edits (click on black, white, or gray) in the Select Foreground Color box. The color you select controls the effect of the edits you will make:

- **White** will reveal more of the layer, decreasing the amount of masked off area.

- **Black** will hide more of the layer, increasing the amount of masked off area.

- **Gray** will create a transparent area on the mask, so the area will be partially visible.

Note: *For solid color, gradient, and pattern fill layers, painting with white has no effect, because the entire layer is revealed. Painting with black hides the portion of the fill that you've painted over.*

5. Click on **OK**. The Color Picker dialog box will close, and the color you selected will become active.

6. Select the tool to use in the toolbox. The tool will become the active tool.

7. Set tool options on the options bar. The options you specify will become active.

8. Draw or paint on the layer. The mask will be altered accordingly.

Note: *A fill layer may jump around a bit onscreen as you edit the mask. It should stabilize after you save your changes.*

9. Right-click on the desired thumbnail in the Layers palette. A shortcut menu will appear.

10. Click on **Discard Layer Mask**. Photoshop removes the layer mask immediately.

Using a Selection from One Layer as a Mask on Another

In some instances, the selection that you want to use to define a mask for a layer may appear on another layer instead of the layer where you want to add the mask. For example, if you have a text layer and a gradient layer, you may want to mask out the gradient layer so that the gradient appears only over the text. The steps below illustrate that case while showing you how to use a selection from one layer to create a mask on another.

1. Click on the **Visibility** button (eye icon) beside any layer to hide in the Layers palette. The eye icon will disappear and the layer will become hidden, making it easier for you to select content on another layer.

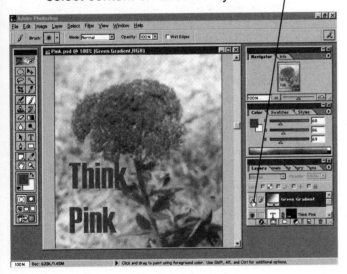

2. Click on the layer with the content to select in the Layers palette. The layer will become the current or active layer.

3. Make a selection on the current layer using the selection method of your choice. The selection marquee will appear.

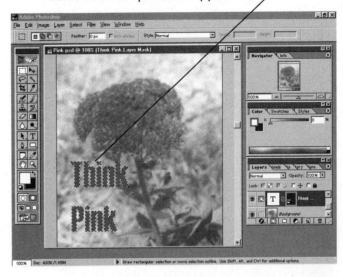

4. Click on the layer to which you want to add the mask in the Layers palette. The layer will become the current or active layer, and it should become visible if you hid it in Step 1.

5. Click on the **Add a mask** button on the bottom of the Layers palette. Photoshop will create the mask immediately.

6. Review the mask thumbnail in the Layers palette. The black area in the thumbnail will show the zone that the mask hides or excludes.

Reviewing the Mask

You can disable and enable a layer mask as needed, so you can see how your image looks with and without the mask applied. The following steps show you the fastest way to control whether or not a mask appears.

1. Right-click on the desired thumbnail in the Layers palette. A shortcut menu will appear.

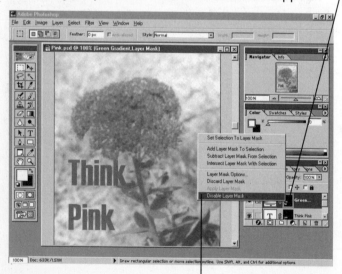

2. Click on **Disable Layer Mask**. Photoshop will disable the mask display immediately and will display a red X through the mask thumbnail.

3. Right-click on the desired thumbnail in the Layers palette. A shortcut menu will appear.

4. Click on **Enable Layer Mask**. Photoshop will reapply the mask immediately, and the image display will be affected accordingly.

Putting a Mask to Work

As noted earlier in this chapter, a layer mask may behave a bit differently or enable you to do different things, depending on the nature of the layer where you added the mask. This section reviews two examples of how you can use layer masks to adjust or enhance selected content in an image.

Crop a Photo

To use this technique, make sure the photo to crop appears on its own layer, not on the background layer.

1. Click on the layer to which you want to add the mask in the Layers palette. The layer will become the current or active layer.

2. Make a selection on the current layer using the selection method of your choice. The selection marquee will appear.

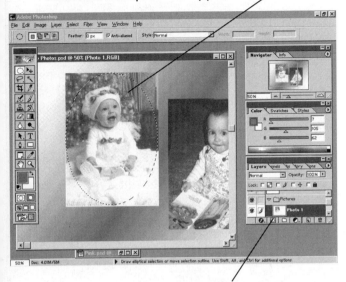

3. Click on the **Add a mask** button on the bottom of the Layers palette. Photoshop will create the mask immediately.

4. Review the mask results in the image. Photoshop will mask out the areas not included within the selection from which you created the mask.

Add a Filter

When you apply a filter, it only affects the currently selected area. Since a mask in effect protects an area like a selection, applying a filter to a layer that has a mask on it filters only the portions of the layer that aren't masked off. This is a particularly vital

technique for text layers; with the mask, Photoshop would prompt you to rasterize the text layer, eliminating your ability to edit the text in the future.

1. Click on the desired layer in the Layers palette. The layer will become the current or active layer.

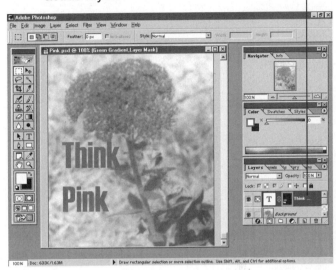

2. Click on **Filter**. The Filter menu will appear.

3. Click on the filter command of your choice. A submenu with specific filter choices will appear.

4. Click on a filter in the submenu. In most cases, a dialog box with options for the filter will appear.

5. Set filter options as needed. A preview in the dialog box will show how the filter will look when applied using the settings you specified.

6. Click on **OK**. The filter settings dialog box will close, and the filter will be applied to the layer contents not hidden or protected by the mask.

7. Review the filter results in the image. Photoshop will display the newly filtered areas.

Recolor Part of the Image

This mask technique works with a special color correction layer (you'll learn more about working with colors in Chapters 15 through 17) called an *adjustment* layer. It enables you to make a color change on part of an image only. This example shows how to make a hue and saturation change, but you can make other changes depending on the nature of the adjustment layer you choose to use.

1. Click on **Layer**. The Layer menu will appear.

2. Click on **New Adjustment Layer**. A submenu with specific layer choices will appear.

3. Click on **Hue/Saturation** in the submenu. The New Layer dialog box will appear.

4. Type a name for the layer into the **Name** text box. The specified name will be used for the layer.

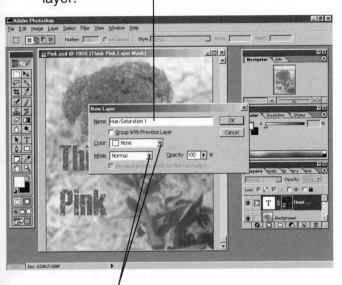

5. Make a choice from the **Color** and **Mode** lists, if needed. Making a color choice will apply a color to the new layer's listing in the Layers palette. Making a Mode choice will apply a layer blending mode, which controls how the individual pixels on the layer blend with pixels on other layers.

6. Type a new entry into the **Opacity** text box, if needed. Photoshop will make the layer's contents more transparent.

7. Click on **OK**. Photoshop will close the New Layer dialog box and open the Hue/Saturation dialog box.

8. Drag the sliders as needed. The image will display the corrected color.

9. Click on **OK**. The Hue/Saturation dialog box will close.

10. Right-click on the thumbnail for the mask for the new hue/saturation layer in the Layers palette. A shortcut menu will appear.

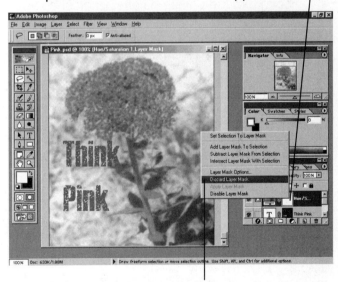

11. Click on **Discard Layer Mask**. Photoshop will remove the layer mask immediately.

12. Make a selection on the layer of your choice using the selection method of your choice. The selection marquee will appear.

13. Click on the **hue/saturation layer** in the Layers palette. It will become the current or active layer.

14. Click on the **Add a mask** button on the bottom of the Layers palette. Photoshop will create the mask immediately.

15. Review the mask results in the image. Photoshop will apply the color correction only to area not blocked by the mask.

Note: If you double-click on the layer thumbnail (to the far left) for the hue/saturation layer, the Hue/Saturation dialog box reopens where you can further adjust the color correction in the areas not blocked by the mask.

Procedures

Change Quick Mask Options

1. Double-click the **Edit Quick Mask Mode** button on the toolbox.

2. Click the desired Color Indicates option:
   a. **Masked Areas** .... Alt + M
   b. **Selected Areas** .... Alt + S

3. Click on the **Color** box.

4. Select the desired color in the Color Picker dialog box.

5. Click **OK** .... Enter

6. Click in **Opacity** and enter the desired opacity percentage.

   OR

   Click the **Opacity** arrow and drag the slider to the desired opacity percentage.

7. Click **OK** .... Enter

   ✓ The settings apply the next time Quick Mask mode is used.

8. Click the **Edit in Standard Mode** button .... Q

Use Quick Mask

1. Make a selection in the image.

2. Click the **Edit Quick Mask Mode** button on the toolbox .... Q

3. Make the desired change to the masked area.

4. Click the **Edit in Standard Mode** button to leave Quick Mask mode .... Q

Create a Layer Mask

1. In the Layers palette, click the layer to be masked.

2. Make a selection in the image.

3. Click the **Add a mask** button ▣ on the Layers palette.

4. A thumbnail of the masked area appears in the Layers palette.

Change Mask

1. In the Layers palette, click the desired layer to be changed.

2. Click the mask thumbnail.

3. Double-click the **Set foreground color** button ▣.

4. Select the desired color in the Color Picker dialog box:

    • White reveals more of the layer.

    • Black hides more of the layer.

    • Gray creates a transparent area on the mask.

5. Click **OK**.. Enter

6. Select the desired tool and options from its options bar.

7. Typically, the mask can be used with drawing or painting tools.

8. Draw or paint on the layer.

Discard Layer Mask

1. Right-click on the desired mask thumbnail in the Layers palette.

2. Click **Discard Layer Mask**.

Use a Selection from One Layer to Mask Another

1. If necessary, click the **Layer visibility** button ▣ in any layer selector in the Layers palette to make it easier to select content on the desired layer.

2. Click the desired layer (masking layer) in the Layers palette.

3. Make a selection in the masking layer.

4. In the Layers palette, click the layer to be masked.

5. Click the **Add a mask** button ▣ on the Layers palette.

Disable a Mask

1. Right-click the desired layer mask thumbnail in the Layers palette.

2. Click **Disable Layer Mask**.

    ✓ *A red X over the thumbnail indicates the mask is disabled.*

Enable a Mask

1. Right-click the desired layer mask thumbnail in the Layers palette.

2. Click **Enable Layer Mask**.

Crop an Image with a Mask

✓ *For this method, the image must appear on its own layer. It cannot be a background layer.*

1. Click the layer to be masked in the Layers palette.

2. Make a selection in the active layer—not the image layer—around the image to the desired shape.

3. Click the **Add a mask** button ▣ on the Layers palette.

    ✓ *The mask crops around the image layer.*

Add a Filter with a Mask

1. Click the layer to be masked in the Layers palette.

2. Click **Filter** .... Alt+T

3. Click on the desired filter command from the submenu:

Artistic ▶
Blur ▶
Brush Strokes ▶
Distort ▶
Noise ▶
Pixelate ▶
Render ▶
Sharpen ▶
Sketch ▶
Stylize ▶
Texture ▶
Video ▶
Other ▶

4. Click on the desired filter's submenu.

5. If necessary, set the filter options in the applicable filter option dialog box.

6. Click **OK** .... Enter

Recolor Part of an Image with a Mask

1. Click **Layer** .... Alt+L

2. Click **New Adjustment Layer** .... J

3. Click **Hue/Saturation** .... H

4. In the **Name** box, type a name for layer .... Alt+N

5. Select the desired layer options:

   a. Click the **Color** arrow and select a color from the drop-down list.

   ✔ *This color is used to identify the new layer in Layers palette. If you don't need a color to identify the new layer, chose None.*

   b. Click the **Mode** arrow and select the desired mode.

   c. Click in **Opacity** and enter the desired opacity percentage.

   OR

   Click the **Opacity** arrow and drag the slider to the desired opacity percentage.

6. Click **OK** .... Enter

7. In the Hue/Saturation dialog box, drag the sliders or enter numbers—or negative numbers—in the **Hue, Saturation**, and **Lightness** boxes to make the desired settings.

8. Click **OK** .... Enter

9. Right-click on the thumbnail for the hue/saturation mask in the Layers palette.

10. Click **Discard Layer Mask**.

11. Make a selection in the layer to be masked.

12. Click the **Hue/Saturation** layer in the Layers palette.

13. Click the **Add a mask** button 🔲 on the Layers palette.

   ✔ *The color applied only to the area not blocked by the mask.*

Exercise 9

A mask works like a selection that you've saved, except that you can combine a mask with layer effects, filters, and other features to achieve effects that wouldn't otherwise be possible. Another benefit of using a mask is that you can hide part of a layer's contents without deleting or erasing that content; then, you could reveal or copy that hidden copy as needed later. While Chapter 9 covers a wide variety of mask techniques—including quick masks, creating a mask from a selection, altering a mask, deleting a mask, copying a mask to another layer, disabling a mask, cropping with a mask, filtering with a mask, and recoloring with a mask—this exercise presents a few of those skills so you can explore the possibilities.

Directions

1. Start Photoshop, if needed.

2. Use the File|Open command to open the ⊙ **PS09** Photoshop file. Zoom the image if needed.

3. Save the file as **PINK**.

4. Use the Magnetic Lasso tool to select the top of the flower.

5. Select the Edit in Quick Mask Mode button near the bottom of the toolbox.

6. Select the Paintbrush tool on the toolbox and select white as the foreground color.

   ✓ *To reverse the default foreground and background colors, click the small bent arrow to the upper-right of the Set Foreground Color and Set Background Color boxes on the toolbox. The top box represents the current foreground color, and the bottom box represents the current background color.*

7. Paint over the stem and some of the leaves of the flower. As you paint, you will be able to see the green color of the stem and leaves revealed, while the mask over the affected areas disappears.

8. Select the Edit in Standard Mode button near the bottom of the toolbox. When the mask disappears, you can see that the selection has been expanded to include the stem and leaves you "painted" out of the mask.

9. Choose Select|Deselect to remove the selection.

10. Click on the Visibility button (eye icon) beside the Background and Flower layers in the Layers palette to hide the layers.

11. Use the Select|Color Range command to select the pink text on the Think Pink layer.

12. Redisplay the Background and Flower layers. You will now be able to see that only the Think Pink text has been selected. Select the Think Pink layer.

13. Click on the Add a mask button at the bottom of the Layers palette. As shown in Illustration 1, the mask will appear immediately beside the Think Pink layer on the palette.

14. Click on the Flower layer in the Layers palette.

15. Click on the Eyedropper tool on the toolbox, then click on a medium green color on a leaf in the image. The specified color will become the current foreground color.

    ✓ *If the selected green becomes the background color instead, click the small bent arrow to the upper-right of the Set Foreground Color and Set Background Color boxes on the toolbox.*

16. Add a new gradient fill layer. The color should blend from transparent at the top of the image to the dark green color at the bottom of the image. Note that when you add the layer, however, the Think Pink text will not appear gradated. To fix this, you need to copy the mask from the text layer to the gradient fill layer.

17. Right-click on the mask thumbnail (not the layer name itself) for the Think Pink layer in the Layers palette, then choose Set Selection to Layer Mask. This selects the pink text once again.

18. Right-click on the mask icon beside the layer name for the new gradient fill layer, then click on Discard Layer Mask. This removes the default mask that was added when you created the fill layer.

19. Click on the gradient fill layer name in the Layers palette to make sure that the layer is selected.

20. Click on the Add a mask button at the bottom of the Layers palette. The mask will be created immediately.

21. If the text doesn't appear gradated from Pink to green, choose Layer|Arrange|Bring Forward so that the effect will be visible.

22. Right-click on the mask thumbnail on the Think Pink layer, then click on Set Selection to Layer Mask. This will once again select the text.

23. Choose Filter|Distort|Glass, and then click on OK. The filter appears on the pink text immediately.

24. Choose Edit|Undo Glass immediately to remove the filter effect.

25. Select the Flower layer in the Layers palette.

26. Select the Elliptical Marquee tool and change the Feather text box setting to 10 px.

27. Make an oval-shaped selection that includes the flower and its stem.

28. Click on the Add a mask button at the bottom of the Layers palette. The mask immediately hides (crops out) the layer content that was outside the selection, as shown in Illustration 2.

29. Save and close the file.

Illustration 1

Add a mask button

Illustration 2

Next
Chapter
▶▶

10

Using
Paths

A *path* is essentially a vector-based selection outline in Photoshop. Because paths are vector-based (an outline rather than a selection of pixels), creating paths in an image file rather than saved selections will have less of a tendency to increase the file size. This can be beneficial if the file is a large scan, has dozens of layers, or is simply large because it's complex. You can use a path as a selection at any time, fill the path or color the path outline, or even use a special type of path to clip image content when you plan to reuse a file. This chapter shows you how to:

※ Create various types of paths

※ View and work with paths

※ Fill a path or color the path outline

※ Use a path to define a selection

※ Use a clipping path to prepare an image for reuse in other files or settings

Creating Paths

You use the Paths palette to save the paths you create, and use the pen tools and shape tools to actually draw each path. The tool you should use to create the path depends on the desired shape for the path.

Note: *Paths do not print unless you fill them with color or color their border.*

Adding a Shape Path

The section titled "Drawing a Rectangle, Oval, or Other Shape" in Chapter 3 explained how to use the Rectangle tool (and the other shape tools you access via the Rectangle tool) to draw shapes on an image. You also can use those tools to create a path for later use, as described here.

1. Right-click on the **Rectangle** tool in the toolbox. Its shortcut menu will appear.

2. Click on the desired shape tool to use in the menu. The selected tool will become the active tool.

    Note: *If you choose the Custom Shape tool, be sure to use the Shape drop-down list on the options bar to specify which kind of shape to draw.*

3. Click on the **Create new work path** button on the options bar. The selected tool will become active for path selection.

4. Drag diagonally on the picture in the work area. Keep the mouse button pressed as you drag in any desired direction. When you release the mouse button, the path will appear.

5. Click on **Window**. The Window menu will appear.

6. Click on **Show Paths**. The Paths palette will become the active tab in the Layers palette window. The Paths tab will show that the path you've drawn appears as a temporary path called a Work Path.

    Tip: *In place of opening the Window menu and choosing Show Paths, you can click on the Paths tab in the Layers palette window.*

7. Click on the **Paths palette menu** button. The palette menu appears.

8. Click on **Save Path**. The Save Path dialog box will open.

   Note: *You don't have to save any temporary work path unless you want to save the path in the file and reuse it later.*

9. Type a name for the path in the Save Path text box. Your new name will replace the temporary name in the text box.

10. Click on **OK**. The Save Path dialog box will close and Photoshop will finish saving the path under the name you specified.

11. Click on the **Dismiss Target Path** button (✓) at the right end of the options bar to accept the path and finish it.

Note: *If you skip this last step when using any tool to create a path, the path will remain selected and further actions you take pertain to that path. For example, if you try to create a path with another tool, it would simply be added into the current path rather than create as a separate work path.*

Note: *You can click on the Layers tab in the Layers palette window at the end of each path creation process to return to the regular view of layers in the image.*

Making a Pen Path

The Pen tool enables you to create paths with straight lines, curves, and angles. Use this tool when you want to create a path that's irregular in shape or has swooping, controlled curves.

Note: *You must be careful in using the mouse with the Pen tool. Different mouse actions have different results. The following steps illustrate the various mouse techniques you need to master when using the Pen tool.*

1. Click on the **Pen** tool in the toolbox. Its options will appear in the options bar.

2. Click on **Create new work path** button on the options bar. The Pen tool will become active for path selection.

   Note: *If you click on the Create new shape layer button on the options bar for any tool described in this chapter, instead, the tool draws a shape or outline on a new layer in the image rather than simply creating a path.*

3. Click on the starting point for the first segment in the path. An anchor point appears at the location where you clicked.

4. Click on the location where you want to end the segment. A straight line segment appears between the anchor points.

5. Click and drag on the location for the end of the next segment. Because you dragged, Photoshop will create a curved segment.

6. Drag the direction point at the end of the direction line, then release the mouse button. Photoshop will adjust the depth and direction of the curved segment based on where you drag the direction point.

7. Click and drag in the opposite direction on the location for the end of the next segment. Because you dragged in the opposite direction, Photoshop will create a segment that curves in the opposite direction.

8. Drag the direction point at the end of the direction line, then release the mouse button. Photoshop will adjust the depth and direction of the curved segment based on where you drag the direction point.

Tip: *To create a point at an anchor point between curved segments, press and hold the Alt key when you set the anchor point for the second segment.*

9. After you create all the needed segments, finish drawing the path in one of two ways:

- Click on the first anchor point to close the path shape. Note that when the mouse pointer is over the first anchor point, a small circle appears along with the pointer to tell you that clicking would then close the path.

- Click on the **Pen** tool in the toolbox to finish the path without closing the shape.

10. Click on **Window**. The Window menu will appear.

11. Click on **Show Paths**. The Paths palette will become the active tab in the Layers palette window. The Paths tab will show that the path you've drawn appears as a temporary path called a Work Path.

12. Click on the **Paths palette menu** button. The palette menu appears.

13. Click on **Save Path**. The Save Path dialog box will open.

14. Type a name for the path in the **Name** text box. Your new name will replace the temporary name in the text box.

15. Click on **OK**. The Save Path dialog box will close and Photoshop will finish saving the path under the name you specified.

16. Click on the **Dismiss Target Path** button (✓) at the right end of the options bar to accept the path and finish it.

Making a Freeform Path

The Freeform Pen tool enables you to create a path by dragging on the image. In addition, you can turn on the Magnetic option with the Freeform Pen tool to have the path outline "snap to" a shape in the image. This tool comes in handy when you want to create a path around a particular item or region in an image.

1. Right-click on the **Pen** tool in the toolbox. Its shortcut menu will appear.

2. Click on **Freeform Pen Tool**. The Freeform Pen tool will become the active tool.

3. Click on the **Create new work path** button on the options bar. The Freeform Pen tool will become active for path selection.

4. Click on the **Magnetic** check box to check it, if desired. Checking this option will cause the Freeform Pen tool to function as the Magnetic Pen tool, and your path will snap to the outline for an item in the image.

   Note: *The Magnetic feature works via color and tone contrast. You can click on the Magnetic Pen Options button on the options bar to display choices for making the Magnetic Pen tool more or less sensitive to contrast.*

5. Drag on the picture in the work area. Keep the mouse button pressed as you drag in any desired direction. When you release the mouse button, the path will appear.

Tip: *If you're using the Magnetic Pen tool, you can click to set specific anchor points, and press Delete to remove the most recent anchor point. However, with the Freeform Pen too, you must keep the mouse pointer pressed as you drag.*

6. Finish drawing the path in one of three ways:

    *   Click on the first anchor point to close the path shape. Note that when the mouse pointer is over the first anchor point, a small circle appears along with the pointer to tell you that clicking would then close the path.

    *   Double-click on the next-to-last anchor point that you want to close the path automatically.

    *   Click on the **Freeform Pen** tool in the toolbox to finish the path without closing the shape.

        Note: *When you're drawing any path, you can click on Select and then click on Deselect Path to stop drawing the path. You can then click on Select and click on Dismiss Path to clear the path.*

7. Click on **Window**. The Window menu will appear.

8. Click on **Show Paths**. The Paths palette will become the active tab in the Layers palette window. The Paths tab will show that the path you've drawn appears as a temporary path called a Work Path.

9. Click on the **Paths palette menu** button. The palette menu appears.

10. Click on **Save Path**. The Save Path dialog box will open.

11. Type a name for the path in the Save Path text box. Your new name will replace the temporary name in the text box.

12. Click on **OK**. The Save Path dialog box will close and Photoshop will finish saving the path under the name you specified.

13. Click on the **Dismiss Target Path** button (✓) at the right end of the options bar to accept the path and finish it.

Viewing and Changing a Path

The Paths palette enables you to view and work with the paths in an image file. When you change a path, you move, add, and delete anchor points.

1. Click on **Window**. The Window menu will appear.

2. Click on **Show Paths**. The Paths palette will become the active tab in the Layers palette window.

   Tip: *In place of opening the Window menu and choosing Show Paths, you can click on the Paths tab in the Layers palette window.*

3. Click on the desired path on the Paths palette tab. The path will become the active path.

4. Use the Navigator to pan the path into view, if needed. The path will become visible in the work area.

5. Right-click on the **Pen** tool in the toolbox. Its shortcut menu will appear.

6. Click on **Add Anchor Point Tool**. The Add Anchor Point tool will become the active tool.

7. Click on the path at the location where you want to add the new anchor point. The anchor point will appear.

8. Drag the new anchor point to the desired location. The path will reshape accordingly.

9. Drag other anchor points to reposition them as needed. Again, the path will reshape accordingly.

10. Right-click on an anchor point to delete. A shortcut menu will appear.

11. Click on **Delete Anchor Point**. The path will reshape accordingly.

12. Right-click on the **Path Component Selection** tool in the toolbox. A shortcut menu will appear.

13. Click on **Direct Selection Tool**. The Direct Selection tool will become the active tool.

14. Click on the path, then drag anchor points to reposition them as needed. Again, the path will reshape accordingly, but in this case, you didn't have to add new anchor points.

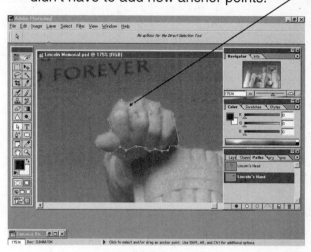

Note: *You can use the Path Component Selection tool to drag the whole path on the image.*

15. Press **Esc**. The path will be deselected, but your changes will remain in the path. From here, you can click on the Layers tab in the Layers palette to resume working with layers.

Filling or Coloring a Path

You can fill a path with color to add a spot of color in an image or "stroke" the path outline with color to add a subtle outline of color in the image. While by default a path doesn't print, it will print after you fill or stroke it with color. These steps explain how to use color with a path.

1. Click on the desired fill or outline color in the color bar at the bottom of the Color palette. The color will become the active foreground color.

2. Click on **Window**. The Window menu will appear.

3. Click on **Show Paths**. The Paths palette will become the active tab in the Layers palette window.

4. Click on the desired path in the Paths palette. The path will become the active path.

5a. Click on **Fills path with foreground color** at the bottom of the Paths palette tab. Photoshop will fill the path with the color you selected in Step 1.

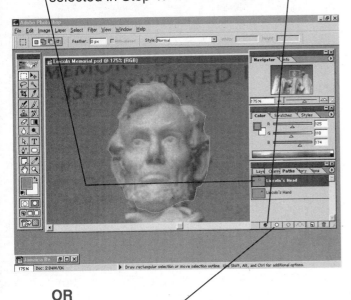

OR

5b. Click on **Strokes path with foreground color**. Photoshop will apply a very thin outline of the foreground color to the path outline.

6. Review the resulting color. This example shows the path filled with color. If you merely stroked the path with color, the result may be fairly subtle and may not appear visible until you finish working with the Paths palette.

Note: *At this point, you can click on the Layers tab in the Layers palette to finish working with paths.*

Using a Path to Make a Selection

As was noted much earlier in the chapter, you can use a path as a selection at any time, making it easy for you to work with the path area later, applying a filter or other effect.

1. Click on **Window**. The Window menu will appear.

2. Click on **Show Paths**. The Paths palette will become the active tab in the Layers palette window.

3. Click on the desired path. The path will become the active path.

4. Click on the **Loads path as a selection** button at the bottom of the Paths palette tab. A selection marquee will appear around the path. You then can work with the selection just as you would any other selection.

Using Clipping Paths

A *clipping path* works much like a mask. You should use one if you plan to save a copy of a file and insert that copy into another file or use the copy in a document. The area outside the clipping path will be transparent in the file copy when you insert it into a file or document. Using a clipping path ensures that other content in the location where you use the file copy—especially when you insert it into another Photoshop file or another type of document—will be able to show through areas made transparent by the clipping path.

Adding a Clipping Path

The fastest way to create a clipping path is to duplicate an existing path in the image and then save it as a clipping path, as the following steps will illustrate.

1. Click on **Window**. The Window menu will appear.

2. Click on **Show Paths**. The Paths palette will become the active tab in the Layers palette window.

3. Right-click on the desired path. A shortcut menu will appear.

Tip: *Use the Navigator to scroll the path into view first, if needed, to verify that you're duplicating the correct path.*

4. Click on **Duplicate Path**. The selection marquee will appear around the path. The Duplicate Path dialog box will appear.

5. Type a name for the clipping path in the Duplicate Path text box. Your new name will replace the temporary name in the text box.

6. Click on **OK**. The dialog box will close and the new path will appear in the Paths palette.

7. With the new path still selected in the Paths palette tab, click the **Paths palette menu** button. The palette menu appears.

8. Click on **Clipping Path**. The Clipping Path dialog box will open.

9. Click on the down arrow beside the **Path** drop-down list, then click on the name of the path you just duplicated. The path will be selected.

10. Click on **OK**. Photoshop will save the duplicated path as a clipping path. You can then return to the Layers palette and continue working if you want. You should save the file to save all of your paths in the original file. To learn to use the clipping path content, proceed to the next section.

Using Clipped Content

Merely creating the clipping path doesn't clip the image. You must save a copy of the image in Photoshop EPS, DCS, or PDF format (or TIFF if you plan to use the image with a non-Postscript printer), then import or place it in another file or document. The steps here show an example of how this process works.

1. Open the file that holds the clipping path. The file will become the active file.

2. Click on **File**. The File menu will appear.

3. Click on **Save As**. The Save As dialog box will open.

4. Use the **Save in** list to choose another save location, if needed. The clipped file will be saved to the designated location.

5. Edit the file name in the **File name** text box, if needed. Photoshop will use the name you specify for the clipped file.

6. Click on the down arrow beside the **Format** list, then click on Photoshop EPS, one of the Photoshop DCS choices, Photoshop PDF, or TIFF. The clipped file will be saved with the specified format.

7. Click on **Save**. Photoshop may display an options dialog box, depending on the file format you selected in Step 6.

8. Choose options as needed in the dialog box. Photoshop will apply your choices when it finishes saving the clipped file.

9. Click on **OK**. Photoshop will save the clipped file and it will stay open, although it will not appear clipped onscreen.

10. Click on **File**. The File menu will appear.

11. Click on **Close**. The clipped file will close.

12. Click on **File**. The File menu will appear.

13. Click on **New**. The New dialog box will open.

14. Specify settings for the new file. The new file will use the designated settings.

15. Click on **OK**. Photoshop will open the new file.

16. Click on **File**. The File menu will appear.

17. Click on **Place**. The Place dialog box will open.

18. Select the file type you used for the clipped file from the Files of type drop-down list. (Also use the Look In list to navigate to the location holding the clipped file, if needed.) The file will appear in the list of files in the dialog box.

19. Click on the clipped file in the list. It becomes the selected file.

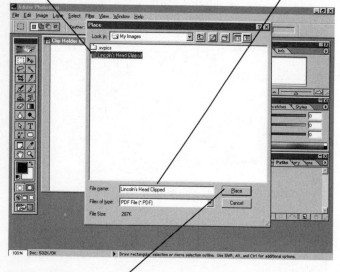

20. Click on **Place**. Photoshop will insert the clipped file in the new file you created.

21. Review the position of the clipped information, then click on the **Commit Place** button (✓) at the right end of the options bar to finish placing the clipped file into the new Photoshop file. The inserted clipped file will appear on its own new layer in the image file.

Procedures

Add Shape Path

1. Click the desired shape tool button in the toolbox .... U

2. Click the **Create new work path** button on the options toolbar.

3. Click the mouse to the left and above the desired position while holding down the mouse button.

4. Drag diagonally to draw the shape to the desired size and shape.

5. Release the mouse button to finalize the shape.

6. Click **Window** .... Alt + W

7. Click **Show Paths** .... P

    OR

    Click the **Paths** tab in the Layers palette.

    ✓ *The Paths palette is selected.*

8. Click the **Paths palette menu** button and select **Save Path**.

9. In the **Name** box, type a name for the path .... Alt + N

10. Click **OK** .... Enter

11. Click the **Commit** button in the options toolbar.

Create a Pen Path

1. Click the **Pen Tool** button 🖊️
   in the toolbox... P

2. Click the **Create new work path** button 🔲
   on the options toolbar.

3. Click on the starting point for the first
   segment in the path.

4. Click the location where the segment ends.

   ✓ *To create curved segments, click the
   location for the end of the curved segment
   and drag. Adjust the, length, depth, and
   direction of the curve by the direction in
   which the segment is dragged.*

5. After creating the needed segments, finish
   the path by:

   • Clicking on the first anchor point (the
     starting point).

     ✓ *A small circle to the right of the mouse
     pointer indicates when the shape can
     be closed.*

   OR

   • Clicking on the **Pen Tool** button 🖊️ in
     the toolbox to finish the path without
     closing the shape.

6. Click **Window** .... Alt + W

7. Click **Show Paths** .... P

   OR

   Click the **Paths** tab in the Layers palette.

   ✓ *The Paths palette is selected.*

8. Click the **Paths palette menu** button ⏵ and
   select **Save Path**.

9. In the **Name** box, type a name
   for the path... Alt + N

10. Click **OK** .... Enter

11. Click the **Commit** button ✓ in the options
    toolbar.

Create a Freeform Pen Path

1. Click the **Freeform Pen Tool**
   button 🖊️ in the toolbox........................... P

2. Click the **Create new work path** button 🔲
   on the options toolbar.

   ✓ *To make the Freeform Pen Tool apply a
   magnetic path that snaps to the outline of
   an item in an image, click the Magnetic
   option in the options toolbar.*

3. Click on the starting point for the first
   segment in the path.

4. Position the mouse pointer at the starting
   point of the path.

5. Drag the path to the desired shape.

6. To finish the path:

   • Click on the first anchor point (the
     starting point).

     ✓ *A small circle to the right of the mouse
     pointer indicates when the shape can
     be closed.*

   OR

   • Double-click on the next-to-last anchor
     point.

   OR

   • Click on the **Freeform Pen Tool** button
     🖊️ in the toolbox to finish the path without
     closing the shape at the starting point.

7. Click **Window** .... Alt + W

8. Click **Show Paths** .... P

   OR

   Click the **Paths** tab in the Layers palette.

   ✓ *The Paths palette is selected.*

9. Click the **Paths palette menu** button ⏵ and
   select **Save Path**.

10. In the **Name** box, type a name
    for the path .... Alt + N

11. Click **OK** .... Enter

12. Click the **Commit** button ✓ in the options
    toolbar.

View (Select) a Path

1. Click **Window** .... Alt + W

2. Click **Show Paths** .... P

   OR

   Click the **Paths** tab in the Layers palette

   ✓ *The Paths palette is selected.*

3. Click the desired path selector in the Paths palette.

Add Anchor Points to Change Path

1. Select the path in the Paths palette.

2. Use the Navigator to enhance the view if needed.

3. If necessary, right-click the **Pen Tool** button in the toolbox .... P

4. Click the **Add Anchor Point** button.

5. Click on the path at the desired location.

6. Drag the new anchor point to a new location to change the path.

7. Drag other anchor points as needed.

Delete Anchor Point in a Path

1. Click the desired path in the Paths palette.

2. Use the Navigator to enhance the view if needed.

3. Right-click on the desired anchor point.

4. Click **Delete Anchor Point**.

Select Anchor Points to Change Path

1. Click the desired path in the Paths palette.

2. Use the Navigator to enhance the view if needed.

3. If necessary, right-click the **Path Component Selection** tool button in the toolbox .... A

4. Click the **Direct Selection Tool** button in the toolbox.

5. Click on the path at the desired location.

6. Drag the anchor points to reposition them as desired.

7. Press **Esc** to deselect the path .... Esc

Add Fill or Color to a Path

1. Select a foreground color.

2. Click **Window** .... Alt + W

3. Click **Show Paths** .... P

   OR

   Click the **Paths** tab in the Layers palette.

   ✓ *The Paths palette is selected.*

4. Click the desired path in the Paths palette.

5. Click the **Fills path with foreground color** button in the Paths palette.

   OR

   Click **Strokes path with foreground color** button in the Paths palette.

Use Path to Make Selection

1. Click **Window** .... Alt + W

2. Click **Show Paths** .... P

   OR

   Click the **Paths** tab in the Layers palette.

   ✓ *The Paths palette is selected.*

3. Click the desired path in the Paths palette.

4. Click the **Loads path as a selection** button in the Paths palette.

Add Clipping Path

1. Click **Window** .... Alt + W

2. Click **Show Paths** .... P

   OR

   Click the **Paths** tab in the Layers palette.

   ✓ *The Paths palette is selected.*

3. Right-click the desired path in the Paths palette.

OR

1. Click the **Paths palette menu** button ▶.

2. Click **Duplicate Path**.

3. In the **Name** box, type a name for the duplicate path .... Alt + N

4. Click **OK** .... Enter

5. With the desired path still selected, click the **Paths palette** menu button ▶.

6. Click **Clipping Path**.

7. Click on the **Path** box arrow and select the name of the path just duplicated.

8. Click **OK** .... Enter

Save Clipped Content for Future Use

1. Open the file that holds the clipping path.

2. Click **File** .... Alt + F

3. Click **Save As** .... A

4. Click the **Save in** arrow if necessary and select a save location I

5. In the **File name** box edit the file name if desired .... N

6. Click the **Format** drop-down arrow .... F

7. Select one of the file formats:
   - **Photoshop EPS**
   - **Any Photoshop DCS format**
   - **Photoshop PDF**
   - **TIFF**

8. Click **Save** .... Enter

9. If necessary, choose any applicable options in the appropriate dialog box.

10. Click **OK** .... Enter

11. Click **File** .... Alt + F

12. Click **Close** C

Place Clipped File in an Image

1. Click **File** .... Alt + F

2. Click **New** .... N

3. Specify the desired settings in the New dialog box.

4. Click **OK** .... Enter

5. Click **File** .... Alt + F

6. Click **Place** L

7. If necessary, click the **Files of type** box arrow and select the desired format of the clipped file.

8. Select the clipped file in Place dialog box window.

9. Click **Place** .... P

10. Click the **Commit** button ✓ in the options toolbar.

167

Exercise 10

So far, you've worked with saving a selection marquee so you can choose the selection again at any time. You've also seen how you can create a mask to hide image content not selecting in the mask. In this exercise, you work with paths, which provide you another way to select and work with image content. The advantage to using paths rather than saved selections is that they consume less file size. Also, you can display multiple paths onscreen at one time, which can be useful in this situation. In this exercise, learn a bit more about paths through a little practice.

Directions

1. Start Photoshop, if needed.

2. Use the File|Open command to open the ☺PS10 Photoshop file.

3. Save the file as LINC.

4. Zoom the image to 100% size and increase the size of the file window.

5. Choose a shape tool like the Rectangle tool or Custom Shape tool.

6. Click on the Create new work path button on the options bar.

7. Drag on the image to create the path.

8. Choose Window|Show Paths to display the Paths tab in the Layers palette.

9. Click on the Paths palette menu button and then click on Save Path.

10. Enter **Shape Path** as the path Name, then click on OK.

11. Click on the Dismiss button (✓) on the options bar to dismiss the new path.

12. Click on Shape Path in the paths palette to redisplay the path.

13. Choose a bright green foreground color using the Color palette.

14. Click on the Fills path with foreground color button at the bottom of the Paths palette. The path will be filled with color, as shown in Illustration1.

    ✓   *The filled color does appear on printouts of the image.*

15. Undo the path fill, and delete the path.

16. Zoom in on Lincoln's head in the image.

17. Choose the Freeform Pen tool.

    ✓   *Right-click on the Pen tool, then click on Freeform Pen Tool.*

18. Check the Magnetic check box on the options bar.

19. Drag to create the path around Lincoln's head.

    ✓   *Press the Delete key to remove the previous anchor point, or press Esc to remove the path. Click with the mouse to place anchor points as desired. Click on the first anchor point (the start of the path) to close the path.*

20. Click on the Paths palette menu button and then click on Save Path.

21. Enter **Head** as the path Name, then click on OK.

22. Click on the Dismiss button (✓) on the options bar to dismiss the new path.

23. Click on the Head path in the Paths palette, then click on the Loads path as selection button near the bottom of the Paths palette. The path becomes a selection in the image, as shown in Illustration 2.

24. Choose Select|Deselect.

25. Right-click on the Head path in the Paths palette, then choose Duplicate Path.

26. Type **Clip** as the Name for the new path, then click on OK.

27. With the Clips path still selected in the Paths palette, click on the palette menu button, then click on Clipping Path.

28. Open the Path drop-down list in the Clipping Path dialog box, then choose the Clip path in the list. Click on OK.

    ✓ *A clipping path works like a mask. It enables you to select part of the file so that when you save the file in a new format, only the selected portion (within the clipping path) is visible.*

29. Save the **LINC** file.

30. Use the File|Save As command to save the file in Photoshop EPS. (You don't have to change the file name itself, as the file name extension will change.) Leave the settings as is in the EPS Options dialog box, and click on OK.

31. Close the **LINC.eps** file.

32. Create a new image file in Photoshop with these settings:

Name	**LINC2**
Width	6 inches
Height	4 inches
Resolution	72 pixels/inch
Mode	RGB Color
Contents	White

33. Choose File|Place.

34. Select the **LINC.eps** file, then click on Place. The clipped image will appear in the **LINC2** file as shown in Illustration 3.

35. Click on the Commit button (✓) on the Options bar. The selection handles and black boundaries around the clipped image will disappear.

36. Save and close the file.

Illustration 1

Palette menu button

Fills Path with foreground color button

Illustration 2

Illustration 3

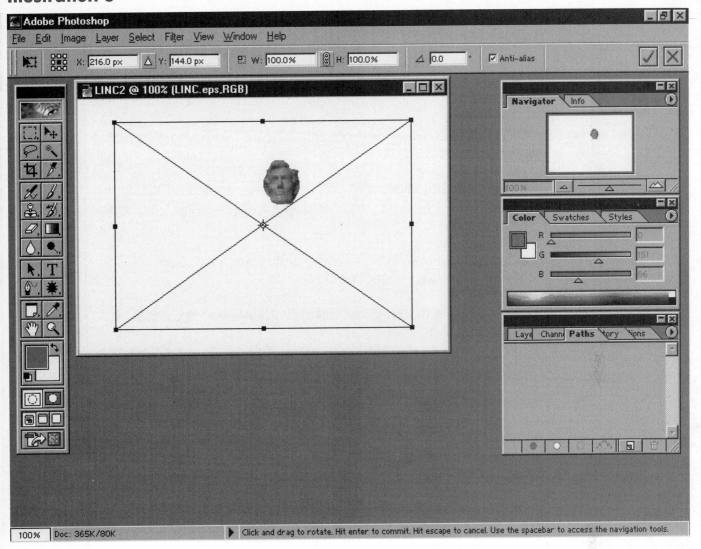

Part III Review Questions

1. How do you add a new layer? *See "Making a New Layer" in Chapter 8.*

2. How do you go to a layer to work with it? *See "Selecting a Layer" in Chapter 8.*

3. What other kinds of layers can you add? *See "Adding a Fill Layer," "Adding a Gradient Layer," and "Adding a Pattern Layer" in Chapter 8.*

4. What do you do if one layer is hiding part of another? *See "Arranging Layer Order" in Chapter 8.*

5. Why do you use a mask? *See "Using Layer Masks" in Chapter 9.*

6. How do you convert a selection to a mask? *See "Using a Selection from One Layer as a Mask on Another" in Chapter 9.*

7. What can you do once you've created a mask? *See "Putting a Mask to Work" in Chapter 9.*

8. How and why do you create a path? *See "Adding a Shape Path," "Making a Pen Path," and "Making a Freeform Path" in Chapter 10.*

9. How do you convert a selection to a path? *See "Using a Path to Make a Selection" in Chapter 10.*

10. How do you create and use a clipping path? *See "Using Clipping Paths" in Chapter 10.*

11

Using Other Editing Tools

Photoshop includes a number of editing tools that you can use to touch up specific areas of an image or layer. Many of the techniques resemble traditional techniques used to correct a photo during development. You can adjust the focus of a particular area, enhance the intensity of an area, or use other techniques such as filling an area with color. In this chapter, you learn how to:

❋ Add blurring or smudging to an area

❋ Sharpen an area

❋ Use the eraser tools to erase to the background color or transparency

❋ Erase all of a particular color on a layer using the magic eraser

❋ Add a gradient or fill an area with color

❋ Dodge, burn, or sponge an area

Blurring an Area

It may seem contrary to your needs in most cases, but blurring part of an image can help camouflage an imperfection or achieve an effect. For example, it's common to blur a portrait to achieve a dreamy effect or downplay skin imperfections. The steps here explain how to blur an area in an image, which reduces the sharpness of any edges or reduces detail in the affected area.

Note: *Photoshop includes filters that correspond with the capabilities of many of the tools described in this chapter. Use a filter when you want to change the appearance of a selection or a layer. Use a tool when you want to "paint" on a particular area to make a correction.*

1. Click on the layer in the Layers palette that holds the content you want to blur. The selected layer will become the active layer.

    Note: *Most of the tools described in this chapter cannot be used on a type layer.*

2. Use the Navigator to zoom in on and display the desired area. The selected area will become more visible.

3. Click on the **Blur** tool in the toolbox. The Blur tool will become the active tool.

4. Choose a **Brush** style on the options bar. The selected brush will become active for the Blur tool.

Note: *To choose a brush for any tool, click on the down arrow beside the Brush choice in the options bar, click on the brush to use, then click on the down arrow beside the Brush choice to close the drop-down palette. If you click on the right arrow button in the palette of brushes, you can use the menu that appears to load other brushes.*

5. Make a choice from the **Mode** drop-down list on the options bar. The selected mode will become active for the Blur tool.

6. Select the **Pressure** text box contents, type a new entry, and press **Enter**. (Alternatively, click on the right arrow beside the Pressure choice, drag the slider, then click on the right arrow again.) The pressure setting will become active for the Blur tool.

7. Click and drag on the desired layer. Blurring will begin to appear.

8. Drag as much as is needed. Photoshop will continue to add more blurring, but it may take quite a bit of dragging. When you finish, you can continue working with another tool or operation in Photoshop.

Note: *The Blur tool can be quite subtle, but if you compare the eyes in the last screen shot with the prior two, you can see the blurring that's been applied to the eyes.*

Smudging an Area

The Smudge tool helps you drag color from one area into another, much as you could with a paintbrush full of wet paint. You can use the smudge tool to add a painted effect in a very specific area of the image, rather than using a filter to achieve the effect over a larger area. Follow the next set of steps to practice smudging.

1. Click on the layer in the Layers palette that holds the desired content. The selected layer will become the active layer.

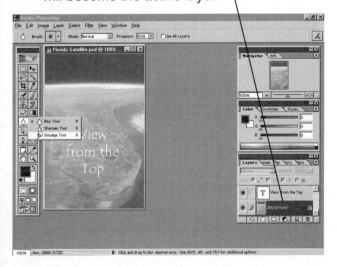

2. Use the Navigator to zoom in on and display the area to smudge. The selected area will become more visible.

3. Right-click on the **Blur** tool in the toolbox. A menu will appear.

4. Click on **Smudge Tool**. The Smudge tool will become the active tool.

5. Choose a **Brush** style on the options bar. The selected brush will become active for the Smudge tool.

6. Make a choice from the **Mode** drop-down list on the options bar. The selected mode will become active for the Smudge tool.

7. Select the **Pressure** text box contents, type a new entry, and press **Enter**. (Alternately, click on the right arrow beside the Pressure choice, drag the slider, then click on the right arrow again.) The pressure setting will become active for the Smudge tool.

Note: *If you click on the Finger Painting check box (in the options bar) to check it, dragging with the Smudge tool will paint using the currently selected foreground color.*

8. Click and drag on the layer over two contrasting colors to make the smudge. Smudging will begin to appear. When you finish creating all the needed smudges, you can continue working with another tool or operation in Photoshop.

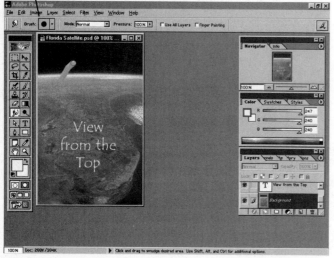

Note: *You can make the effects of the Blur, Smudge, or Sharpen tool partially transparent after you use the tool. To do so, click on Edit, then click on Fade (Tool Name). Specify an Opacity setting in the Fade dialog box that appears, then click on OK.*

Sharpening an Area

The Sharpen tool works in the opposite way as the Blur tool: it tries to improve the focus of edges that are soft so that the image appears clearer. So, for example, you might want to use this tool if one small spot on a layer looks out of focus.

1. Click on the layer in the Layers palette that holds the content you want to sharpen. The selected layer will become the active layer.

2. Use the Navigator to zoom in on and display the area to sharpen. The selected area will become more visible.

3. Right-click on the **Blur** tool in the toolbox. A menu will appear.

4. Click on **Sharpen Tool**. The Sharpen tool will become the active tool.

5. Choose a **Brush** style on the options bar. The selected brush will become active for the Sharpen tool.

6. Make a choice from the **Mode** drop-down list on the options bar. The selected mode will become active for the Sharpen tool.

7. Select the **Pressure** text box contents, type a new entry, and press **Enter**. (Alternatively, click on the right arrow beside the Pressure choice, drag the slider, then click on the right arrow again.) The pressure setting will become active for the Sharpen tool.

8. Click or drag on the desired layer. Sharpening will begin to appear. When you finish adding all the needed sharpening, you can continue working with another tool or operation in Photoshop.

> *Note:* Note that if you use a large, sharp brush and a higher Pressure setting with the Sharpen tool, clicking or dragging can have unwanted effects beyond sharpening—the color of pixels outside the area to be sharpened may be changed dramatically. Even though the impact of sharpening can be subtle, you still want to use the Sharpen tool sparingly to avoid those unwanted changes.

Erasing Image Content

Photoshop offers three different eraser tools so that you can achieve exactly the erasing effect that you need in any particular situation.

Using the Eraser

The standard Eraser tool erases color or content on a layer, enabling the background layer in the image to show through to varying degrees, depending on the opacity you specify. If you're working on the background layer itself, using the standard Eraser actually paints or draws on the currently selected background color rather than erasing layer content. The following steps show an example of each of these uses for the Eraser.

1. Click on the layer in the Layers palette that holds the content you want to erase. (In this case, click on any layer except the background layer.) The selected layer will become the active layer.

2. Use the Navigator to zoom in on and display the area to erase. The selected area will become more visible.

3. Click on the **Eraser** tool. The Eraser tool will become the active tool.

4. Make a choice from the Mode drop-down list on the options bar. The selected mode will become active for the Eraser tool.

> *Note:* Because the Mode choice affects the available Brush choices in this case, choose the Mode first.

5. Choose a **Brush** style on the options bar. The selected brush will become active for the Eraser tool.

6. Select the **Pressure** text box contents, type a new entry, and press **Enter**. (Alternatively, click on the right arrow beside the Pressure choice, drag the slider, then click on the right arrow again.) The pressure setting will become active for the Eraser tool.

7. Click or drag on the desired layer. Photoshop will erase the current layer's content and reveal the content on the background layer.

   Note: *Checking Erase to History on the options bar makes the Eraser tool restore the area over which you drag to the state (appearance) it had when you last saved the file.*

8. Click on the background layer in the Layers palette. The background layer will become the active layer.

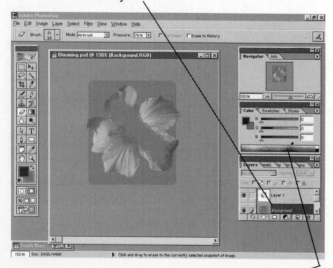

9. Press and hold the **Alt** key, then click on the desired background color in the color bar at the bottom of the Color palette.

Note: *If pressing Alt and clicking selects the foreground color instead, click on the Set Background Color color chip or box near the left side of the Color palette, then Alt+click on the desired background color.*

10. Drag on the background layer. The Eraser tool will paint the selected background color on the background layer. When you finish using the Eraser tool, you can continue working with another tool or operation in Photoshop.

Using the Background Eraser

The Background Eraser tool erases the content on any layer, including both the foreground and background colors on the background layer. Areas you erase with this tool become transparent, so that content on other layers in the image can show through. If the image only has one layer, then the areas erased with this tool will be transparent if the image file is placed in a document.

1. Click on the layer in the Layers palette that holds the content you want to erase. The selected layer will become the active layer.

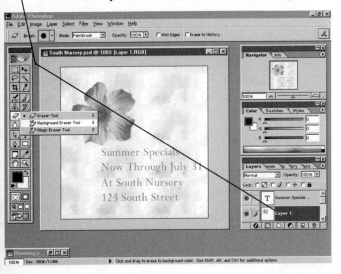

2. Use the Navigator to zoom in on and display the area to erase. The selected area will become more visible.

3. Right-click on the **Eraser** tool. A menu will appear.

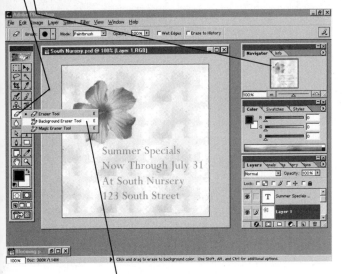

4. Click on **Background Eraser Tool**. The Background Eraser tool will become the active tool.

5. Choose a **Brush** style on the options bar. The selected brush will become active for the Background Eraser tool.

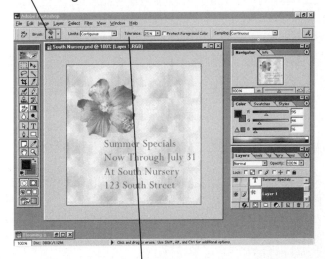

6. Make **Limits**, **Tolerance**, and **Sampling** choices on the options bar. The selected choices will affect the erasing as follows:

   - **Limits**. Controls how far the erasing can spread, based on dragging over similar colors.

   - **Tolerance**. Controls whether the eraser will erase only pixels of alike colors (lower settings) or similar colors.

   - **Sampling**. Determines whether erasing tests matching colors continuously or by the color initially selected.

   Tip: *To make a Tolerance entry, drag over the contents of that text box, type a new entry, and press Enter.*

7. Click or drag on the desired layer. Photoshop will erase the current layer's content, leaving a transparent area behind.

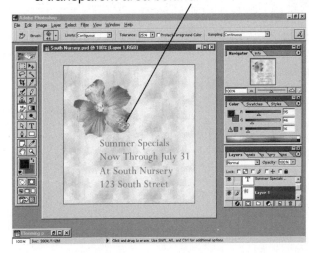

Using the Magic Eraser

Use the Magic Eraser tool when you want to erase a contiguous area of color on a layer. You can either completely erase the area of color, or make the erasure less opaque so that only part of the color area is erased.

1. Click on the layer that holds the content to erase in the Layers palette. The selected layer will become the active layer.

2. Use the Navigator to zoom in on and display the area to erase. The selected area will become more visible.

3. Right-click on the **Eraser** tool. A menu will appear.

4. Click on **Magic Eraser Tool**. The Magic Eraser tool will become the active tool.

5. Make a **Tolerance** entry on the options bar. The specified setting will become active for the Magic Eraser tool. Lower settings will tell the tool to erase only colors that are a closer match; higher settings will enable the tool to also erase less similar colors.

6. Select the **Opacity** text box contents, type a new entry, and press **Enter**. (Alternatively, click on the right arrow beside the Opacity choice, drag the slider, then click on the right arrow again.) The Opacity setting will become active for the Magic Eraser tool.

7. Click or drag on the desired area on the current layer. Photoshop will erase the selected color and any matching adjacent areas, applying transparency if specified.

Adding a Gradient

You can add a gradient onto most layers, except for layers that hold text. The gradient blends the colors you specify, so you may have a bit more flexibility when you use this method to add a gradient, as opposed to inserting a gradient fill layer as described in Chapter 8 in the section called "Adding a Gradient Layer." These steps describe how to use the Gradient tool.

Note: *No matter what types of changes you're making, don't forget to save your file from time to time.*

1. Click on the desired foreground color for the gradient on the color bar in the Color palette. The selected color will become the foreground color (first color) for the blend.

2. Press and hold the **Alt** key, and click on the desired background color on the color bar in the color palette.

3. Click on the desired layer in the Layers palette. The selected layer will become the active layer.

4. Click on the **Gradient** tool in the toolbox. The Gradient tool will become the active tool.

   Tip: *If you want to fill a particular area with a gradient, select the area first (either manually or with a path) or use a mask to prevent Photoshop from displaying the gradient in the affected area.*

5. Click on a gradient style button. Photoshop will apply the selected style.

   Note: *If needed, click on the down arrow beside the Gradient Picker box, and then click on a new gradient to use, Photoshop will apply the selected gradient and its colors. If you click on the Gradient Picker box itself, the Gradient Editor dialog box opens. You can use it to edit the gradient style, or click on the arrow button at the top right of the Presets section of the dialog box and then click on a choice at the bottom of the submenu that appears to see other gradient possibilities.*

6. Select the **Opacity** text box contents, type a new entry, and press **Enter**. (Alternatively, click on the right-arrow beside the Opacity choice, drag the slider, then click on the right arrow again.) The Opacity setting will become active for the Gradient tool.

   Note: *Changing the Mode setting can have the Gradient tool (and the Paint Bucket tool, described in the next section) apply different behavior, such as dissolving the image.*

7. Drag on the layer to set the angle or center point for the gradient (depending on the style you selected in Step 5). Photoshop applies the gradient immediately.

8. Review the results. As with other types of effects you create, the gradient interacts with other content on the layer, blending with that content if the gradient wasn't 100% opaque. Note that in this instance, because the flower image appears on its own layer and that layer is in the front of the image, the gradient doesn't fill or overlay the flower. After you finish the gradient, you can work with another tool or operation in Photoshop.

Filling with the Paint Bucket

Use the Paint Bucket tool to fill a contiguous (adjoining) area of color (or similar colors) with the current foreground color.

1. Click on the foreground color for the fill on the color bar in the Color palette. The selected color will become the fill color for the Paint Bucket tool.

2. Click on the layer in the Layers palette that includes the area you want to fill. The selected layer will become the active layer.

   Tip: *If you want to fill a particular area with the selected color, select the area first (either manually or with a path) on the layer, then click in the selection later to fill it.*

3. Right-click on the **Gradient** tool in the toolbox. A menu will appear.

4. Click on **Paint Bucket Tool**. The Paint Bucket tool will become the active tool.

5. Select the **Opacity** text box contents, type a new entry, and press **Enter**. (Alternatively, click on the right arrow beside the Opacity choice, drag the slider, then click on the right arrow again.) The Opacity setting will become active for the Paint Bucket.

6. Select the **Tolerance** text box contents, type a new entry, and press **Enter**. The Tolerance setting will become active for the Paint Bucket tool. (Remember, Tolerance refers to how carefully a tool must match the color of the area you click on in order to identify which pixels to fill or erase.)

Note: *If you want to use the Paint Bucket to fill an area with a pattern, choose Pattern from the Fill drop-down list, then choose a pattern from the Pattern drop-down list. The steps in the section called "Adding a Pattern Layer" in Chapter 8 explain how to save a pattern choice based on an image selection.*

7. Click on the area to fill with the foreground color you selected. Photoshop applies the gradient immediately. Even if the layer includes other areas with the same color, those areas will not be filled if they are not contiguous. After you finish filling, you can work with another tool or operation in Photoshop.

Using Photo Techniques

One of the past benefits of using a professional photographer was the photographer's (or the photo lab's) ability to manipulate lighting—both when shooting the initial photo and creating the prints. The Dodge, Burn, and Sponge tools in Photoshop help you mimic a photographer's tricks in correcting lighting in an image.

Dodging an Area

Use the Dodge tool to lighten an area that's too dark in your image. In the case of scanned content or a photo downloaded from a digital camera, dodging can actually reveal detail that previously wasn't visible in the image. Follow these steps to work with dodging.

1. Open the image to correct and select the desired layer, if needed. The image (and layer) will become active or current.

2. Click on the **Dodge** tool in the toolbox. The Dodge tool will become the active tool.

3. Choose options on the options bar as needed. The options for the Dodge tool are:

    *   **Brush**. Designates the brush style for the tool.

    *   **Range**. Specifies whether the Dodge tool affects shadows, midtones, or highlights in the areas over which you drag.

    *   **Exposure**. Identifies how much of a change the Dodge tool makes as you drag.

4. Click on or drag over on the desired area(s). Photoshop makes the corrections immediately. After you finish dodging, you can work with another tool or operation in Photoshop.

Burning an Area

The Burn tool has the opposite impact as the Dodge tool. Burning an area darkens an area in the image, as if more light were directed to that area when the "photo" was being developed. You can use burning to help balance an area that seems week or too light in an image, or to emphasize a particular area. In the case of a color image, burning can intensify the color in an area and make it stand out from its background a bit more.

1. Open the desired image and select the layer to burn, if needed. The image (and layer) will become active or current.

    Tip: Use the Navigator whenever you need to zoom in on the area to correct with a tool.

2. Right-click on the **Dodge** tool in the toolbox. A menu will appear.

3. Click on the **Burn Tool**. The Burn tool will become the active tool.

4. **Choose options** on the options bar as needed. The options for the Burn tool are:

    *   **Brush**. Designates the brush style for the tool.

    *   **Range**. Specifies whether the Burn tool affects shadows, midtones, or highlights in the areas over which you drag.

    *   **Exposure**. Identifies how much of a change the Dodge tool makes as you drag.

5. Click on or drag over on the area(s) to burn. Photoshop makes the corrections immediately. After you finish burning, you can work with another tool or operation in Photoshop.

Sponging an Area

The Sponge tool (sponging) changes color saturation in a color image and contrast in a grayscale image. In either case, using the Sponge tool helps make the area you're correcting appear more bright or crisp, to help it stand out from surrounding content in the image.

1. Open the desired image and select the layer to correct, if needed. The image (and layer) will become active or current.

2. Right-click on the **Dodge** tool in the toolbox. A menu will appear.

3. Click on **Sponge Tool**. The Sponge tool will become the active tool.

4. Choose options on the options bar as needed. The options for the Sponge tool are:

   - **Brush**. Designates the brush style for the tool.

   - **Mode**. Specifies whether the Sponge tool saturates (adds more color intensity) or desaturates (decreases color intensity) in the area you drag over.

   - **Pressure**. Identifies how much of a change the Sponge tool makes as you drag.

5. Click on or drag over on the area(s) to sponge. Photoshop makes the corrections immediately. After you finish sponging, you can work with another tool or operation in Photoshop.

Procedures

✓ *Unless otherwise noted, "layer" in these procedures also includes the background layer.*

Use the Blur Tool

1. If necessary, click on the desired layer in the Layers palette.

2. If necessary, use the Navigator to zoom in on and display the desired area.

3. Click the **Blur Tool** button ⬟ from the toolbox.. Ⓡ

4. Select the desired options from the Blur Tool options bar:

   a. Click **Brush** and select a brush size and style.

      ✓ *For further brush options, click the Brush menu arrow ⓓ and click the desired option.*

   b. Click the **Mode** arrow and select the desired mode.

   c. Click in the **Pressure** box and enter the desired pressure percentage.

      OR

      Click the **Pressure** arrow and drag the slider to the desired pressure percentage.

5. Position the mouse pointer in the desired area of the layer.

6. Click or drag to create the desired blur effect.

7. Release the mouse button to cease blurring as needed.

   ✓ *Use Undo, Step Backward, and Step Forward if necessary to get the desired effect.*

8. Repeat steps 4–7 as needed.

   ✓ *To fade the effects of this tool, click **Edit** and then click **Fade** [tool name] (Ctrl+Shift+F).*

Use the Smudge Tool

1. If necessary, click on the desired layer in the Layers palette.

2. If necessary, use the Navigator to zoom in on and display the desired area.

3. Click the **Smudge Tool** button 👌 from the toolbox.. Ⓡ

4. Select the desired options from the Smudge Tool options bar:

   a. Click **Brush** and select a brush size and style.

      ✓ *For further brush options, click the Brush menu arrow ⓓ and click the desired option.*

   b. Click the **Mode** arrow and select the desired mode.

   c. Click in the **Pressure** box and enter the desired pressure percentage.

      OR

      Click the **Pressure** arrow and drag the slider to the desired pressure percentage.

   d. Select the **Finger Painting** checkbox to smudge with the foreground color.

5. Position the mouse pointer in the desired area of the layer.

6. Drag over different colors to create the desired smudge effect.

   ✓ *If using the Finger Painting option, each time you click the mouse adds some foreground to the "smudge" mix.*

7. Release the mouse button to cease smudging as needed.

   ✓ *Use Undo, Step Backward, and Step Forward if necessary to get the desired effect.*

8. Repeat steps 4–7 as needed.

   ✓ *To fade the effects of this tool, click **Edit** and then click **Fade** [tool name] (Ctrl+Shift+F).*

Use the Sharpen Tool

1. If necessary, click on the desired layer in the Layers palette.

2. If necessary, use the Navigator to zoom in on and display the desired area.

3. Click the **Sharpen Tool** button 🔺 from the toolbox .... Ⓡ

4. Select the desired options from the Sharpen Tool options bar:

   a. Click **Brush** and select a brush size and style.

      ✔ *For further brush options, click the Brush menu arrow ⓓ and click the desired option.*

   b. Click the **Mode** arrow and select the desired mode.

   c. Click in the **Pressure** box and enter the desired pressure percentage.

      OR

      Click the **Pressure** arrow and drag the slider to the desired pressure percentage.

5. Position the mouse pointer in the desired area of the layer.

6. Click or drag to create the desired sharpening effect.

7. Release the mouse button to cease sharpening as needed.

   ✔ *Use Undo, Step Backward, and Step Forward if necessary to get the desired effect.*

8. Repeat steps 4–7 as needed.

   ✔ *To fade the effects of this tool, click **Edit** and then click **Fade** [tool name] (Ctrl+Shift+F).*

Use Eraser Tool

1. If necessary, click on the desired layer in the Layers palette.

2. If necessary, use the Navigator to zoom in on and display the desired area.

3. Click the **Eraser Tool** button 🖉 from the toolbox .... Ⓔ

4. Select the desired options from the Eraser Tool options bar:

   a. Click the **Tolerance** box and enter the desired percentage.

      OR

      Click the **Tolerance** arrow and drag the slider to the desired percentage.

   b. Click in the **Anti-aliased** checkbox to select or deselect it.

   c. Select the **Contiguous** checkbox to select or deselect it.

   d. Select the **Use All Layers** checkbox to select or deselect it.

   e. Click in **Opacity** and enter the desired opacity performance.

      OR

      Click the **Opacity** arrow and drag the slider to the desired opacity percentage.

5. Position the mouse pointer in the desired area of the layer.

6. Click or drag to erase the desired area.

7. Release the mouse button to cease erasing as needed.

   ✔ *Use Undo, Step Backward, and Step Forward if necessary to get the desired effect—or use the Erase to History option.*

8. Repeat steps 4–7 as needed.

   ✔ *To fade the effects of this tool, click **Edit** and then click **Fade** [tool name] (Ctrl+Shift+F).*

Use the Background Eraser Tool

1. If necessary, click on the desired layer in the Layers palette.

2. If necessary, use the Navigator to zoom in on and display the desired area.

3. Click the **Background Eraser Tool** button 🖉 from the toolbox .... Ⓔ

4. Select the desired options from the Background Eraser Tool options bar:

   a. Click **Brush** and select a brush size and style.

✓ *For further brush options, click the Brush menu arrow ⊙ and click the desired option.*

b. Click the **Limits** arrow and select the desired setting.

c. Click in the **Tolerance** box and enter the desired percentage.

   OR

   Click the **Tolerance** arrow and drag the slider to the desired percentage.

d. Select the **Protect Foreground Color** checkbox if needed to keep foreground color from being erased.

e. Click the **Sampling** arrow and select the desired setting.

5. Position the mouse pointer in the desired area of the layer.

6. Click or drag to erase the desired area.

7. Release the mouse button to cease erasing as needed.

   ✓ *Use Undo, Step Backward, and Step Forward if necessary to get the desired effect.*

8. Repeat steps 4–7 as needed.

   ✓ *To fade the effects of this tool, click Edit and then click Fade [tool name] (Ctrl+Shift+F).*

Use the Magic Eraser Tool

1. If necessary, click on the desired layer in the Layers palette.

2. If necessary, use the Navigator to zoom in on and display the desired area.

3. Click the **Magic Eraser Tool** button 🖾 from the toolbox...................... E

4. Select the desired options from the Magic Eraser Tool options bar:

a. Click in the **Tolerance** box and enter a number from 1–255.

b. Click the **Anti-aliased** checkbox to select or deselect it.

c. Select the **Contiguous** checkbox to select or deselect it.

d. Click the **Use All Layers** checkbox to select or deselect it.

e. Click in **Opacity** and enter the desired opacity percentage.

   OR

   Click the **Opacity** arrow and drag the slider to the desired opacity percentage.

5. Position the mouse pointer in the desired area of the layer.

6. Click or drag to erase the desired area.

7. Release the mouse button to cease erasing as needed.

   ✓ *Use Undo, Step Backward, and Step Forward if necessary to get the desired effect.*

8. Repeat steps 4–7 as needed.

   ✓ *To fade the effects of this tool, click Edit and then click Fade [tool name] (Ctrl+Shift+F).*

Use Gradient Tool

✓ *See Chapter 3 for the procedure to choose a foreground and background color in the Color palette or with the Eyedropper tool.*

1. Select a foreground color.

2. Select a background color.

3. Click the **Gradient Tool** button 🎨 in the toolbox................................... G

4. Select the desired options from the Gradient Tool options bar:

a. Click on the **Gradient** box arrow and select a preset gradient.

   OR

   Click in the **Gradient** box, create a custom gradient in the Gradient Editor dialog box, and click **OK**.

b. Choose a gradient style button:

   • **Linear Gradient** 🎨.

   • **Radial Gradient** ⬤.

   • **Angle Gradient** 🔲.

   • **Reflected Gradient** ▬.

OR

Diamond Gradient .

c. Click the **Mode** arrow and select the desired mode.

d. Click in **Opacity** and enter the desired opacity percentage.

   OR

   Click the **Opacity** arrow and drag the slider to the desired opacity percentage.

e. Select the **Reverse** checkbox to select or deselect it.

f. Select the **Dither** checkbox to select or deselect it.

g. Select the **Transparency** checkbox to select or deselect it.

5. Depending on the style of gradient selected, drag on the layer to set angle or center point if necessary.

Use Paint Bucket Tool

✓ *See Chapter 3 for the procedure to choose a foreground color in the Color palette or with the Eyedropper tool.*

1. Select the desired foreground color.

   ✓ *Skip step 1 if a pattern fill is desired, which can be selected from the Paint Bucket Tool options bar.*

2. If necessary, click on the desired layer in the Layers palette.

3. Click the **Paint Bucket Tool** button in the toolbox .... G

4. Select the desired options from the Paint Bucket Tool options bar:

   a. If a pattern fill is desired, click on the **Fill** box arrow, click **Pattern**, and then select the desired pattern from the Pattern menu.

   b. Click the **Mode** arrow and select the desired mode.

   c. Click in **Opacity** and enter the desired opacity percentage.

   OR

   Click the **Opacity** arrow and drag the slider to the desired opacity percentage.

d. Click in the **Tolerance** box and enter a number from 1–255.

e. Click the **Anti-aliased** checkbox to select or deselect it.

f. Select the **Contiguous** checkbox to select or deselect it.

g. Select the **All Layers** checkbox to select or deselect it.

5. Click on the area in the layer to fill.

Use the Dodge Tool

1. If necessary, click on the desired layer in the Layers palette.

2. Click the **Dodge Tool** button on the toolbox .... O

3. Select the desired options from the Dodge Tool options bar:

   a. Click **Brush** and select a brush size and style.

      ✓ *For further brush options, click the Brush menu arrow and click the desired option.*

   b. Click the **Range** arrow and select:

      • **Shadows**

      • **Midtones**

      OR

      Highlights

   c. Click in the **Exposure** box and enter the desired exposure percentage.

   OR

   Click the **Exposure** arrow and drag the slider to the desired exposure percentage.

4. Click or drag to dodge the desired area.

5. Release the mouse button to cease dodging as needed.

   ✓ *Use Undo, Step Backward, and Step Forward if necessary to get the desired effect.*

6. Repeat steps 3–5 as needed.

   ✓ *To fade the effects of this tool, click **Edit** and then click **Fade** [tool name] (Ctrl+Shift+F).*

Directions

1. Start Photoshop, if needed.

2. Use the File|Open command to open the ⊘ **PS11** Photoshop file.

3. Save the file as **SUN**.

4. Zoom the image to 100% size and increase the size of the file window.

5. Choose the Background layer.

   ✓ *In fact, make sure the Background layer is selected unless otherwise instructed in this exercise.*

6. Choose the Blur tool, change the Brush setting if desired, press and hold the left mouse button, and drag it back and forth over the left eye in the sun face. Compare the left and right eyes to see the blurring.

7. Undo the blurring.

8. Choose the Smudge tool, change the Brush setting if desired, and change the Pressure setting to 60-70%. Press and hold the left mouse button, and drag from the black area near the top of the layer down over the tan clapboard area. The black color should be smudged down in the tan, with the black gradually becoming lighter, as in Illustration 1.

9. Undo the smudging.

10. Choose the Sharpen tool, change the Brush setting if desired, press and hold the left mouse button, and drag it back and forth a few times over the left eye in the sun face. Compare the left and right eyes to see the sharpening, as shown in Illustration 1.

    ✓ *In this case, the sharpening will cause the highlights to have a more definite outline, making them appear brighter. Use the sharpen tool sparingly, as it can quickly make an area appear pixellated or blocky.*

11. Undo the sharpening.

12. Choose the Eraser tool and change its settings, if needed. Also choose the background color of your choice by using Alt+click on the Color or Swatches palette.

Drag in a circle around the sun face. In this case, the tool will paint with the background color, because the regular Eraser tool can't erase on the Background layer.

13. Undo the erasure (painting).

14. Choose the Background Eraser tool and change its settings, if needed. Drag in a circle around the sun face. This tool will erase all content on the layer, revealing a transparent background as shown in Illustration 2.

    ✓ *By default, you should see a gray and white checkerboard pattern in the transparent areas. If not, you can use the Edit|Preferences|Transparency & Gamut settings to turn on the grid so that you can verify the transparency.*

15. Undo the erasure.

16. Choose the Magic Eraser tool and change its Tolerance setting to 20. Click on the black shadow below the sun face. This will erase the black shadow and all contiguous black areas, including many of the shadows on the sun face itself.

17. Undo the erasure.

18. Use the Color or Swatches palette to choose new foreground and background colors.

19. Chose the Gradient tool, choose a gradient style, and change the Opacity setting to 75%. Drag from the center of the sun face's nose to the upper-left corner of the image area. The gradient will appear over the image immediately. Note that in this case, the gradient will appear right on the current layer; Photoshop will not create a new layer for it.

20. Undo the gradient.

21. Chose the Paint Bucket tool. Change its Opacity to 50% and Tolerance to 25, then click on a highlight on the sun face. The highlight will be filled with the foreground color.

22. Undo the paint bucket fill.

23. Choose the Dodge tool, change its settings if needed, press and hold the left mouse button, and drag repeatedly back and forth over the bottom right area of the sun face, where it adjoins its shadow. The edge of the sun face will become more obvious and the adjoining shadow will be lightened.

    ✓ *Dodging lightens an area in a photo (scanned image or image from a digital camera) that's too dark, often revealing hidden detail. Burning darkens an area, fixing or blending a too-light area. Sponging helps you work specifically with the color or contrast in an area.*

24. Undo the dodging.

25. Choose the Burn tool, change its settings if needed, press and hold the left mouse button, and drag repeatedly back and forth over the top left of the sun face, where it adjoins the clapboard background. The edge of the sun face will darken, so it's more consistent with the rest of the sun face.

26. Undo the burning.

27. Choose the Sponge tool, change the Pressure setting to 100%, press and hold the left mouse button, and drag repeatedly back and forth over the center of the sun face. The effect will be very subtle, but the colors will even out in the image. The coppery color will be toned down on the face.

28. Undo the sponging.

29. Use the three tools of your choice (or more) to enhance the image.

    ✓ *If required by your instructor for grading purposes, write down what tools you've used and what part of the image you've corrected.*

30. Save and close the image.

Illustration 1

Illustration 2

Erased area

Next
Chapter
▶▶

12

Working with Image Size and Orientation

When you create a new image file, you specify its size. When you import an image from a scanner or digital camera, you have less control over the size and orientation of the image. In either case, you can use some tricks to tweak the size and orientation of the image so that it suits your purpose. In this chapter, you'll learn how to:

❋ Use the Crop tool to crop an image

❋ Resize the image

❋ Adjust the image canvas

❋ Rotate the entire canvas

❋ Trim the edges of the image

Cropping the Image

When you crop the image, you select the area of the image that you want to keep, and then have Photoshop hide or remove the unselected portions of the image. You can crop if an image's subject is off-center, if you need to eliminate a distracting element from the image, or if you need to fit the image to a particular height and width.

1. Click on the **Crop** tool on the toolbox. The Crop tool will become active.

2. Make entries in the **Width** and **Height** text boxes, if needed. When you use these text boxes, Photoshop will resize the cropped material to the specified dimensions (in addition to performing the crop).

   Note: *Enter the abbreviation for inches, in, in the Width and Height text boxes unless you want to specify the measurement in pixels (px). Clicking on Front Image loads the current image dimensions into the text boxes.*

3. Make an entry in the Resolution text box, if needed. If you make an entry, Photoshop will resample the cropped material to the specified resolution.

4. Drag on the image. This will select the area to keep; the area outside the selection will be shielded or grayed out.

5. Adjust shielding settings, if needed. Photoshop will change the temporary shading used to mask the areas to be cropped out of the image.

6. Click on the **Perspective** check box, if needed. This will enable perspective cropping, so that you can add perspective while cropping.

7. Drag the crop selection to resize or rotate the crop zone. Dragging a corner will resize the crop zone, and dragging a side will rotate the crop zone.

8. Click on the **Commit** button (✓) on the options bar or press **Enter**. Photoshop will crop the image to the specified zone.

Note: If you've selected part of the image with a selection tool, you can click on Image and then click on Crop to display the Crop dialog box. Click on an option button to determine whether the cropped out areas should be Hidden or Deleted, then click on OK to apply the crop.

Changing the Image Size

You can resize an image file when you want to both fit the image to a particular size and keep all of the content in the image. Resizing the image also gives you the opportunity to resample it, or change the resolution (pixels per inch) in the image.

Tip: Although both increasing and decreasing the resolution can degrade image quality, in general more pixels per inch leads to better image quality.

1. Click on **Image**. The Image menu will appear.

2. Click on **Image Size**. The Image Size dialog box will open.

Tip: To see the current image size before you display the Image Size dialog box, press and hold the Alt key, and click and hold on the Doc size indicator near the bottom-left corner of the Photoshop window.

3. Enter a new width or height under either Pixel Dimensions or Document Size. Photoshop will adjust the other three text box entries to keep them proportional.

Tip: Click on the Constrain Proportion check box to clear the check if you want to resize only one image dimension. Otherwise, changing a Height entry automatically adjusts the Width, and vice versa.

4. Enter a new **Resolution**. Photoshop will apply the new resolution setting.

Tip: *Use the Resample Image drop-down list to choose another resampling method for faster (but less accurate) resampling. Alternatively, click on the Resample Image check box to clear it and disable resampling.*

5. Click on **Auto**. The Auto Resolution dialog box will open.

6. Make a new **Screen** text box entry and choose another measure from the **Screen** drop-down list, if needed. Photoshop will apply the designated line screen settings when you finish resizing the image.

Note: *The settings in the Auto Resolution affect the image if you plan to include it in a document to be professionally printed. These settings are less important if you'll be using the image online or merely printing it from your own printer.*

7. Click on a **Quality** option. Photoshop will apply the new quality setting.

8. Click on **OK**. The Auto dialog box will close.

9. Click on **OK**. The Image Size dialog box will close and Photoshop will resize and resample the image as specified.

Changing the Canvas Size

The canvas size and image size always use the same dimensions. Thus, changing the canvas size changes the image size, but not in the same way that using the Image Size command does. When you change to a canvas size that's smaller than the current image/canvas size, Photoshop crops out part of the image. When you change to a canvas size that's larger than the current image/canvas size, Photoshop adds white space to the image. (If the image has a filled background, the fill color fills the added space.)

1. Click on **Image**. The Image menu will appear.

2. Click on **Canvas Size**. The Canvas Size dialog box will open.

3. Enter a new **Width** and/or **Height**, and choose another measurement unit for each, if needed. Photoshop will display the projected new size for the image above those measurements.

4. Click another **Anchor** point, if needed. When you're increasing the canvas size, the selected anchor point will control where white space will be added around the image. When you're decreasing the canvas size, the selected anchor point will designate which part of the image to keep and which to crop out.

5. Click on **OK**. Photoshop will apply the new canvas size, unless it needs to display a warning regarding the size change, as shown in Step 6.

6. Click on **Proceed** in the warning dialog box, if it appears. Photoshop will finish resizing the canvas.

Rotating the Canvas

You can rotate the canvas to rotate the entire image—all the content on all the layers. Photoshop provides these rotation options:

- **180°**. Rotates the canvas so that the top of the image becomes the bottom.

- **90° CW**. Rotates the canvas one quarter turn in the clockwise direction.

- **90° CCW**. Rotates the canvas one quarter turn in the counterclockwise direction.

- **Arbitrary**. Displays the Rotate Canvas dialog box so that you can specify a precise rotation amount and direction.

- **Flip Horizontal**. Flips the image right to left.

- **Flip Vertical**. Flips the image top to bottom.

Use the following steps when you're ready to rotate the image.

1. Click on **Image**. The Image menu will appear.

2. Click on **Rotate Canvas**. The Rotate Canvas submenu will appear.

3. Click on a rotation choice. If you chose anything but Arbitrary, Photoshop will apply the rotation immediately. Otherwise, the Rotate Canvas dialog box will appear.

4. Type an entry in the **Angle** text box. Your entry will specify how much rotation Photoshop applies.

5. Click on the **CW** or **CCW option**. Your choice will specify either the clockwise or counter-clockwise rotation direction.

6. Click on **OK**. Photoshop will rotate the image as specified by the rotation settings you entered.

Trimming the Canvas

You can use the trim feature to crop out unneeded information around the edge of an image, such as a white photo print border; blank canvas space that's no longer needed; or discolored areas around an image from a contact sheet, fading, or folding. For the trim feature to work, the area to be trimmed must all be the same color.

1. Click on **Image**. The Image menu will appear.

2. Click on **Trim**. The Trim dialog box will open.

3. Click on a **Based On** option button. Photoshop will use the specified setting to identify which pixels to trim from the image.

4. Click on **Trim Away** check boxes as needed. Clearing a Trim Away check box tells Photoshop not to trim the designated portion of the image.

5. Click on **OK**. Photoshop will perform the image trim.

Procedures

Crop an Image

✓ The term "cropped area" in these procedures means the area to be deleted or hidden. The term "crop selection" means the area selected by the Crop Tool that is left after the crop.

1. Click the **Crop Tool** button 🔲 from the toolbox .... ⓒ

2. For cropping with specified dimensions:

   a. In the Crop Tool options bar, enter a width and a measurement abbreviation (**in** for inches or **px** or nothing for pixels) in the **Width** box.

   b. In the Crop Tool options bar, enter a height and a measurement abbreviation (**in** for inches or **px** or nothing for pixels) in the **Height** box.

3. Select the desired options from the Crop Tool options bar:

   a. Click in the **Resolution** box and enter a number between 1–30,000.

   b. Click the **Resolution** box arrow and select a resolution type:

      ● **Pixels/inch**

      ● **Pixels/cm**

✓ If you have made setting you don't want in the Crop Tool options bar, click the Clear button .

4. Click the mouse a little to the left and above the desired cropping position and hold down the mouse button.

5. Drag diagonally to select the crop selection to the desired size and shape.

6. After making the crop, the Crop Tool options bar provides customizable viewing options:

   a. Click the **Shield cropped area** checkbox to select or deselect the shield.

   b. Click the **Color** box to change the shield color in the Color Picker dialog box.

   c. Click in the **Opacity** box and enter the desired percentage.

      OR

      Click the **Opacity** arrow and drag the slider to the desired percentage.

   d. Click the **Perspective** checkbox to select or deselect the cropping with added perspective.

   e. Click the **Cropped Area Delete** or **Hide** option buttons to choose between the two options.

7. Use the handles on the crop selection to make any other adjustments.

8. To complete the crop:
   - Click the **Commit** button ✔ in the options toolbar.

   OR

   - Press **Enter** .... `Enter`

   OR

   - Right-click the crop selection and click **Crop**.
     - ✓ To cancel a crop, click the **Cancel** button ✖ or right-click the crop selection and click **Cancel**.

Change Image Size

1. Click **Image** .... `Alt`+`I`

2. Click **Image Size** .... `I`
   - ✓ Choose to resize the image under Pixel Dimensions or Document Size. The new size will be reflected in both settings.
   - ✓ The new size will adjust proportionally for either method unless the Constrain Proportions checkbox is cleared.

3. To change the size of the document under Pixel Dimensions:
   - Enter a new width in the **Width** box .... `Alt`+`W`

   OR

   - Enter a new height in the **Height** box .... `Alt`+`H`

   OR

   To change the document size of the image, under Document Size:
   - ✓ Click the arrows in the Width and Height box to change the type of measurement (percent, inches, cm, points, picas, and columns).
   - Enter a new width in the **Width** box .... `Alt`+`D`

   OR

   - Enter a new height in the **Height** box .... `Alt`+`G`
     - ✓ To change the image resolution, see steps 3-4 in "Change Image Resolution."

4. Click **OK** .... `Enter`

Change Image Resolution

1. Click **Image** .... `Alt`+`I`

2. Click **Image Size** .... `I`

3. Enter a new resolution in the **Resolution** box .... `Alt`+`R`
   - ✓ Click the Resolution box arrow to select between pixels/in or pixels/cm.

4. Click **OK** .... `Enter`

Use Auto Resolution

1. Click **Image** .... `Alt`+`I`

2. Click **Image Size** .... `I`

3. Click the **Auto** button .... `Alt`+`A`

4. Enter the desired screen line setting in the **Screen** box .... `Alt`+`S`
   - ✓ Click the Screen box arrow to select between lines/in or lines/cm.

5. Click the desired quality button:
   - **Draft** .... `Alt`+`D`
   - **Good** .... `Alt`+`G`
   - **Best** .... `Alt`+`B`

6. Click **OK** .... `Enter`

7. Click **OK** .... `Enter`

Change Canvas Size

1. Click **Image** .... `Alt`+`I`

2. Click **Canvas Size** .... `S`

3. Under New Size:

a. Enter a new width in the
   Width box.................................... `Alt`+`W`

b. Enter a new height in the
   Height box................................... `Alt`+`H`

   ✓ *Click the arrows in the Width and
   Height box to change the type of
   measurement (percent, inches, cm,
   points, picas, and columns).*

4. Click an **Anchor** button to select a new
   anchor point if desired.

5. Click **OK**.................................... `Enter`

Rotate Canvas

1. Click **Image**.............................. `Alt`+`I`

2. Click **Rotate Canvas** .... `E`

3. Click the desired rotation in the submenu:

   > 180°
   > 90° CW
   > 90° CCW
   > Arbitrary...
   >
   > Flip Horizontal
   > Flip Vertical

4. If you clicked Arbitrary:
   a. Enter the degrees in the
      Angle box................................ `Alt`+`A`

b. For a clockwise angle, click
   the **CW** option .... `Alt`+`C`

c. For a counterclockwise angle,
   click the **CCW** option.................... `Alt`+`W`

5. Click **OK** .... `Enter`

Trim Canvas

1. Click **Image** .... `Alt`+`I`

2. Click **Trim**................................... `R`

3. Select an option under Based On:
   a. **Transparent Pixels** .... `Alt`+`A`
   b. **Top Left Pixel Color** .... `Alt`+`O`

   OR

   Bottom Right Pixel Color........... `Alt`+`M`

4. Click on the desired Trim Away checkbox
   options:
   • **Top**.. `Alt`+`T`
   • **Bottom**.................................... `Alt`+`B`
   • **Left**.. `Alt`+`L`
   • **Right** .... `Alt`+`R`

5. Click **OK** .... `Enter`

Exercise 12

In an earlier exercise, you saw how to use a mask to hide or crop out part of the information on a layer. That technique affected the selected layer only. This exercise presents the alternate techniques that you need to use to crop the entire image or even increase the image size. You can select part of the image and discard the rest of it—called *cropping*. To keep all of the image content but change its size, you can either specify new image dimensions or resample the image. Resampling increases or decreases the number of pixels per inch, affecting the image's dimensions, clarity, and file size. To rotate the image, you rotate the canvas (the imaginary space that all the layers rest on). You also can trim the canvas to remove part of the image or increase the size of the canvas to make room for more image content. Get started now with these various techniques.

Directions

1. Start Photoshop, if needed.

2. Use the File|Open command to open the ⊙ **PS12** Photoshop file.

3. Save the file as **CAP**.

4. Zoom the image to 100% size, increase the size of the file window, and display approximately the center of the image.

    ✓   *Notice that the original image file is about 2.73M in size. The near lower-left area of the Photoshop status bar displays the file size by default.*

5. Choose the Image|Image Size command. The Image Size dialog box will appear.

6. In the Document Size area of the dialog box, change the Width setting to 4 inches and change the Resolution setting to 125 pixels/inch, and then click OK. Photoshop immediately resamples the image. Note the newly-calculated file size.

7. Use the Rectangular Marquee tool to select an area near the center of the image that includes the Capitol Building, as shown in Illustration 1.

8. Choose Image|Crop. Photoshop will immediately crop the image file, as shown in Illustration 2.

9. Choose Image|Rotate Canvas|90° CW. Photoshop will immediately rotate the image.

10. Undo the rotation.

11. Choose Image|Canvas Size. The Canvas Size dialog box will appear.

12. Change the Width and Height settings to 2 inches, then click on OK. The expanded canvas will appear immediately, as in Illustration 3.

    ✓   *When you add extra canvas space like this, you can then add text in the white border area to caption the image, for example. Added canvas area will be opaque if the layer is.*

13. Save and close the image.

Illustration 1

Illustration 2

Illustration 3

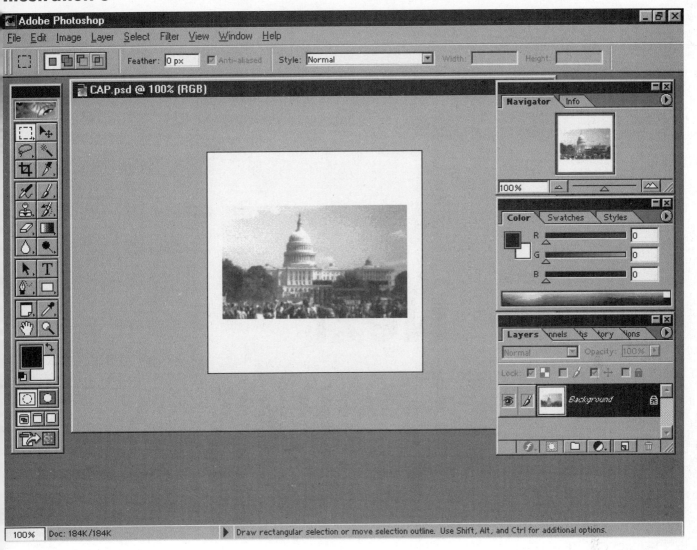

Next Chapter ▶▶

13

Using a Filter

You can think of a filter as a special effect. When you apply the filter, Photoshop makes changes to the image or selection that might otherwise take you numerous steps to create or that may not even be possible. This chapter enables you to:

❋ Understand the available filters

❋ Apply a filter when you need it

❋ Adjust the filter

❋ Use the last filter again

chapter

Previewing the Filters

The default Photoshop installation installs dozens of filters. The filter menu groups the filters on several submenus. The table below lists the submenus and gives a description of the types of filters found in each submenu group.

Group	Includes Filters That
Artistic	Make the image look like it was created with watercolors or pastels, has a film grain, has poster edges, and so on.
Blur	Add blurs to simulate movement, such as in a single direction or rotation.
Brush Strokes	Apply a brush stroke effect in one of various available shapes.
Distort	Give the appearance of natural or artificial distortions caused by shape and light, such as a ripple, glass, or twirl effect.
Noise	Apply noise (white speckling) to affect the image appearance, or fix spots and scratches.
Pixelate	Apply one of several dotted effects to the image.
Render	Let you change the fill, add a lighting effect, apply 3D, and more.
Sharpen	Improve image sharpness.
Sketch	Apply a drawing effect in one of various available techniques.
Stylize	Make a number of changes that lend a modern effect like glowing edges or embossing.
Texture	Convert the image's appearance to make it consistent with the selected texture.
Video	Change the color method used in a video still.
Other	Create a custom filter or work with other custom filters.

Note: *Plug-ins are generally additional filters that you can install. See Chapter 18, "Working with Plug-Ins," to learn more about installing and using plug-ins.*

Applying a Filter

Applying some filters merely requires selecting the appropriate filter command. The vast majority of filters display a dialog box with a preview that enables you to adjust and preview the filter before applying it. Because the filter settings vary to such a degree, the following steps provide an overview of using a filter.

Tip: *After you apply one filter, you can apply another to blend filter effects.*

1. Open the image you want to adjust. The image will open in a window in Photoshop.

2. Display the layer that holds the desired image content to filter and use a selection tool to select the desired image area, if needed. The selected layer's content will appear, and a selection marquee will appear.

Tip: *Photoshop applies the filter effect only to the current layer and current selection (if any).*

3. Click on **Filter**. The Filter menu will appear.

4. Point to a filter submenu name. The submenu will appear.

5. Click on a filter in the submenu. Photoshop will either apply the filter immediately, or display the settings dialog box for the filter.

6. Adjust dialog box settings as needed. The preview in the dialog box adjusts to show what the filter will do to the image or selection when applied.

7. Click on **OK**. The dialog box will close and Photoshop will apply the filter.

   Note: *If the image doesn't use RGB color or is a bitmapped, indexed, or 16-bit per channel image, Photoshop won't allow you to apply a filter to it. Consult Chapter 15, "Understanding Colors and Channels," to learn more about image color modes.*

Fading a Filter

Note: *The Fade command may not be available for all filters. However, it is available for some of the painting tools in Photoshop and works for those just as described here.*

Fading a filter enables you to make the filter effect more transparent or adjust the light or color density for the filter effect. Using the Fade capability gives you even greater control over how the filter affects the image.

1. Open the image to adjust. The image will open in a window in Photoshop.

2. Display the layer that holds the image content to filter and select the filtered area, if needed. The selected layer's content will appear, and a selection marquee will appear.

   Tip: *Save and name the selection area before applying a filter. (See "Saving a Selection" and "Loading a Selection" in Chapter 6.) Then, you can easily reload the selection to fade or adjust the filter settings.*

3. Click on **Edit**. The Edit menu will appear.

4. Click on **Fade (Filter Name)**. The Fade dialog box will open.

5. Drag the **Opacity** slider. The Opacity setting will adjust accordingly.

6. Click on the down arrow beside the **Mode** list. The Mode list will open.

7. Click on a mode in the list. The image or selection will preview the selected Opacity and Mode settings.

8. Click on **OK**. The dialog box will close and Photoshop will apply the fade.

Reapplying the Last Filter

You can apply the most recently used filter to another selection or image. Using this shortcut applies the filter using the settings for the filter that you selected when you previously used the filter.

1. Open the image to adjust. The image will open in a window in Photoshop.

2. Display the layer that holds the image content to filter and use a selection tool to select the desired image area, if needed. The selected layer's content will appear, and a selection marquee will appear.

3. Click on **Filter**. The Filter menu will appear.

4. Click on the filter at the top of the menu. Photoshop will apply the filter immediately.

    Note: *If you're applying the filter to an entire layer and the image is large, it can take a few minutes for Photoshop to process the filter application.*

Procedures

Apply a Filter

1. If necessary, click on the layer with the desired image content in the Layers palette.

2. Select the desired area in the layer.

    ✓ *If no selection is made, the filter is applied to the entire image.*

3. Click **Filter** .... Alt + T

4. Click the desired filter set in the Filter menu:

Artistic	▶
Blur	▶
Brush Strokes	▶
Distort	▶
Noise	▶
Pixelate	▶
Render	▶
Sharpen	▶
Sketch	▶
Stylize	▶
Texture	▶
Video	▶
Other	▶

5. Click the desired filter in the submenu.

    ✓ *Some filters require further settings. If so, perform steps 6 and 7.*

6. Select the desired settings in the selected filter's dialog box.

7. Click **OK** .... Enter

    ✓ *Hint: Before deselecting the selection marquee, save the selection so that it can be loaded again for future image editing. See the procedures for saving and loading a selection in Chapter 6.*

Fade a Filter (Shift+Ctrl+F)

1. With the filtered area still selected after applying the filter, click **Edit** .... Alt + E

2. Click **Fade [filter name]**.

3. Click in the **Opacity** box and enter the desired percentage....................... Alt + O

    OR

    Click the **Opacity** arrow and drag the slider to the desired percentage.

4. Click on the **Mode** box arrow and select the desired mode.

5. Click **OK** .... Enter

Reapply Last Filter (Ctrl+F)

1. If necessary, click on the layer with the desired image content in the Layers palette.

2. Select the desired area in the layer.

    ✓ *If no selection is made, the filter is applied to the entire image.*

3. Click **Filter**... Alt + T

4. At the top of the menu, click **[Filter name]**.

Exercise 13

Photoshop comes with a number of filters, arranged for you on submenus of the Filters menu. Most filters enable you to apply some special effect to selected content on a layer. For example, you could add a motion blur to a portion of an image that contains a car, to simulate the appearance of movement. Or, you can use one of the artistic or stylistic filters to make an ordinary scanned image look more like a work of art. In this exercise, practice using a few filters.

Directions

1. Start Photoshop, if needed.

2. Use the File|Open command to open the ⊙ PS13 Photoshop file.

3. Save the file as **STAT**.

4. Zoom the image to 100% size and scroll up to the top of the image.

5. Use the Rectangular Marquee tool to select the head and shoulders area of the statue.

6. Choose Filter|Stylize|Glowing Edges. The Glowing Edges dialog box will appear.

7. Adjust the filter settings until the preview looks as you want it to, then click on OK. Illustration 1 shows an example of how the filter might look.

8. Choose Edit|Fade Glowing Edges. The Fade dialog box will appear.

9. Change the Opacity setting to 50%, then click on OK. The filtering effect will become more subtle.

10. Undo the filter fading, and then step backward to undo the Glowing Edges filter.

11. Choose Filter|Distort|Twirl. The Twirl dialog box will appear.

12. Chang the Angle setting to 75, then click on OK. Illustration 2 shows an example of how your image might look at this point.

13. Undo the Twirl filter.

14. Choose Filter|Artistic|Sponge. The Sponge dialog box will appear.

15. Change the Brush Size setting to 5, change the Definition setting to 15, and change the Smoothness setting to 1. Click on OK. Illustration 3 shows an example of how the filter should look.

16. Undo the Sponge filter.

17. Choose Filter|Sponge to reapply the Sponge filter with the settings you most recently selected.

18. Save and close the file.

Illustration 1

Illustration 2

Illustration 3

14

Printing Your Image

In most environments, you'll use a local or network printer to print your image file so you can check your work. Photoshop adds a number of printing features that you may not have seen before if your previous computer experience has been limited to word processors and spreadsheets. This chapter helps you explore the printing possibilities in Photoshop and shows you how to:

❋ Choose the printer to use

❋ Choose a screen setting for traditional printing

❋ Use transfer settings to correct certain color problems

❋ Add a border, bleed, or background for the printout

❋ Print with other special marks and features

❋ Choose print scaling options

❋ Send the print job

Choosing a Printer

Stating the obvious, different printers offer different capabilities. You may have a black-and-white laser printer for basic document printouts and image proofing and a color printer for sales documents and final image printouts. You need to select the printer to use to print the current image from among those installed on your system, as described here.

1. Click on **File**. The File menu will appear.

2. Click on **Page Setup**. The Page Setup dialog box will open.

3. Click on the down arrow beside the **Name** drop-down list. The Name drop-down list will open.

4. Click on the desired printer in the list. The printer will become the active printer.

5. Click on **Properties**. The properties dialog box for the selected printer will appear.

6. Choose options for the printer as needed. The choices will become the active choices.

7. Click on **OK**. Your printer settings will take effect and the Properties dialog box will close.

8a. Click on **OK** to finish at this time. The printer settings (and any other Page Setup settings) will take effect.

OR

8b. Choose other settings as described in the next section, then click on **OK** to finish. The new settings you've selected will take effect.

Changing the Page Setup

Other settings in the Page Setup dialog box have an impact on how Photoshop prepares an image for printing from your printer for output by a professional print shop (or for inclusion in a document that will be output professionally). This section shows you how to find the various settings you may need to prepare the current image for printing.

Working with Screens

Note: *You must save an image to save your Page Setup choices for it. Use the Save As command on the File menu to save a Photoshop file as an EPS file. The section called "Saving to Another Format" in Chapter 2 explains how to save a Photoshop file in another format.*

A *screen* (*or halftone screen*) controls the size, shape, and alignment of the dots of black or colors that print during a printout. For full-color printing, the CMYK (**C**yan, **M**agenta, **Y**ellow, and blac**K**) screens each must be set to a particular angle, so that the screens don't

overlap but do align properly. When printing to your own printer, you typically will not need to change screen settings, as your printer will handle screening for you according to its individual capabilities. However, if you plan to have the image professionally printed or will be saving the image as an EPS file for professional printing or printing from a PostScript printer, you may need to adjust the screens as described next. Consult the print shop you'll be using for the correct screen settings.

1. Click on **File**. The File menu will appear.

2. Click on **Page Setup**. The Page Setup dialog box will open.

3. Click on **Screens**. The Halftone Screens dialog box will open.

4. Click on the **Use Printer's Default Screens** check box to clear it. The other screen settings in the dialog box will become active.

5. Choose an ink color from the **Ink** drop-down list. The settings you set next will apply to the selected color.

6. Choose screen settings for the selected ink as follows:

- **Frequency**. Your entry in this text box (and your selection from the accompanying measurement drop-down) will determine how large or fine the screen size (ink dots) are. A higher Frequency setting results in a more fine screen for smoother printing.

- **Angle**. Your entry in this text box will specify the alignment of the screen for the selected color. Each color screen must use a different angle.

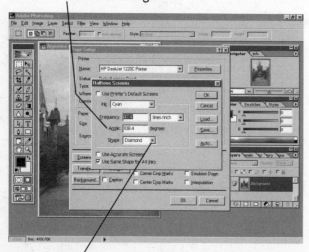

- **Shape**. Your choice from this drop-down list will control the shape of the ink (toner) dots created by the screen.

7. Repeat Steps 5 and 6 to choose screen settings for other ink colors. The choices you make will become active for the current image.

8. Click on **OK**. The Halftone Screens dialog box will close.

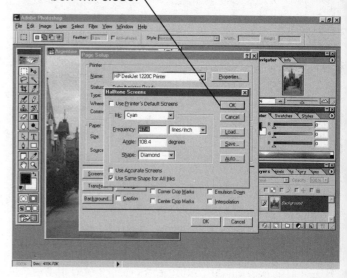

9a. Click on **OK** to finish at this time. The printer settings (and any other Page Setup settings) will take effect.

OR

9b. Choose other settings as described in the rest of this section, then click on **OK** to finish. The new settings you've selected will take effect.

Adjust Transfer Settings

The transfer settings are for use only when you're printing an image to film for professional full-color printing or saving a Photoshop file to the EPS format for that purpose, so most users will never need to change these settings. You would change the transfer settings if the ultimate output device has problems with dot gain and dot loss (ink color dots growing or shrinking), meaning that the device isn't calibrated properly. If your print shop asks you to change the transfer settings for an image, the following steps lead you through the choices for doing so.

1. Click on **File**. The File menu will appear.

2. Click on **Page Setup**. The Page Setup dialog box will open.

3. Click on **Transfer**. The Transfer Functions dialog box will open.

Note: Make sure that the Override Printer's Default Functions check box in the Transfer Functions dialog box is checked so that your changes will apply.

4. Click on the **All Same** check box to clear it. The color options buttons below that check box will become active.

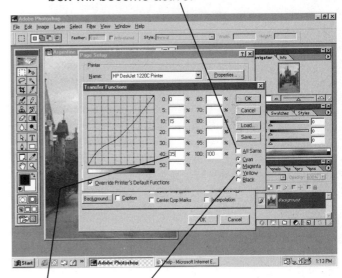

5. Click on an ink color option button. The settings you set next will apply to the selected color.

6. Enter transfer settings for the color into the appropriate text box(es). The graph at the left side of the dialog box will change to reflect your changes.

Note: Your print shop can provide the needed transfer settings.

7. Repeat Steps 5 and 6 to choose transfer settings for other ink colors. The choices you make will become active for the current image.

8. Click on **OK**. The Transfer dialog box will close.

9a. Click on **OK** to finish at this time. The printer settings (and any other Page Setup settings) will take effect.

OR

9b. Choose other settings as described in the rest of this section, then click on **OK** to finish. The new settings you've selected will take effect.

Adding a Border

If you prefer, you can specify that the image print with a black border around it, for a more finished edge appearance. Use the Page Setup as described next to add the border.

1. Click on **File**. The File menu will appear.

2. Click on **Page Setup**. The Page Setup dialog box will open.

3. Click on **Border**. The Border dialog box will open.

4. Choose a measurement unit from the right-drop-down list. The type of units you select will become active.

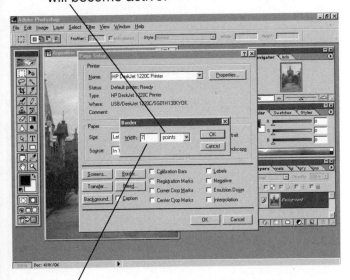

5. Enter a value in the **Width** text box. The value you enter will set the border width.

Note: *The Width setting can be 0 to 3.5 mm, 0 to 10 points, or 0 to .150 inches.*

Tip: *Don't forget that if a text box already contains an entry, you can double-click on the entry to select it, then type a replacement entry.*

6. Click on **OK**. The Border dialog box will close.

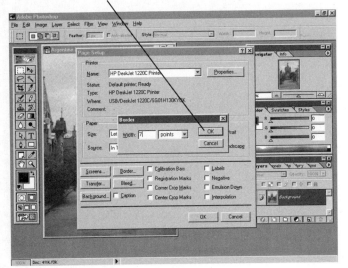

7a. Click on **OK** to finish at this time. The printer settings (and any other Page Setup settings) will take effect.

OR

7b. Choose other settings as described in the rest of this section, then click on **OK** to finish. The new settings you've selected will take effect.

Note: *You can preview a border, bleed, or background color in the Print Options dialog box. To display this dialog box, click on File, then click on Print Options.*

Specifying a Bleed

Adding a bleed enables you to set up the image so that a small part of it along each edge prints outside the crop area. (See "Using Page Settings" to see how to add crop marks to a printout.) This ensures that when you trim the image to the actual crop size, there won't be any unwanted white areas. Specifying a bleed resembles specifying a border, as described next.

1. Click on **File**. The File menu will appear.

2. Click on **Page Setup**. The Page Setup dialog box will open.

3. Click on **Bleed**. The Bleed dialog box will open.

4. Choose a measurement unit from the right-drop-down list. The type of units you select will become active.

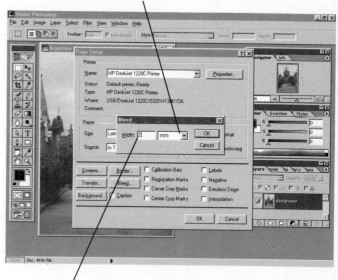

5. Enter a value in the **Width** text box. The value you enter will set the border width.

    Note: *The width setting can be 0 to 3.18 mm, 0 to 9.01 points, or 0 to .125 inches.*

6. Click on **OK**. The Bleed dialog box will close.

7a. Click on **OK** to finish at this time. The printer settings (and any other Page Setup settings) will take effect.

OR

7b. Choose other settings as described in the rest of this section, then click on **OK** to finish. The new settings you've selected will take effect.

Choosing a Background Color

If needed, you can print a background color on the areas of the page (paper) that the image itself doesn't fill. This can create a nice "frame" around the image and lend a more finished appearance to the printout. Follow the next set of steps to add a background color to a printout.

1. Click on **File**. The File menu will appear.

2. Click on **Page Setup**. The Page Setup dialog box will open.

3. Click on **Background**. The Color Picker dialog box will open.

4. Click on a color in the narrow band of colors near the middle of the dialog box. Photoshop will display a different range of colors in the Pick a Solid Color box.

5. Click on a color in the Select Background Color box. The color you click on will become the active mask color.

6. Click on **OK**. The Color Picker dialog box will close.

7a. Click on **OK** to finish at this time. The printer settings (and any other Page Setup settings) will take effect.

OR

7b. Choose other settings as described in the rest of this section, then click on **OK** to finish. The new settings you've selected will take effect.

Using Other Page Settings

The Page Setup dialog box includes a number of other settings that you can apply to control the appearance of your printout. You can change the paper size and orientation, as well as enabling a number of other features via check boxes. The table below details those check box choices, and the steps following the table review how to choose additional page setup settings.

Option	Effect When Checked
Caption	If you've entered a caption for the image in the File Information dialog box as described in the section "Adding File Info" in Chapter 2, the caption prints.
Calibration Bars	Prints a one (grayscale) or two (CMYK) color or tint comparison bars if blank area is available on the page outside the edges of the image. This helps a professional print shop check the image tone or color versus other comparable images or other images used in the same print job.
Registration Marks	Prints marks (again in the available white space outside the edges of the image) used to align color plates in professional full-color printing.
Corner Crop Marks	Prints crop marks specifying the corner of each image. Any bleed you specified extends beyond the area bounded by the crop marks.
Center Crop Marks	Prints crop marks specifying the center of each edge of the image. Any bleed you specified extends beyond the area bounded by the crop marks.
Labels	Adds the image file name to the printout, typically at the center top, in the blank area of the page outside the image.
Negative	Generates a negative image when printing to film. This feature is most likely to be used by a print shop for generating film separations, but you may need to choose it if you're saving the image to EPS format for later use by a print shop. Your print shop can tell you if you need to use this option.
Emulsion Down	Another setting typically only used when generating film, as by a print shop, this setting adjusts the type so that it's readable when the photosensitive layer of the film or photo paper faces away. Again, consult your print shop to see if this feature is needed.
Interpolation	If an image has low resolution that may appear jaggie when printed, this option attempts to correct the problem by resampling to increase the resolution while printing.

1. Click on **File**. The File menu will appear.

2. Click on **Page Setup**. The Page Setup dialog box will open.

3. Click on the down arrow beside the **Size** drop-down list in the Paper area. The Size drop-down list will open.

4. Click on the paper size to use in the list. The paper size will become the size.

Note: *The available paper sizes vary depending on the printer selected in the Name drop-down list. You also can change the paper size in the properties dialog box for your printer, which you open by clicking on the Properties button beside the selected printer. Notice that you don't need to change the Source drop-down list choice unless your printer has multiple paper trays or doesn't switch trays automatically.*

5. Click on an options button in the Orientation area. Choose **Portrait** to print with the short sides of the paper along the top and bottom and **Landscape** to print with the long sides of the paper along the top and bottom. Photoshop will rotate the image on the printout accordingly.

6. Click on other options to check them as needed. The selected features will be applied to the printout.

7. Click on **OK**. The Page Setup dialog box will close.

Note: *As noted earlier, save the image to preserve your Page Setup choices for it.*

Specifying Print Options

The Print Options dialog box enables you to control a few more details of how your printout looks. For example, you can choose how to position the image on the paper, or scale the image to a larger size so it better fits the paper. The next steps review the Print Options choices.

1. Click on **File**. The File menu will appear.

2. Click on **Print Options**. The Print Options dialog box will open.

3. Click on the **Center Image** check box to clear it. The Top and Left choices will become active.

4. Specify **Top** and **Left** entries and measurement units. The image will reposition on the paper as specified.

Note: *In this example, the image is set up to print with a background color, its label (file name), and crop marks. Note that if you do change the image position on the paper, it looks best to allow a little more space below the image than above it.*

5. Change the **Scale** text box entry if you want to increase or decrease the size of the image in the printout. The image will resize accordingly.

Note: *If you check Show Bounding Box, a selection box appears around the image on the preview so that you can drag to resize the image. Checking Show More Options displays a number of the options from the Page Setup dialog box in the Print Options dialog box.*

6. Click on **OK**. The Print Options dialog box will close.

Print the Image

You should at last be ready for the moment of truth—sending your final image to the printer. Follow these steps to get the job done, so to speak.

1. Click on **File**. The File menu will appear.

2. Click on **Print**. The Print dialog box will open.

Tip: *You also can click on the Print button in the Print Options dialog box to open the Print dialog box.*

Note: *You only need to click on the Proof Setup option under Source Space first if you've set up the image to display with proof colors rather than the default monitor colors onscreen. Chapter 15 will discuss how to proof colors.*

6. Click on **OK**. Photoshop will send the print job to the printer and close the Print dialog box.

3. Click on the option identifying what to print in the Print Range area:

   - **All**. Will print the entire current image.

   - **Selected**. Will print only the area that's selected in the current image.

   - **Pages**. Will print only the pages you identify by making entries in the From and To text boxes.

4. Change the **Copies** text box entry if needed. Photoshop will print multiple copies of the image if you change this setting.

Note: *Check Print to File if you want to "print" the file to a special disk file that you can then provide directly to your print shop.*

5. Make choices from the Print Space drop-down lists, if needed. During printing, Photoshop will adjust the image color to work best with the color management scheme or capabilities for your printer our output device.

Procedures

Choose a Printer (Shift+Ctrl+P)

1. Click **File** .... `Alt`+`F`

2. Click **Page Setup** .... `G`

3. Click on the **Name** box arrow and select the desired printer from the drop-down list .... `Alt`+`N`

4. If desired, click the **Properties** button ` Properties... ` and select the desired options from the printer's properties dialog box .... `Alt`+`P`

   ✓ *For example, the print quality of the image file document can be changed to create a draft printout for review.*

5. Click **OK** .... `Enter`

6. Click **OK** .... `Enter`

Change Printer's Screens

1. Click **File** .... `Alt`+`F`

2. Click **Page Setup** .... `G`

3. Click the **Screens** button ` Screens... ` .... `Alt`+`S`

4. If necessary, deselect the **Use Printer's default screens** checkbox .... `Alt`+`P`

5. Choose the desired options in the Halftone Screens dialog box.

6. Click **OK** .... `Enter`

7. Click **OK** .... `Enter`

Adjust Transfer Settings

1. Click **File** .... `Alt`+`F`

2. Click **Page Setup** .... `G`

3. Click the **Transfer** button ` Transfer... ` .... `Alt`+`F`

4. a. To set settings for individual colors, deselect the **All Same** checkbox .... `Alt`+`A`

   b. Click the ink color option underneath the All same checkbox.

5. Choose the desired options in the Transfer Functions dialog box.

6. If necessary, repeat steps 4b and 5 to create transfer settings for other ink colors.

7. Click **OK** .... `Enter`

8. Click **OK** .... `Enter`

Add a Border

1. Click **File** .... `Alt`+`F`

2. Click **Page Setup** .... `G`

3. Click the **Border** button ` Border... ` .... `Alt`+`B`

4. Type a width in the **Width** box .... `Alt`+`W`

   ✓ *By default, the width can be set from 0–10 points—or its equivalent in inches or mm by clicking the Width box arrow and changing the measurement unit. If the number entered is too large, an error window will appear with the allowable width that can be entered in the Width box.*

5. Click **OK** .... `Enter`

6. Click **OK** .... `Enter`

Specify a Bleed

1. Click **File** .... `Alt`+`F`

2. Click **Page Setup** .... `G`

3. Click the **Bleed** button ` Bleed... ` ...... `Alt`+`D`

4. Type a width in the **Width** box .... `Alt`+`W`

   ✓ *By default, the width can be set from 0–3.18 mm—or its equivalent in inches or points by clicking the Width box arrow and changing the measurement unit. If the number entered is too large, an error window will appear with the allowable width that can be entered in the Width box.*

5. Click **OK** .... `Enter`

6. Click **OK** .... `Enter`

Choose a Background Color for Printout

1. Click **File** .... `Alt`+`F`

2. Click **Page Setup** .... `G`

3. Click the **Background** button
   `Background...` .... `Alt`+`K`

4. Select the desired color in the Color Picker dialog box.

5. Click **OK** .... `Enter`

6. Click **OK** .... `Enter`

Change Paper Size/Orientation

1. Click **File** .... `Alt`+`F`

2. Click **Page Setup** .... `G`

3. If needed, click the **Size** box arrow and select the desired size .... `Alt`+`Z`

4. To change the page orientation:
   - **Portrait** .... `Alt`+`O`
   - **Landscape** .... `Alt`+`E`

   ✓ *If the paper is being fed from a source other than the printer's tray, click in the Source box arrow and choose the desired paper source.*

5. Click **OK** .... `Enter`

Select Other Printout Options

1. Click **File** .... `Alt`+`F`

2. Click **Page Setup** .... `G`

3. Select the desired option(s):
   a. **Caption** .... `Alt`+`C`
   b. **Calibration Bars** .... `Alt`+`A`
   c. **Registration Marks** .... `Alt`+`T`
   d. **Corner Crop Marks** .... `Alt`+`M`
   e. **Center Crop Marks** .... `Alt`+`R`
   f. **Labels** .... `Alt`+`L`
   g. **Negative** .... `Alt`+`G`
   h. **Emulsion Down** .... `Alt`+`W`
   i. **Interpolation** .... `Alt`+`I`

4. Click **OK** .... `Enter`

Specify the Printout Size and Position on the Page (Alt+Ctrl+P)

1. Click **File** .... `Alt`+`F`

2. Click **Print Options** .... `T`

3. Enter the desired printout options for the position and size of the printout.

   ✓ *To change the printout's position on the page, deselect the Center Image checkbox.*

   ✓ *To use the Print Options dialog box preview window to change the image's size or position by dragging, select the Show Bounding Box checkbox. (The Center Image checkbox must be deselected to drag the image into a different position.)*

4. Click **OK** .... `Enter`

Print an Image (Ctrl+P)

1. Click **File** .... `Alt`+`F`

2. Click **Print** .... `P`

3. Enter the desired printout options in the Print dialog box.

4. Click **OK** .... `Enter`

Exercise 14

Once you've used Photoshop's tools and features to make an image look the way that you want it to, you're ready to prep it for output—printing. You may have to change the page setup and print settings for two different types of output: saving an image file in another format (often EPS) for use in a larger document file or printing directly to a printer connected to your computer or network. In either case, once you make many page setup changes and save your file, Photoshop preserves those page setup choices so that you don't have to choose them again later. In this exercise, practice choosing some page setup and printing choices, as well as printing an image, if applicable.

Directions

1. Start Photoshop, if needed.

2. Use the File|Open command to open the ⊚PS14 Photoshop file.

3. Save the file as **MON**.

4. Choose File|Page Setup. The Page Setup dialog box will appear.

5. Open the Name drop-down list in the Printer area and click on the name of the printer your instructor specifies that you should use.

6. Click on the Screens button. The Halftone Screens dialog box will appear.

7. Make sure that Use Printer's Default Screens is checked, then click on OK.

8. Click on the Border button. The Border dialog box will appear.

9. Specify 5 points as the Width, then click on OK.

   ✓ *You won't be able to specify a Background color for the printout unless the printer you selected in Step 5 is a color printer.*

10. Click on the Bleed button. The Bleed dialog box will appear.

11. Specify 2 mm as the Width, then click on OK.

    ✓ *The bleed extends the edges of the image beyond the actual image size (crop area). You add a bleed when the image will be trimmed to its precise size. The bleed provides some extra printed area to be trimmed away, ensuring there won't be any unwanted white edges around the trimmed image.*

12. Click to check the Caption option button. This will print the Caption entered in the File Info dialog box with the image.

13. Click to check the Corner Crop Marks check box. This will add crop marks at each corner of the image to help with trimming.

14. Click on OK to close the Page Setup dialog box.

15. Save the file.

16. Choose File|Print Options. The Print Options dialog box appears, giving you a preview of the printout.

17. Review the preview, then click on OK.

18. Choose File|Print. The Print dialog box will appear.

19. Click on OK to print the file.

    ✓ *If your instructor tells you not to print the file, click on Cancel instead in Step 19.*

20. Save and close the file.

21. Reopen the file.

22. Redisplay the Page Setup dialog box and verify that the settings you chose earlier are still applied.

23. Close the Page Setup dialog box and then close the file.

Part IV Review Questions

1. How can you correct an area that's too sharp or fuzzy? *See "Blurring an Area," "Smudging an Area," and "Sharpening an Area" in Chapter 11.*

2. How do you fill a selection? *See "Filling with the Paint Bucket" in Chapter 11.*

3. Which toolbox tool enables you to access photo correction techniques? *See "Using Photo Techniques" in Chapter 11.*

4. How do you remove unwanted parts of the image? *See "Cropping the Image" in Chapter 12.*

5. How do you change the image orientation? *See "Rotating the Canvas" in Chapter 12.*

6. How do you resize the image? *See "Changing the Image Size" in Chapter 12.*

7. What kinds of filters are available? *See "Previewing the Filters" in Chapter 13.*

8. How do you apply a filter to an image? *See "Applying a Filter" in Chapter 13.*

9. What print choices can you adjust before printing? *See "Changing the Page Setup" and "Specifying Print Options" in Chapter 14.*

10. How do you finish a print job? *See "Print the Image" in Chapter 14.*

Next
Chapter

▶▶

chapter

15

Understanding Colors and Channels

When you're preparing images for professional printing, color management becomes an important issue. That's because there are differences between how colors are composed onscreen (out of light) and when printed (out of ink). This chapter helps you explore issues surrounding working with color in Photoshop, including how to:

❋ Understand the available color modes

❋ Calibrate your monitor

❋ View and use color channels

❋ Convert an image to another type of color

❋ Prepare the image for professional output

❋ Proof the image color

Reviewing the Color Modes

As you learned in Chapter 2, when you create a new image in Photoshop, you can choose the color mode that it should use. When you're creating an image for onscreen use, you can typically stick with the default mode, RGB color. However, you may want to choose another of the color modes for special situations. Alternatively, you can convert an image to a particular color mode later, after you've created or scanned it. The table below details the available color modes in Photoshop, so you can understand color basics while working with color choices in this chapter.

Mode	Description
Bitmap	This mode enables you to create a black and white image only. Because it provides for only two tones, you can't convert a full-color image to this mode, because too much image information would need to be discarded.
Grayscale	This mode provides for 256 shades of gray in the image, offering enough variation to facilitate clear detail in the image.
RGB	This mode mimics visual—composing images of red, green, and blue—and works best for images to be viewed onscreen, such as those ultimately to be saved for use in a presentation or Web page.
CMYK (Cyan, Magenta, Yellow, and blacK)	This mode optimizes images to be printed, as those are the ink colors used for color printing. This mode tries to compensate for the fact that paper absorbs some of the ink, affecting the appearance of colors.
Lab	This mode uses luminance and brightness settings to help balance the image for all types of devices—printers, monitors, and scanners.
Multichannel	You can convert color images to this mode for special printing situations. This mode converts the various color channels to channels with 256 colors of gray, with each channel having variations in the distribution of gray tones, according to the original colors.

Mode	Description
Indexed Color	When you apply it, this mode converts an image to a more limited palette of 256 colors, using the matching or lookup system that you specify. You may want to convert to indexed color, for example, for images to be used on a Web page or in a presentation, as this mode dramatically decreases the file size while maintaining image appearance.
Duotone	This mode prepares an image for traditional duotone printing, which uses two solid ink colors, such as a dark gray and a blue, yielding a nicely tinted image. You also can construct images with three ink colors (tritones) and four ink colors (quadtones).

Adjusting Your Display

When you install Photoshop, by default the Adobe Gamma utility installs as well in the Windows Control Panel. You can use this utility to calibrate the monitor, a process that saves a color profile that you can apply so images will display using exactly the same tones on other systems with similarly calibrated monitors or in other applications using color controls. Follow these steps to create the calibration profile for your monitor, starting from the Windows desktop.

1. Click on **Start**. The Start menu will appear.

2. Point to **Settings**. The Settings submenu will appear.

3. Click on **Control Panel**. The Control Panel window will open.

4. Double-click on the **Adobe Gamma** icon. The Adobe Gamma dialog box will open.

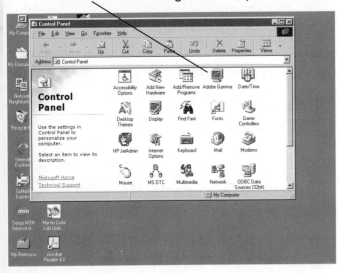

Note: If you're using Windows Millennium Edition, you may need to click on the View All Control Panel Options link at the left side of the Control Panel window to see the Adobe Gamma icon.

5. Click on the **Step By Step (Wizard)** option button. The option button will be selected.

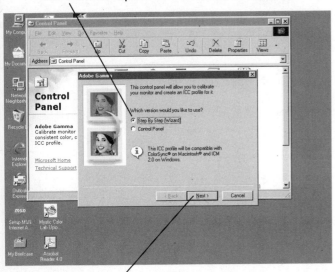

6. Click on **Next**. The next wizard dialog box will appear.

7. Select the contents of the **Description** text box and type a new name, if needed. The name you enter will be applied to the calibration (ICC) profile created for the monitor.

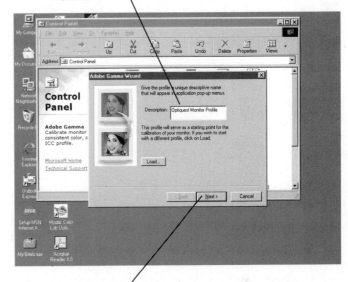

8. Click on **Next**. The next wizard dialog box will appear.

9. Adjust the monitor's brightness and contrast controls as directed, then click on **Next**. The settings will be read and the next wizard dialog box will appear.

237

10. Click on the down arrow beside the **Phosphors** drop-down list, then click on another choice in the list, if needed. The selected phosphors setting will be used for the calibration.

Note: *Make a change in Step 10 only if the documentation for your monitor indicates that it uses phosphors other than those suggested by the wizard. If you choose Custom, the Custom dialog box will appear to prompt you for settings.*

11. Click on **Next**. The next wizard dialog box will appear.

12. Drag the slider until the center box becomes about the same tone as the light parts of the patterned frame, as instructed next. The selected gamma setting will be used for the calibration.

13. Click on **Next**. The next wizard dialog box will appear.

14. Click on the down arrow beside the **Hardware White Point** drop-down list, then click on another choice in the list, if needed. The selected hardware white point setting will be used for the calibration.

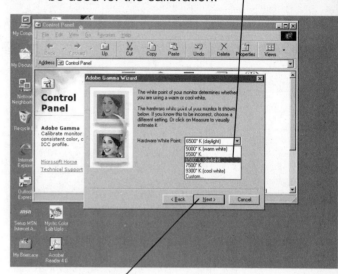

15. Click on **Next**. The next wizard dialog box will appear.

16. Click on **Finish**. The Save As dialog box will appear.

17. Type a name for the calibration file in the File Name text box. The name you type will appear.

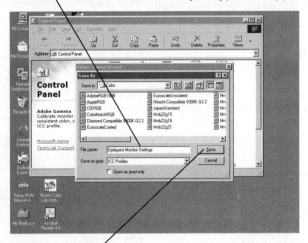

18. Click on **Save**. Adobe Gamma calibrates the monitor according to the settings you specified and saves the calibration settings for future use.

Note: At this point, you can click on the window Close button to close the Control Panel window.

Applying a Color Profile

Once you've used the calibration process to save a color profile, you can apply that color profile (or one of the profiles available by default within Photoshop) to the current image file, as described here, so that Photoshop will display the image using the correct calibration settings. This ensures that any color changes you make will appear correctly on other calibrated displays and devices.

1. Click on **Image**. The Image menu will appear.

2. Click on **Mode**. The Mode submenu will appear.

3. Click on **Assign Profile**. The Assign Profile dialog box will open.

4. Click on the **Profile** option button. The Profile option becomes active.

5. Click on the down arrow beside the **Profile** option, then click on another choice in the list, if needed. The selected profile's settings will be used to display the image.

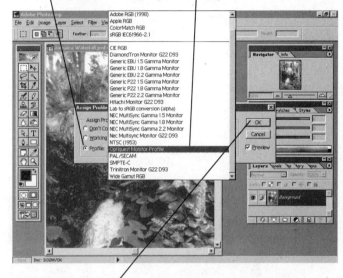

6. Click on **OK**. The selected profile will be applied to the image.

Using Color Channels

When an image uses one of the color modes that has color (for example, not bitmap or grayscale mode), Photoshop displays each color to be displayed or printed as a separate channel. You can work with the image information for a particular channel to edit only that color in the image. This section shows you how to display a channel and gives an example of working with channel content.

Note: Bitmap, grayscale, duotone, and indexed images have a single channel. You can add more channels called alpha channels to any type of image but bitmaps. (See "Adding an Alpha Channel" in the next chapter to learn how to add an alpha channel.) The alpha channels you add can hold masks or add separate colors to be printed in the image.

Changing to a Channel

You use the Channels palette to work with the various color channels in a Photoshop image. Follow these steps when you want to display a particular channel only.

1. Click on the **Channels** tab in the Layers palette. The Channels palette will become the active palette.

   Tip: *In place of Step 1, you also can click on the Window menu and then click on Show Channels.*

2. Click on the down scroll arrow in the Channels palette. The color channels will scroll into view.

3. Click on the desired channel. The channel will become the current or active channel, and its content will appear in the image window.

Working on a Channel

You can edit the content on a single color channel just as you can edit the content of a single layer. You can make a selection on the channel, use editing tools such as the Airbrush, delete selected channel content, apply a filter, and so on. The following steps show just one example of the editing possibilities.

Tip: *To hide a channel, click on the Visibility button (eye icon) to the left of the channel name. To redisplay the change, click on the empty box to redisplay the Visibility button.*

1. Make a selection on the current channel using the tool of your choice, if needed. The selection will become active.

2. Make changes to the channel content using the tool or filter of your choice. This example shows a filter being selected. The changes will appear on the channel immediately.

3. Click on the up scroll arrow. The composite channel that represents the combination of the separate color channels will scroll into view.

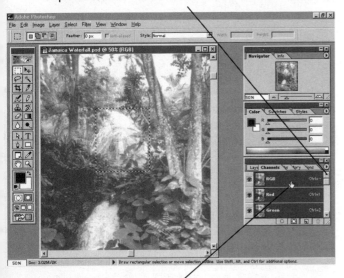

4. Click on the composite channel. The composite channel will become the current or active channel, and all the image color content will reappear in the image window. From this point, you can continue working with other Photoshop tools.

Converting Images

Images you create don't have to remain in the original color mode. Photoshop makes it easy to convert to another color mode when needed. This section walks you through a few of the more common color mode conversion scenarios.

Note: If you experiment with color channel changes, you'll find they can be very subtle. While the average person might not catch all your channel changes, being able to control and manipulate colors is essential if you plan to use your images for professional-level output.

Choosing CMYK Color

Adobe recommends that you perform most of color corrections (and other edits) to an image before you convert the image to CMYK color for professional printing. (Adobe also recommends that you save a copy of the image file before converting to CMYK, so that you can work with the original colors in the image later, if needed.) You convert to CMYK when the image is ready to facilitate a print shop creating color separations—a separate piece of film for each ink color, used for creating a plate to print each color

ink. Typically, you'll convert to CMYK color from RGB color, as in the following steps.

1. Click on **Layer**. The Layer menu will appear.

2. Click on **Flatten Image**. Photoshop will merge all the separate layers onto a single layer, so that you can convert the image to CMYK color. (This is another reason why you should complete your edits in RGB color before converting to CMYK.)

3. Click on **Image**. The Image menu will appear.

4. Click on **Mode**. The Mode submenu will appear.

5. Click on **CMYK Color**. Photoshop will convert the image to CMYK color immediately; if you display the Colors palette, you will see the new channels.

Note: You use the Mode submenu of the Image menu to convert between all color modes.

Working with Bit Depth

In Photoshop, the bit depth refers to the amount of color information each pixel can hold per color channel. (Grayscale images also have a bit depth, given their tonal variations.) Thus, an image set to 16 bits per channel (the default for many scanners) would have an overall color depth of 48 bits (16 x 3) for an RGB image. The higher the bit depth, the greater the possible variation of colors in the image, and the more detail the image can appear to have. On the other hand, an image set to 8 bits per channel lends a much smaller file size, which may work best for certain publications and applications. The following steps show you how to convert from 8 bits per channel to 16 bits per channel and back again.

Tip: *In some cases, when you add layers and masks to a scanned image, Photoshop automatically converts the image from 16 bits to 8 bits, so you have to manually adjust the bit depth later.*

1. Click on **Layer**. The Layer menu will appear.

2. Click on **Flatten Image**. Photoshop will merge all the separate layers onto a single layer, so that you can convert an image from 8 bits per channel to 16 bits per channel.

3. Click on **Image**. The Image menu will appear.

4. Click on **Mode**. The Mode submenu will appear.

5. Click on **16 Bits/Channel**. Photoshop will convert the image to 16 bits of color information per channel immediately.

6. Click on **Image**. The Image menu will appear.

7. Click on **Mode**. The Mode submenu will appear.

8. Click on **8 Bits/Channel**. Photoshop will convert the image to 8 bits of color information per channel immediately.

Note: *Some tools and features, such as the Text tool, don't work in an image set to 16 bits of color. If you try to use an unavailable tool or feature while the image is set to 16 bits, Photoshop will display a message telling you to convert the image to 8 bits per channel.*

Converting to Grayscale

Another common scenario involves converting a color image to grayscale. Most of us take color photos with either our traditional or digital cameras. When you want to use one of those images in a black-and-white publication, convert the image to grayscale mode using Photoshop, as described here.

1. Click on **Image**. The Image menu will appear.

2. Click on **Mode**. The Mode submenu will appear.

3. Click on **Grayscale**. A dialog box will appear to ask you whether you want to complete the conversion by discarding color information.

   Note: *If you are prompted to flatten the image, click on the Flatten button to do so.*

4. Click on **OK**. Photoshop will complete the grayscale conversion.

Prepping for Color Separations

Note: *Obviously, if you convert from grayscale back to one of the color modes, Photoshop won't be able to recreate the original color information. For that reason, it's a good idea to save a copy of your image file before converting to grayscale, so that you can continue working with the color version of the image whenever you need it.*

You need to use trapping only if your image will be output via traditional printing methods from CMYK color. Because the process literally lays down the ink colors in separate passes (on many printing presses), slight shifting in the paper or the printing plates can result in white gaps where the ink colors don't abut as needed. To avoid this problem, you can use trapping to cause colors to overlap slightly so that there is no gap during printing.

Note: *Most images only need trapping when they use large blocks or areas of solid color. Trapping an image with more variation, like a scanned photo, can actually cause problems with the color separations and ultimate print job. To see whether you need to use trapping in an image and to get some guidance about what trapping settings to use, consult your print shop.*

1. After converting the image to CMYK color, click on **Image**. The Image menu will appear.

2. Click on **Trap**. The Trap dialog box will appear.

3. Type a new **Width** entry, and change the measurement unit in the accompanying drop-down list, if needed. The settings will determine how much the colors overlap by when printed.

4. Click on **OK**. Photoshop will finish adding the specified trapping.

Proofing Colors

Photoshop provides you the means to proof the appearance of the various color plates (cyan, magenta, yellow, and black) once you've converted an image to CMYK color. You might want to do this, for example, to look for small specs of color that you may want to clean up by erasing them from the applicable channel. The following steps explain how to get started proofing a color plate.

1. Click on **View**. The View menu will appear.

2. Click on **Proof Colors** (to check it). The color proofing feature will become active.

3. Click on **View**. The View menu will appear.

4. Click on **Proof Setup**. The Proof Setup submenu will appear.

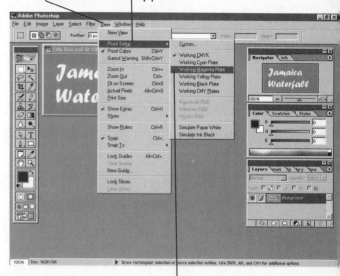

5. Click on one of the **Working (Color) Plate** choices.

   Note: *You can repeat Steps 3 through 5 to proof other plates.*

6. Click on **View**. The View menu will appear.

7. Click on **Proof Colors** (to uncheck it). The color proofing feature will be disabled, and all the colors will reappear in the image.

Procedures

Adjust Screen Display and Create a Color Profile

1. Click the **Start** button [Start] on the Windows taskbar.......................... ⊞

2. Click **Settings** .... [S]

3. Click **Control Panel**................................. [C]

4. Click the **Adobe Gamma** icon Adobe Gamma ·

5. Click the **Step By Step (Wizard)** option button.

6. Click **Next** .... [Alt]+[N]

7. Type a new name in the **Description** box if desired.

8. Click **Next** .... [Alt]+[N]

9. Adjust the monitor's brightness and contrast controls.

10. Click **Next** .... [Alt]+[N]

11. Click the **Phosphors** list arrow and select the desired choice from the drop-down list.

   ✓ *Check the documentation of your monitor to see if it uses a phosphor type different from the one suggested by the wizard.*

12. Click **Next** .... [Alt]+[N]

13. Adjust the gamma setting by dragging the slider control until the center box is about the same shade as its patterned frame.

14. Click **Next** .... [Alt]+[N]

15. Click the **Hardware White Point** list arrow and select the desired choice from the drop-down list.

   ✓ *Check the documentation of your monitor to see if it uses a different setting from the one suggested by the wizard.*

16. Click the **Finish** button [Finish].

17. Type a name for the color profile in the **File name** box .... [Alt]+[N]

18. Click **Save** .... [Enter]

Apply Color Profile

1. Click **Image** .... [Alt]+[I]

2. Click **Mode** .... [M]

3. Click **Assign Profile**.......................... [P]

4. Click the **Profile** option button........... [Alt]+[R]

5. Click the **Profile** box arrow and select the desired color profile from the list.

6. Click **OK** .... [Enter]

Change to a Color Channel

1. Click **Windows** .... [Alt]+[W]

2. Click **Show Channels** .... [H]

   OR

   Click the **Channels** tab in the Layers palette.

3. Click the desired color channel .... [Ctrl]+[Number]

   ✓ *Scroll to view the desired color channel if necessary.*

   ✓ *By default, color channels appear in grayscale. To change them to their color, click Edit, Preferences, and then Display & Cursors. Then select the Color Channels in Color option and click OK.*

Work on a Channel

1. Select the desired area in the active color channel.

   ✓ *See Chapter 5 for making selections.*

   ✓ *If no selection is made, the filter is applied to the entire image.*

2. Make the desired change using the desired tool(s) or filter.

3. To view the change in the composite (RGB) channel, click on the composite channel selector in the Channels palette.

  ✓ *Scroll up to view the composite color channel if necessary.*

Convert to a Different Color Mode

1. Click **Layer** .... Alt + L

2. Click **Flatten Image** .... F

3. Click **Image** .... Alt + I

4. Click **Mode** .... M

5. Click the desired color mode.

  ✓ *For example, convert RGB to CMYK color for preparing a print job.*

Set Bit Depth

1. Click **Layer** .... Alt + L

2. Click **Flatten Image** .... F

3. Click **Image** .... Alt + I

4. Click **Mode** .... M

5. Click the desired big depth:

  • **8 Bits/Channel** .... A

  • **16 Bits/Channel** .... N

Convert to Grayscale

1. Click **Image** .... Alt + I

2. Click **Mode** .... M

3. Click **Grayscale** .... G

4. Click **OK** .... Enter

Set Trapping for a CYMK Image

1. If necessary, convert the image to a CYMK image.

2. Click **Image** .... Alt + I

3. Click **Trap** .... M

4. Type a width in the **Width** box .... Alt + W

  ✓ *By default, the width can be set from 0–10 pixels—or its equivalent in points or mm by clicking the Width box arrow and changing the measurement unit. If the number entered is too large, an error window will appear with the allowable width that can be entered in the Width box.*

5. Click **OK** .... Enter

Enable Color Proofing for a CMYK Image (Ctrl+Y)

1. Click **View** .... Alt + V

2. Select **Proof Colors** L

3. Click **View** .... Alt + V

4. Click **Proof Setup** .... U

5. Select the desired color plate.

Disable Color Proofing (Ctrl+Y)

1. Click **View** .... Alt + V

2. Click **Proof Colors** to deselect it L

Exercise 15

Photoshop's ability to manage colors has long set it apart from competing graphics programs. By default, color images in Photoshop use RGB (Red, Green, Blue) color. Because your monitor (as well as projectors and television sets) compose colors out of red, green, and blue light, RGB color provides the most realistic work when you're working onscreen. Photoshop divides the image into separate color channels. RGB color images have a Red channel, a Green channel, and a Blue channel, plus a composite channel that combines the three other channels. If you find that the colors in an RGB image (especially a scanned image or digital camera image) don't look right onscreen, you can choose another color profile for the image to correct the display.

Among other color mode possibilities, Photoshop also enables you to convert an image to grayscale (shades of gray) for black and white printing and CMYK (Cyan, Magenta, Yellow, and blacK) for full color printing. Full-color printing blends cyan, magenta, yellow, and black inks to produce other colors. You must convert a color image to CMYK color for full-color printing or color separations. This can alter the image appearance, as the colors will then be composed from four color channels (Cyan, Magenta, Yellow, and Black, with a composite channel showing how they appear when blended). So, in addition to converting an image before printing, you need to preview and check it.

Not only can you change the color mode, but you can choose a color channel and edit the content on the selected channel only. This exercise enables you to get started with image color management skills.

Directions

1. Start Photoshop, if needed.

2. Use the File|Open command to open the ☉ **PS15** Photoshop file.

3. Save the file as **WATER**.

4. Zoom the image to 100% size and resize the image window as needed.

5. Choose Image|Mode|Assign Profile. The Assign Profile dialog box will appear.

6. Click on the Profile option button to choose it, then open the accompanying drop-down list and click on ColorMatch RGB. Notice that the onscreen color of the image will change immediately.

   ✓ *The color profile controls how the RGB image displays onscreen. If you're preparing images to be displayed on another computer with a particular type of monitor or with a projector attached, you would choose and apply the color profile that helps the image appear best on that destination display.*

7. Click on Cancel to close the Assign Profile dialog box without applying the new profile. The image colors will revert to their previous appearance.

8. Click on the Channels tab in the Layers palette or choose Window|Show Channels. The color channels for the image will appear on the Channels palette.

9. Click on the Green channel in the palette. The channel will be selected, and only the channel content will appear in the image window.

10. Choose Select|All to select all the content on the channel.

    ✓ *Of course, you could select only part of the channel content to filter that selection.*

11. Choose Filter|Brush Strokes|Crosshatch, and then click on OK in the Crosshatch dialog box. The filtered channel content will resemble Illustration 1.

Chapter 15: Reviewing the Color Modes

12. Click on the Red channel. Its content will appear, showing that the filter was not applied to the Red channel.

13. Click on the composite (RGB) channel at the top of the Channels palette. The image will reappear, with the Crosshatch filter applied.

14. Undo the Crosshatch filter and deselect the Green channel content.

15. Choose Image|Mode|Grayscale, then click on OK in the dialog box that asks whether you want to discard color information. The image will appear in grayscale, and the Channels palette will show a single, gray channel.

16. Undo the grayscale conversion.

17. Choose Image|Mode|CMYK color. The color change will occur immediately, and the Channels palette will display the Cyan, Magenta, Yellow, Black and CMYK (composite) channels.

    ✓ *Because the image has a single layer, in this case you can directly convert it to CMYK color or to change the bit depth. If the RGB image had multiple layers, you would need to flatten the image (with the Layer|Flatten Image command) before you could convert it to CMYK color for full-color printing or color separations. If you failed to flatten the image first, a message would remind you to do so.*

18. Choose Image|Mode|16 Bits/Channel. You won't be able to see the increased bit depth, but the image will have more colors (16 versus 8) per channel.

    ✓ *Note that some tools become available when an image is converted to 16 bits/channel, so you should only make this conversion if you've finished editing the image.*

19. Choose View|Proof Colors. The color proofing feature will become active.

20. Choose View|Proof Setup|Working Cyan Plate. The areas of the image that will print in Cyan ink appear.

21. Choose View|Proof Colors to turn off onscreen proofing.

22. Save and close the file.

Illustration 1

248

16

Correcting Image Color

In addition to working with the color information on individual channels, you can use some commands to adjust and correct the overall color in an image. By using a few straightforward commands, you can make color corrections that once required quite a bit of time in the photo lab. This chapter introduces you to basic color correction techniques in Photoshop, including how to:

❋ Adjust image tones

❋ Rebalance the image color

❋ Change image brightness and contrast

❋ Use a special color effect

❋ Create an alpha channel

Changing the Tonal Quality

The *tonal quality* settings in Photoshop enable you to manipulate the image appearance by adjusting highlights or shadows. This can make the image appear a bit lighter or darker if you adjust all the colors in the image, or can make more subtle changes if you adjust one channel only. Follow these steps to work with the image tone:

1. Click on **Image**. The Image menu will appear.

2. Click on **Adjust**. The Adjust submenu will appear.

3. Click on **Levels**. The Levels dialog box will open.

4. Click on the down arrow beside the **Channel** drop-down list, then click on the desired channel in the list. The selected channel will be selected for tonal adjustments.

5. Drag the **Input Levels** sliders as needed to adjust the tone. The left slider affects shadows, the middle slider affects midtones, and the right slider affects highlights. The image window will preview the changes.

6. Drag the **Output Levels** sliders as needed to further adjust the tone for the selected channel. The left slider adjusts shadows and the right slider adjusts highlights. The image window will preview the changes.

7. Click on **OK**. Photoshop will close the Levels dialog box and apply the tonal changes.

Correcting the Color Balance

The color balance in an image refers to the overall proportion of various colors in the image. For example, if a photo looks too yellow to you, you can make a color balance adjustment as described next to correct that problem. Color balance changes make a general correction to the image color.

1. Click on **Image**. The Image menu will appear.

2. Click on **Adjust**. The Adjust submenu will appear.

Note: *You also can make various color corrections and apply various color special effects by adding an adjustment layer into the image. The adjustment layer enables you to display the color correction or effect when needed, or hide it when not needed. Use the New Adjustment Layer submenu of the Layer menu to add an adjustment layer.*

Correcting Brightness and Contrast

Brightness generally refers to the amount of light (overall lightness) in the image, and contrast refers to the difference between the lightest points and darkest points in the image. Adding brightness to an image can soften its appearance, while increasing contrast can make image objects appear a bit better defined. You adjust both brightness and contrast in the same dialog box, as shown next.

3. Click on **Color Balance**. The Color Balance dialog box will open.

4. Click on the option button for the tonal range to correct in the Tone Balance area, if needed. The color balance changes you make will be applied to the specified tonal range.

5. Drag **Color Balance** sliders as needed to change the amount of color in an image. The image window will preview the changes.

1. Click on **Image**. The Image menu will appear.

2. Click on **Adjust**. The Adjust submenu will appear.

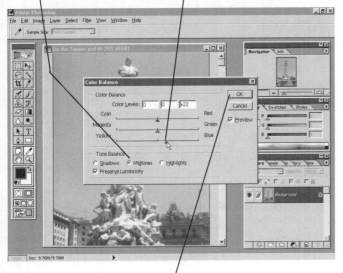

3. Click on **Brightness/Contrast**. The Brightness/Contrast dialog box will open.

6. Click on **OK**. Photoshop will close the Color Balance dialog box and apply the color changes.

4. Drag the **Brightness** slider. The image window will preview the changes.

5. Drag the **Contrast** slider. The image window will preview the changes.

6. Click on **OK**. Photoshop will close the Brightness/Contrast dialog box and apply the changes.

Applying a Special Color Effect

Some of the commands on the Adjust submenu of the Image menu—specifically the Invert, Equalize, Threshold, and Posterize choices—apply special color effects. Each of these commands works a bit differently and applies a slightly different effect, so the following steps provide an example of using one of them—the Posterize choice.

Note: The posterizing effect reduces the number of colors used in the image, so that the image becomes composed of larger color areas, much like the way posters used to be designed and printed or like paint-by-number pictures.

1. Click on **Image**. The Image menu will appear.

2. Click on **Adjust**. The Adjust submenu will appear.

3. Click on **Posterize**. The Posterize dialog box will open.

4. Type a new **Levels** text box entry, if needed. The image window will preview the specified degree of posterization.

5. Click on **OK**. Photoshop will close the Posterize dialog box and apply the special effect.

Adding an Alpha Channel

An alpha channel is an extra channel you use to store a selection in an image. Then, you can easily reload the selection from the channel, or even convert the channel to a spot color treatment as described in the section called "Adding Spot Color" in the next chapter. The steps that follow explain the easiest way to save a spot channel—by saving a selection as a spot channel.

1. Make a selection on a layer using the selection tool of your choice. The selection will appear in the image.

2. Click on the **Channels** tab in the Layers palette window. The Channels palette will become active.

3. Click on the **Save selection as channel** button at the bottom of the palette. The new channel will appear immediately in the Channels palette.

4. Click on the new channel in the palette. The new channel will be selected.

5. Click on the **Channels palette menu** button. The palette menu appears.

6. Click on **Channel Options**. The Channel Options dialog box will open.

7. Type a name for the channel in the Name text box. Your new name will replace the temporary name in the text box.

8. Click on **OK**. The New Channel dialog box will close and Photoshop will finish saving the channel under the name you specified.

   Note: *To load the selection from a channel, click on the channel in the Channels palette, then click on the Load channel as selection button at the bottom of the Channels palette.*

Procedures

Change Tonal Quality (Ctrl+L)

1. Click **I**mage .... `Alt`+`I`

2. Click **A**djust... `A`

3. Click **L**evels... `L`

4. Click the **Channel** drop-down list arrow and choose the desired color channel:
   - **RGB** (composite)........................ `Ctrl`+`~`
   - **Red**... `Ctrl`+`1`
   - **Green** .... `Ctrl`+`2`
   - **Blue**.. `Ctrl`+`3`

5. Drag the **Input Levels** sliders to the desired setting.

   OR

   Type the desired value in the **I**nput Levels boxes .... `Alt`+`I`

   ✓ *If the integer or number exceeds the proper value range, an error message will appear with the correct range.*

6. Drag the **Output Levels** sliders to the desired setting.

   OR

   Type the desired value between 0–255 in the **O**utput Levels boxes .... `Alt`+`O`

7. Click **OK** .... `Enter`

Correct Color Balance (Ctrl+B)

1. Click **I**mage .... `Alt`+`I`

2. Click **A**djust... `A`

3. Click **Color B**alance................................ `B`

4. Click the desired tonal balance option channel:
   - **S**hadows .... `Alt`+`S`
   - **Mi**d**tones** .... `Alt`+`D`
   - **H**ighlights .... `Alt`+`H`

5. Drag the **Cyan, Magenta,** and **Yellow** sliders to the desired settings.

   OR

   Type a value between −100 to +100 in the **Color L**evels boxes .... `Alt`+`L`

   ✓ *The first box is Cyan, the second Magenta, and the third Yellow.*

6. Repeat steps 4–5 as needed to set the desired options.

7. Click **OK** .... `Enter`

Correct Brightness and Contrast

1. Click **I**mage .... `Alt`+`I`

2. Click **A**djust .... `A`

3. Click **Brightness/C**ontrast .... `C`

4. Drag the **Brightness** slider to the desired setting.

   OR

   Type a value between −100 to +100 in the **B**rightness box .... `Alt`+`B`

5. Drag the **Contrast** slider to the desired setting.

   OR

   Type a value between −100 to +100 in the **C**ontrast box .... `Alt`+`C`

6. Click **OK** .... `Enter`

Apply Color Effects

1. Click **Image**...................................... Alt + I

2. Click **Adjust**..................................... A

3. Click the desired special color effect:

   • **Invert**... I

   • **Equalize** .... E

   • a. **Threshold** .... T

     b. Type a value between
        1–255 in the **Threshold**
        Level box .... Alt + T

     c. Click **OK** .... Enter

   • a. **Posterize**........................... P

     b. Type a value between
        2–255 in the **Levels** box........ Alt + L

     c. Click **OK** .... Enter

Add Alpha Channel

1. Make a selection in the desired layer.

2. Click the **Channels** tab.

   OR

   Click **Windows** .... Alt + W

3. Click **Show Channels** .... H

4. Click the **Save selection as channel** button
   [icon] on the Channels palette.

5. Click the new channel's selector in the
   Channel palette.

6. Click the **Channels palette** menu button .

7. Click **Channel Options**.

8. Click in the **Name** box and type a name for
   the new channel .... Alt + N

9. Click **OK** .... Enter

Exercise 16

In the last exercise, you practiced various ways to view and convert the colors in an image. Those techniques are useful, but they only adjust existing image colors. They do not correct problems with an image's color or enhance the image's appearance. In this exercise, you'll practice a few techniques for improving an image's colors, such as changing the overall image tone or working with the color balance.

Directions

1. Start Photoshop, if needed.

2. Use the File|Open command to open the ⊙PS16 Photoshop file.

3. Save the file as **STAT2**.

4. Choose Image|Adjust|Levels. The Levels dialog box will appear.

5. Open the Channel drop-down list and choose one of the channels. (The RGB choice represents the composite channel, or all the colors.)

6. Adjust the Input Levels and Output Levels sliders, watching how the image's appearance changes as you do so.

7. When the image color takes on the desired appearance, click on OK.

8. Undo the Levels command changes.

9. Choose Image|Adjust|Color Balance. The color balance dialog box will appear.

10. Click on one of the option buttons in the Tone Balance area to specify whether you want your changes to apply primarily to the Shadows, Midtones, or Highlights.

   ✓ *Changing the color balance provides a great way to tint the highlights or shadows in an image, and can be faster than selecting those areas and tinting them individually.*

11. Drag the sliders in the Color Balance dialog box as needed to adjust the image colors. Watch image to see the effect of your changes.

12. When the image color takes on the desired appearance, click on OK.

13. Undo the Color Balance changes.

14. Choose Image|Adjust|Brightness/Contrast. The Brightness/Contrast dialog box appears.

15. Drag the Brightness and Contrast sliders, watching the image to see the results of your changes.

   ✓ *Brightness makes an image darker or lighter overall, while contrast increases or decreases the relative difference between the lightest and darkest areas in the image. In particular, increasing the contrast can help a somewhat fuzzy or flat image appear more sharp and three-dimensional.*

16. When the image color takes on the desired appearance, click on OK.

17. Undo the Brightness/Contrast change.

18. Choose Image|Adjust|Posterize. The Posterize dialog box appears.

   ✓ *As noted in the book, the Invert, Equalize, Threshold, and Posterize choices of the Image|Adjust submenu apply special color effects.*

19. Change the Levels setting to 5, then click on OK. Illustration 1 shows how your image should look at this point.

20. Use the Magnetic Lasso tool to select the figure standing on the statue pedestal.

21. Go to the Channels palette by clicking on its tab in the Layers palette or by choosing Window|Show Channels.

22. Click on the Save selection as channel button at the bottom of the palette.

   ✓ *Saving the selection in this way creates an alpha channel. You can use the channel to apply spot color, as illustrated in the next exercise.*

23. Scroll down the list of channels until you see the new alpha channel (Alpha 1), then click on it to select it.

24. Click on the palette menu button, then choose Channel Options in the menu. The Channel Options dialog box appears.

25. Type **Top** as the channel Name, then click on OK. You'll see the channel as shown in Illustration 2.

26. Scroll up and click on the composite (RGB) channel. The image content will reappear.

27. Save and close the image file.

Illustration 1

STAT2.psd @ 66.7% (RGB)

Illustration 2

Save selection as
channel button

17

Having Fun with Color

You've probably seen old photos from the 1940s and 50s, where photographers hand-painted tints onto black and white images, or warmer brown and ivory images called sepia prints. You can achieve similar effects in Photoshop, as well as creating your own special treatments such as duotones for printing. This chapter reveals these three tricks, showing you how to:

❋ Add spot color to an image

❋ Make an image to be printed as a duotone

❋ Convert a color image to sepia tones

Adding Spot Color

Typically, you would add spot color to enhance or colorize an area on a grayscale image, but you can really add spot color to any image that allows multiple channels. You can use an alpha channel to create the spot color, as described in the following example, or you can make another selection and then start with Step 4 to finish adding the spot color.

1. Click on the **Channels** tab in the Layers palette window. The Channels palette will become active.

2. Click on the alpha channel that you want to use to apply the spot color in the palette. The channel will be selected.

3. Click on the **Load channel as selection** button at the bottom of the palette. The selection appears immediately in the channel.

4. Click on the **Channels palette menu** button. The palette menu appears.

5. Click on **New Spot Channel**. The New Spot Channel dialog box will open.

6. Type a name for the spot channel in the Name text box. Your new name will replace the temporary name in the text box.

7. Click on the **Color** box. The Color Picker dialog box will open.

8. Click on a color in the narrow band of colors near the middle of the dialog box. Photoshop will display a different range of colors in the Select Spot Color box.

9. Click on a color in the Select Spot Color box. The color you click on will become the active spot color.

10. Click on **OK**. The Color Picker dialog box will close.

11. Make a new entry in the Solidity text box, if needed. An entry greater than 0 will make the spot color more opaque.

12. Click on **OK**. The New Spot Channel dialog box will close, finishing the spot color channel.

13. Click on the composite channel in the Channels palette. The image will reappear in the image window.

14. Click on the **Visibility** button (eye icon) beside the spot channel so that the icon appears in it. The spot color will appear in the image.

15. Convert the image to RGB or CMYK color. After you make the conversion, the image will print with the spot color. (If you skip the conversion, the image will still print in grayscale.)

Creating a Duotone Image

As noted in an earlier chapter, a duotone image typically is a grayscale image to which you add a second printed color to tint the image overall. (You can add two tint colors to create a tritone image, and three tint colors to create a quadtone image.) The steps here illustrate an example of converting a grayscale image to a duotone for a nicely tinted printout.

Note: Remember, some tools and conversions aren't available for images using 16 bits of color information per channel, so convert to 8 bits per channel. To convert to a duotone, the image must be set to 8 bits per channel. Refer to "Working with Bit Depth" in Chapter 15 to see how to make this change.

1. Click on **Image**. The Image menu will appear.

2. Click on **Mode**. The Mode submenu will appear.

3. Click on **Duotone**. The Duotone dialog box will appear.

4. Click on the down arrow beside the **Type** drop-down list, then click on **Duotone** in the list. The second ink color will become active for the image.

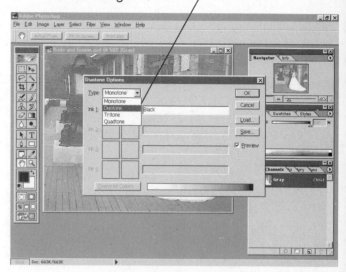

Note: Of course, you would click on Tritone or Quadtone to add more than one tint color to the image.

5. Click on the white **Ink 2** box. The Custom Colors dialog box will open.

6.   Click on a color in the narrow band of colors near the middle of the dialog box. Photoshop will display a different selection of colors in the list at the left side of the dialog box.

Note: *You actually can choose colors from a number of different color sets. To view colors in another set, make another choice from the Book drop-down list.*

7.   Click on a color in the list at the left side of the dialog box. The color you click on will become the active tint color, and the image window will preview the selected tint.

8.   Click on **OK**. The Custom Colors dialog box will close.

9.   Type a color plate name in the Ink 2 text box. (Enter Cyan, Magenta, or Yellow.) The name will tell Photoshop to use a separate color plate for the tint ink color.

Tip: *If the duotone will be included in a document to be printed by a professional printer, it's best to write down the Pantone Color name so you can tell the printer the exact tint ink color.*

10. Click on **OK**. The Duotone Options dialog box will close, finishing the duotone creation.

11. Click on **Image**. The Image menu will appear.

12. Click on **Mode**. The Mode submenu will appear.

13. Click on **Multichannel**. Photoshop separates the single duotone color channels into multiple channels, so you can preview individual colors.

14. Click on the color channel to preview in the Channels palette. Photoshop will display the ink areas to be printed with that color in the image window.

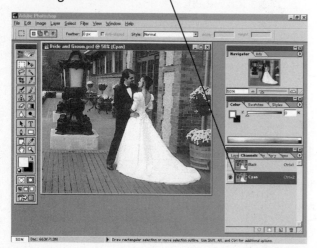

15. Click on **Edit**. The Edit menu will appear.

16. Click on **Undo Multichannel**. Photoshop removes the multichannel mode and redisplays the single duotone color channel.

Making a Sepia Image

You'll typically work in the opposite direction when you create a sepia image, working from a color image to one that appears more like a creamy brown grayscale. (But you can make a "sepia" image with any mix of color that you prefer.) Use the following steps to make your favorite color image appear as a traditional sepia image.

Tip: *You can convert a grayscale image to RGB color and then use the techniques described here to make it a sepia image.*

Note: *Photoshop includes an action you can use to create a sepia tone on a layer (choose File, Automate, Batch, then choose Sepia Toning from the Action drop-down list, and use the other Batch dialog box settings to finish applying the Automation). There are also automations for applying other color effects, and you can download actions for applying sepia tone and other effects from the Internet. See Chapter 19 to learn more about actions, and Appendix C for sources for downloadable resources, including actions.*

1. Click on **Image**. The Image menu will appear.

2. Click on **Adjust**. The Adjust submenu will appear.

3. Click on **Channel Mixer**. The Channel Mixer dialog box will appear.

4. Click on the **Monochrome** check box. Photoshop checks the check box.

5. Click on the **Monochrome** check box. Photoshop unchecks the check box.

Note: *You have to check and uncheck the Monochrome check box to be able to blend channels separately.*

6. Choose a channel from the Output Channel drop-down list. The selected color channel will be ready for adjustment.

7. Drag the **Source Channels** slider for the selected color. The image window will preview the color change in the image.

8. After you adjust the mix for each channel, click on **OK**. The Channel Mixer dialog box will close, so that you can review the final tint.

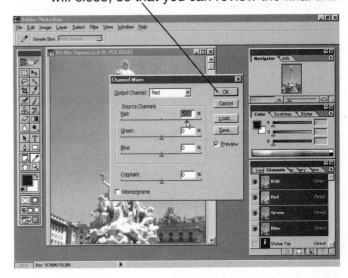

Procedures

Add Spot Color

1. Click the **Channels** tab in the Layers palette.

   OR

   a. Click **Windows** .... Alt + W

   b. Click **Show Channels** .... H

2. Click on the desired alpha channel.

   ✓ *To create an alpha channel, see the procedures for Chapter 16.*

3. Click the **Load channel as selection** button ⬚ on the Channels palette.

4. Click the **Channels palette** menu button ▶.

5. Click **New Spot Channel.**

6. Click in the **Name** box and type a name for the spot channel .... Alt + N

7. Click on the **Color** box.

8. Select the desired color in the Color Picker dialog box.

9. Click **OK** .... Enter

10. Click in the **Solidity** box if desired and type a percentage from 0–100..... Alt + S

11. Click **OK** .... Enter

12. Click on the **RGB** (the composite) channel in the Channels palette .... Ctrl + ~

13. Click the deselected **eye icon box** ⬚ on the new spot channel's selector in the Channels palette.

14. Convert the image from RGB to CMYK color.

Create a Duotone Image from a Grayscale Image

1. Click **Image** .... Alt + I

2. Click **Mode** .... M

3. Click **Duotone** .... D

4. Click the **Type** box arrow and select **Duotone** in the drop-down list.

   ✓ *The Duotone Options dialog box also has selections for Monotone (one tint color), Tritone (three tint colors), and Quadtone (four tint colors).*

5. Click the **Ink 2** box.

6. In the ink color scroll bar, click on, scroll, or click the scroll buttons at the top or bottom of the bar to select the approximate desired color in the color selector.

   OR

   Type the number of the desired ink color in known.

7. If necessary, click the desired ink color swatch in the ink color sample window to the left of the ink color scroll bar.

8. Click **OK** .... Enter

9. Click **OK** .... Enter

Create Multichannel(s) for Editing Duotone

1. Click **Image** .... Alt + I

2. Click **Mode** .... M

3. Click **Multichannel** .... M

4. If necessary, click the **Channels** tab in the Layers palette.

   OR

   a. Click **Windows** .... Alt + W

   b. Click **Show Channels** .... H

5. Click the desired ink color channel in the Channels palette.

   ✓ *Double-clicking the ink color channel selector launches the Spot Channel Options dialog box.*

Create a Sepia Image from a Color Image

✓ *To create a sepia image from a grayscale image, convert the grayscale image to RGB color.*

1. Click **Image** .... Alt + I

2. Click **Adjust** .... U

3. Click **Channel Mixer** X

4. Click the **Monochrome** checkbox to deselect it if necessary .... Alt + H

5. Click on the **Output Channel** box arrow and select a color channel from the drop-down list.

   • **Red** .... Ctrl + 1

   • **Green** .... Ctrl + 2

   • **Blue** .... Ctrl + 3

6. Make the desired color setting for each color to create the sepia tone:

   a. Drag the **Red** slider to the desired setting.

      OR

      Type the desired percentage between −200 to +200 in the **Red** box .... Alt + R

   b. Drag the **Green** slider to the desired setting.

      OR

      Type the desired percentage between −200 to +200 in the **Green** box .... Alt + G

   c. Drag the **Red** slider to the desired setting.

      OR

      Type a percentage between −200 to +200 in the **Blue** box .... Alt + B

✓ *Hint: For the Red channel, increase the Red slider to +120%. For the Green channel, decrease the Green slider to –10%. For the Blue channel, decrease the Blue slider to –20%.*

7. Repeat steps 5–6 for each color channel until the desired sepia tone is achieved.

8. Click **OK** ....

Exercise 17

While you practiced making color corrections in the last exercise, here you get to have a little fun. In this exercise, practice adding some special color effects to an image. You'll learn how to use an alpha channel to add spot color to an area in the image. You'll see how to create a duotone—an image that uses only two colors for printing. Typically, a duotone is a grayscale image overprinted with a second color that "tints" the image. Finally, you'll try out one method for creating a sepia image. That's a grayscale image adjusted so that it looks more ivory and brown than black and white, lending an antique feel to the image. These are great effects you can use to enhance your personal photos. (In this instance, you'll be practicing with a wedding photo of the author and her husband.)

Directions

1. Start Photoshop, if needed.

2. Use the File|Open command to open the ☉**PS17** Photoshop file.

3. Zoom the image to 100% size and resize the image window. You'll be able to better see the impact of the changes you'll be making.

4. Click on the Channels tab or choose Window|Show Channels.

5. Click on the Dress channel. This is an alpha channel that was already added into the image for you.

   ✓ *You learned how to create an alpha channel in the exercise for Chapter 16.*

6. Click on the Load channel as selection button at the bottom of the Channels palette.

7. Click on the palette menu button, then click on New Spot Channel. The New Spot Channel dialog box appears.

8. Type Dress Spot, then click on the Color box under Ink Characteristics.

9. In the Color Picker dialog box, click on a pale pinkish gray color, then click on OK.

10. Change the Solidity setting to 25%, then click on OK again to close the New Spot Channel dialog box.

11. Click on the composite (Gray) channel in the Channels palette to redisplay the image, then click on the Visibility button (eye icon) beside the Dress Spot spot color channel to display it.

12. Choose Image|Mode|CMYK Color.

   ✓ *You must convert from grayscale mode to a color mode like RGB color or CMYK color so that the spot color will print from your color printer. For professional color printing, consult your print shop to see whether the file should be converted to a color mode. The print shop may prefer to handle the conversion itself.*

13. Save the file as **WED1.** The image should resemble Illustration 1 at this point. Close the file.

14. Reopen the **PS17** file and zoom and resize it as before.

15. Choose Image|Mode|Duotone. The Duotone Options dialog box will appear.

16. Open the Type drop-down list and click on Duotone. A second ink color will appear in the dialog box.

17. Click on the white box beside the Ink 2 color. The Custom Colors dialog box will appear.

18. Click on a color in the narrow band near the center of the dialog box, then click on the desired color in the list at the left. Click on OK to return to the Duotone Options dialog box.

19. Click on OK to close the dialog box and apply the duotone color.

✓ *For the sake of clarity, you can change the name of the selected Ink 2 color to use the name of one of the three CMYK ink colors (not black). If you use this approach but want to have the image professionally separated or printed, be sure to write down the name of the ink or Pantone color that you selected, so you can tell the printer what ink color to use.*

20. Choose Image|Mode|Multichannel. The Channels palette displays the separate black channel and color channel, as shown in Illustration 2.

✓ *Displaying the multiple channels helps prep the image for your printer. You can undo that change if you wish.*

21. Save the file as **WED2** and close the file.

22. Reopen the **PS17** file and zoom and resize it as before.

23. Choose Image|Mode|RGB Color. You have to convert the grayscale image to color to be able to convert it to sepia using the technique described here.

24. Choose Image|Adjust|Channel Mixer. The Channel Mixer dialog box will appear.

25. Click on the Monochrome check box twice to check it and then uncheck it.

26. Select each channel form the Output Channel drop-down list, then drag the three Source Channel sliders as needed to tint the image.

✓ *Hint: For the Red channel, increase the Red slider to +120%. For the Green channel, decrease the Green slider to –10%. For the Blue channel, decrease the Blue slider to –20%.*

27. Click on OK. The image will appear in sepia, ready for printing on a color printer.

28. Save the file as **WED3** and close the file.

Illustration 1

Illustration 2

18

Working with Plug-Ins

Simply stated, a plug-in is a mini-program that extends the capabilities of Photoshop (or its companion program ImageReady). Each plug-in functions in one of three ways: as a filter, as an additional import or export choice, or as a file format choice in the Save As or Open dialog box. This chapter shows you how to take advantage of plug-ins, including how to:

❋ Install a plug-in you've purchased or downloaded

❋ Use a plug-in (that's not a filter)

Installing Plug-Ins

By default, the plug-ins that come with Photoshop install to various subfolders of the C:\Program Files\Adobe\Photoshop 6.0\Plug-Ins\ folder. You can purchase additional plug-ins or download a variety of freeware and shareware plug-ins from a variety of sources online. (See Appendix C, which lists some Web sites where you can begin your search for available plug-ins.)

If you download a particular type of plug-in, you typically can just move or copy the plug-in file (after decompressing it, unzipping it, or renaming it, if indicated per the instructions accompanying the plug-in) to the folder that holds similar plug-in files, assuming the plug-in doesn't include its own installer program. In other cases, you may want to store your third-party plug-ins in a separate folder to distinguish them from the plug-ins provided with Photoshop. If you choose this route, you need to specify the alternate plug-in location, as described next.

Note: *If a plug-in was written for Photoshop only, copy it to the appropriate subfolder of C:\Program Files\Adobe\Photoshop 6.0\Plug-Ins\Adobe Photoshop Only\. If a plug-in was written for ImageReady only, copy it to the appropriate subfolder of C:\Program Files\Adobe\Photoshop 6.0\Plug-Ins\Adobe ImageReady Only\.*

1.   Click on **Edit**. The Edit menu will appear.

2.   Click on **Preferences**. The Preferences submenu will open.

3.   Click on **Plug-Ins & Scratch Disks**. The Preferences dialog box will appear, with its Plug-Ins & Scratch Disks settings displayed.

Note: *In ImageReady, you would choose Edit, Preferences, Plug-Ins to start specifying another plug-ins folder.*

4.   Click on the **Additional Plug-Ins Directory** check box. The check box will become checked.

5.   Click on **Choose**. The Browse for Folder dialog box will open.

6.   Select the folder that holds the plug-ins in the folder tree. The specified folder will become active as a plug-in folder.

7.   Click on **OK**. The Browse for Folder dialog box will close.

8. Click on **OK**. The Preferences dialog box will close.

9. Click on **File**. The File menu will open.

10. Click on **Exit**. Photoshop will close.

    Note: *When you close Photoshop, save changes to any open file, if prompted. You must exit and restart Photoshop (or ImageReady) for the new plug-ins folder to take effect.*

11. In the newly specified plug-ins folder, decompress or rename the plug-in file, or run its installer as required. The appropriate plug-in files will decompress or appear in the appropriate folder location.

12. Click on **Start**. The Start menu will appear.

13. Click on **Programs**. The Programs submenu will appear.

14. Point to **Adobe**. The Adobe submenu will appear.

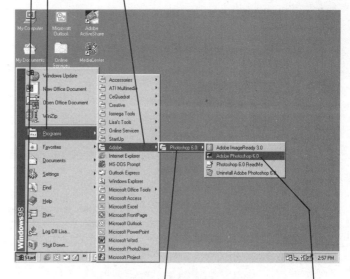

15. Point to **Photoshop 6**. The Photoshop 6 submenu will appear.

16. Click on **Adobe Photoshop 6**. The Photoshop program will load, with the added plug-ins newly active. From there, you can open files as needed and use the plug-ins.

Applying a Plug-In to a File

As noted at the very beginning of the chapter, plug-ins generally work in limited ways, enabling you to open or save files in different formats, or to apply custom filters to an image. This section shows an example of using a filter that falls into each category.

Note: *In some cases, you will need to copy additional files to the folder that holds the Photoshop program or to the \Windows\System\ folder. Be sure to read any Readme file that comes with a plug-in to verify how to install it, particularly if the plug-in creates one or more folders when you unzip or decompress it.*

Applying by Opening or Saving

If a filter enables you to use Photoshop to work with files of different formats, the filter typically adds the format into the Files of type list of the Open dialog box or the Format list of the Save As dialog box. The following steps show one example—using a filter that enables you to save files in the Windows icon format (.ICO). Before you begin the steps, be sure you have open the file to which you want to apply the plug-in.

Note: *In other cases, plug-ins that work with file formats appear on the Import or Export submenus of the File menu.*

1. Click on **File**. The File menu will appear.

2. Click on **Save As**. The Save As dialog box will appear.

3. Click on the down arrow beside the **Format** drop-down list, then click on the file format provided by the plug-in (in this case, IconFormat). The selected format will be used for the save operation.

4. Change the File name and Save in location, if needed. The newly saved file will use the name and location you specify.

5. Click on **Save**. The Save As dialog box will close and Photoshop will save the file in the new format.

Applying a Filter Plug-In

In most cases, installing a plug-in installs a new filter or group of filters. Photoshop typically adds the new filter choices or groups (submenus) to the bottom of the Filter menu, making added filters as easy to access as default filters. Like the default filters, some plug-in filters will display a dialog box prompting you to choose additional settings, and others will take effect immediately. The following steps show an example freeware plug-in filter.

Note: *In this case, after you save a file in the .ICO format, you can close the file in Photoshop and then assign the file as the icon for a desktop item. (Right-click on the desktop, then click on Properties. Use the Effects tab in the Display Properties dialog box to select the icon file.) You also can right-click on any shortcut icon, click on the Shortcut tab, and click on Change Icon to specify another icon file.*

1. With the file to filter open, click on **Filter**. The Filter menu will appear.

   Note: As with other commands and effects in Photoshop, many filters require that an image be using a particular color mode. For example, the grayscale image shown here had to be converted to RGB color before the plug-in filter could be used.

2. Point to the name for the filter group, if needed. The group submenu will appear.

3. Click on a filter. The filter will appear, or the filter dialog box will appear.

4. Adjust filter settings as needed. Either a preview area in the filter dialog box or the image window itself will preview the filter changes.

5. Click on **OK**. Photoshop will apply the filter settings to the image.

Procedures

Create Alternate Plug-In Location

1. Click **Edit** .... Alt + E

2. Click **Preferences** .... N

3. Click **Plug-Ins & Scratch Disks** .... Ctrl + 7

4. Click the **Additional Plug-Ins Directory** checkbox to select it .... Alt + A

5. Click the **Choose** button Choose... ... Alt + O

6. Navigate to the desired folder in the Browse in Folder dialog box.

7. Select the folder.

8. Click **OK** .... Enter

9. Click **OK** .... Enter

   ✓ *You must close Photoshop and launch it again for the new plug-in folder setting to activate.*

10. a. Click **Edit** .... Alt + E

    b. Click **Exit** .... E

    OR

    Click the **Close** button X .

    ✓ *Extract (decompress or unzip) new plug-ins files to the alternate plug-in location folder.*

Exercise 18

Plug-ins are custom modules that extend Photoshop's capabilities. Plug-ins fall into two different types or categories. The first type of plug-in enables Photoshop to save, open, import, or export in a file format not offered by default. The second type of plug-in adds a new filter or set of filters to the Filters menu. This exercise shows you how to install and use new plug-ins. These are optional plug-ins from the Photoshop 6.0 CD-ROM, but you can download free and commercial plug-ins from a variety of Web sites. In this exercise, practice installing and using those custom plug-ins.

Directions

1. Start Photoshop, if needed.

2. Choose Edit|Preferences|Plug-Ins & Scratch Disks.

3. Click on the Additional Plug-Ins Directory check box to check it, then click on the Choose button that becomes active.

4. In the Browse for Folder dialog box that appears, choose the C:\Temp folder, then click on OK.

5. Click on OK again to close the Preferences dialog box and apply your changes.

6. Exit Photoshop.

   ✓ *When it starts up, Photoshop searches its default plug-ins folders as well as the optional folder that you specify for installed plug-ins. That's why you need to close Photoshop, install new plug-ins, then restart the program so that it will find and load the plug-ins.*

7. Use My Computer or the Windows Explorer to navigate to the \Sample Plug-Ins folder. Consult your instructor if you can't find the folder.

8. Select or highlight the three files in the folder (**Ffactory.8bf**, **Ffexamp.afs**, and **GIF89a Export.8be**), then use the method of your choice to copy them.

9. Navigate to the C:\Temp folder, then use the method of your choice to paste the files into the folder.

✓ *This exercise shows a simple plug-in installation example. Some plug-ins come with their own installation routine, while others have multiple files that must be copied to specific folders on the system. Consult the **Readme** file that comes with a plug-in for installation details.*

10. Start Photoshop.

11. Use the File|Open command to open the ⊙**PS18** Photoshop file.

12. Choose Filter|Synthetic|Filter Factory. The Filter Factory dialog box appears.

13. Click on the Load button, click on the **Ffexamp.afs** file in the Open dialog box that appears, then click on OK. Photoshop applies the filter to the image, as shown in Illustration 1.

14. Choose File|Export|GIF89a Export. The Options dialog box for this plug-in appears, as shown in Illustration 2.

15. Click on OK in the dialog box to proceed with the export operation.

16. Type **WED4** as the File Name, then click on Save. The filter saves the file, but you will not see it onscreen. The previous will remain open, instead.

17. Close the **PS18** file without saving changes to it, and exit Photoshop.

Illustration 1

Illustration 2

Next
Chapter

▶▶

19

Working with Actions

You can see that the possible combinations of Photoshop features and filters you can use is endless, let alone the specific settings you use with each feature or filter. In Photoshop, you can create actions and droplets to store a series of commands and settings that you choose. This chapter shows you how to save yourself some work in Photoshop, including how to:

❋ Record an action

❋ Play an action

❋ Make a droplet from an action

❋ Use a droplet

Creating an Action

If you've ever created a macro in an application, then you'll have an easy time creating an action. Like a macro, an action is a series of steps and settings that you save so that you can repeat them quickly later. Saving and using the action eliminates the necessity to remember the filter settings you prefer, for example, or the color adjustment choices to use. Actions come in handy when you need to prepare multiple images using the same settings; for example, if you're converting a series of grayscale images to duotones using a particular pantone color for inclusion in the same publications. The steps that follow show you how to use the Actions palette to record a new action.

1. Click on the **Actions** tab in the Layers palette. The Actions palette will become the active palette.

   Tip: *In place of Step 1, you also can click on the Window menu and then click on Show Actions.*

2. Click on the **Create new set** button at the bottom of the palette. The New Set dialog box will appear.

3. Type a name for the new set. The name you type will replace the placeholder entry in the Name text box.

4. Click on **OK**. The new set will appear in the Actions palette and will be selected by default.

   Note: *To add a new action to an existing set, click on the set name in the Actions palette and then follow the rest of the steps here.*

5. Click on the **Create new action** button at the bottom of the palette. The New Action dialog box will appear.

6. Type a name for the new action. The name you type will replace the placeholder entry in the Name text box.

7. Specify other settings in the dialog box, such as adding a Function Key (shortcut key combination) to play back the action. The remaining settings will be added for the function.

8. Click on **Record**. Recording will start.

9. Perform the steps to record. The steps will be added to the named action.

   Note: *If a particular feature can't be recorded, it will either be unavailable or you'll see a warning message.*

10. Click on the **Stop playing/recording** button at the bottom of the Actions palette. Photoshop will stop recording your steps, finishing the action.

Using an Action

Note: *As with plug-ins, you can download a number of free action (.ATN) files from various Web sites, such as those listed in Appendix C. Decompress or unzip the action file, if needed, then copy it to the C:\Program Files\Adobe\Photoshop 6.0\Presets\Photoshop Actions. Click on the Actions palette menu button, and then click on Load Actions. The Load dialog box will appear. Select the newly copied action, then click on Load. To save a set of actions you've created in a .ATN file (necessary only to back up your actions or share them with others), select the set in the Actions palette, click on the Actions palette menu button, then click on Save Actions. Use the Save dialog box that appears to finish the save.*

Much as you use a recording process to create an action, you use a playback process to run the action. Before you run the action, open the file to which you want to apply the action, and perform any preliminary steps to prepare for the action, such as making a selection or converting to the proper color mode. Then use the steps that follow.

1. Click on the **Actions** tab in the Layers palette. The Actions palette will become the active palette.

2. Scroll to display the set that holds the action to perform in the palette. The actions will appear in the palette.

   Note: *Click on the right-arrow to the left of the set name if you don't see its actions.*

3. Click on the action to perform. The action will be selected.

4. Click on the **Play selection** button at the bottom of the palette. The action plays immediately.

Making a Droplet

You can save an action as a droplet, a mini-program you can use to process image files even when Photoshop isn't running. Use the following steps to create a droplet using default droplet settings.

1. Click on **File**. The File menu will open.

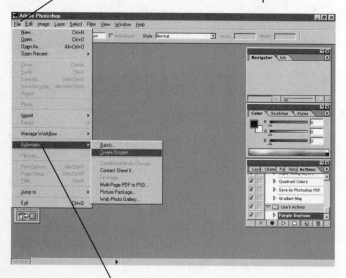

2. Click on **Automate**. The actions will appear in the palette.

Note: *The Automate submenu also includes a number of preset automations—mini-programs you can use to process a batch of images. For example, you can use the Contact Sheet automation to create a contact sheet image file from all the images stored in a particular folder.*

3. Click on **Create Droplet**. The Create Droplet dialog box will open.

4. Choose the set that holds the action to convert from the **Set** drop-down list. The set's actions will become available from the **Action** drop-down list.

5. Choose the action to save as a droplet from the **Action** drop-down list. The selected action appears.

6. Click on **Choose**. The Save dialog box will open.

7. Type a name for the new droplet file. The name you type will replace the placeholder entry in the File name text box.

8. Click on **Save**. The Save dialog box will close and the name you specified will appear in the Create Droplet dialog box.

9. Click on **OK**. Photoshop will close the Create Droplet dialog box and finish saving the droplet.

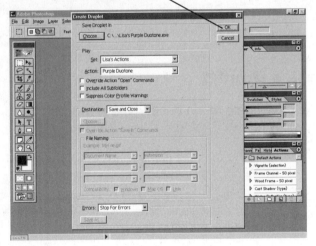

Using a Droplet

As you saw in the last section, Photoshop saves a droplet you create as an .EXE file. The Photoshop program doesn't have to be open for you to use the droplet. You can use the droplet from the folder where you saved it (C:\Program Files\Adobe\Photoshop 6.0\Presets\Photoshop Actions\ by default), or copy the .EXE file to any other folder, including the Windows desktop—shown in the next set of steps—for convenient use. Because you don't have to open Photoshop, the droplet provides a fast alternative for making changes to a number of files, because you also don't have to open the individual image files in Photoshop. Using the droplet is an easy drag-and-drop operation, as illustrated next.

1. Open the folder that holds the file to process with the automation. The folder will appear in Windows.

2. Drag the file to process from its folder and drop it onto the icon for the droplet file (on the desktop or in another folder). The droplet's actions will be performed on the file. You can repeat the process for as many files as need to be processed.

Note: *Of course, the file(s) to be processed must use the correct color mode and other settings, or the droplet will stop and display an error message.*

Procedures

Create an Action

1. Click the **Actions** tab in the Layers palette.

    OR

    a. Click **Windows**............................. `Alt`+`W`

    b. Click **Show Actions**............................. `S`

2. Click the **Create new set** button `▭` in the Actions palette.

3. Click in the **Name** box and type a name for the new set .... `Alt`+`N`

4. Click **OK** .... `Enter`

5. Click the **Create new action** button `▣` in the Actions palette.

6. Click in the **Name** box and type a name for the new action .... `Alt`+`N`

7. Click the **Record** button `Record` .

8. Perform the desired steps to record.

9. To finalize the action, click the **Stop playing/recording** button `■` in the Actions palette.

Use an Action

1. Click the **Actions** tab in the Layers palette.

    OR

    a. Click **Windows**............................. `Alt`+`W`

    b. Click **Show Actions**............................. `S`

2. If necessary, scroll in the Actions palette to display the desired set.

3. If necessary, click the action set arrow button `▷` to show the actions contained in the set.

4. Click the desired action.

5. Click the **Play selection** button `▷` in the Actions palette.

Make a Droplet

1. Click **File** ....`Alt`+`F`

2. Click **Automate** ....`U`

3. Click **Create Droplet**................................`C`

4. Click the **Set** box arrow and select the desired set in the drop-down list.... `Alt`+`S`

5. Click the **Action** box arrow and select the desired action from the drop-down list .... `Alt`+`A`

6. Click the **Choose** button `Choose...` ... `Alt`+`C`

7. Click in the **File name** box and type a name for the new droplet.......... `Alt`+`N`

8. Click the **Save** button `Save` .... `Enter`

9. Click **OK** .... `Enter`

Use a Droplet

1. Navigate to the desired file to process using Windows Explorer or My Computer.

2. Drag the desired file into the droplet icon on the Windows desktop.

    ✓   *If the file or files to be processed are not compatible with the color mode and other settings for the droplet action, the droplet will stop and display an error message.*

Exercise 19

You need programming skills to create your own plug-ins, so unless you want to become a serious Photoshop user, you probably won't be creating your own plug-ins any time soon. However, any Photoshop user can create an action, with only a minimal learning curve. An action is like a macro in other programs; you record a set of steps, then you can replay them on another file to save time. Further, you can convert any action into a droplet. You place the droplet .EXE file on the Windows desktop or on the folder of your choice, and then you can drag Photoshop files onto it to apply the action's steps without even opening Photoshop. The steps in this exercise show you examples of creating and using actions and droplets.

Directions

1. Start Photoshop, if needed.

2. Use the File|Open command to open the ⊚ PS19 Photoshop file.

3. Click on the Actions tab in the Layers palette or choose Window|Show Actions.

4. Click on the Create new set button at the bottom of the palette, type **Student** as the Name in the New Set dialog box, then click on OK.

5. Click on the Create new action button at the bottom of the palette, type **My Duotone** as the Name for the action in the New Action dialog box, then click on Record.

   ✓ *As when you create macros in many other applications, you simply record the steps that you take in Photoshop to create an action.*

6. Choose Image|Mode|Duotone. Change the settings and colors in the Duotone Options dialog box as desired, then click on OK.

   ✓ *Refer back to Chapter 17 for information on creating duotones.*

7. Click on the Stop Playing/Recording button at the bottom of the Actions palette. This will finish the action recording.

8. Recording the action also applied the duotone to the image, so undo the Duotone.

9. Click on the **My Duotone** action in the Actions palette, then click on the Play selection button at the bottom of the palette. (See Illustration 1.) Photoshop reapplies the duotone to the image.

10. Undo the Duotone.

11. Save the file as LINC3, then close the file.

12. Choose File|Automate|Create Droplet.

13. Make sure **Student** and **My Duotone** are selected for the Set and Action choices, respectively, then click on the Choose button.

14. Click on the View Desktop button at the top of the Save dialog box to navigate to your system's Windows Desktop. Type **My Duotone Droplet** as the File name, then click on Save.

15. Click on OK back in the Create Droplet dialog box.

16. Close Photoshop.

17. Open a My Computer or Windows Explorer window, and navigate to the folder that holds the LINC3 file.

18. Drag the file from its folder over the icon for your droplet on the Desktop, as shown in Illustration 2. Drop the file onto the droplet. Photoshop will open, open the file, and apply the droplet (action) choices.

19. Open the LINC3 file in Photoshop to verify that the droplet applied the duotone, then close the file.

Illustration 1

Illustration 2

Part V Review Questions

1. How do I choose what type of image colors to use? *See "Reviewing the Color Modes" in Chapter 15.*

2. What's a color channel, and how do I select one? *See "Using Color Channels" in Chapter 15.*

3. What are the most common color mode conversions? *See "Converting Images" in Chapter 15.*

4. What do I do if my image is too dark? *See "Correcting Brightness and Contrast" in Chapter 16.*

5. How do you add spot color to an image? *See "Adding Spot Color" in Chapter 17.*

6. What's a duotone, and how do you create one? *See "Creating a Duotone Image" in Chapter 17.*

7. How do you add plug-ins to Photoshop? *See "Installing Plug-Ins" in Chapter 18.*

8. What methods do you use to employ a plug-in? *See "Applying a Plug-In to a File" in Chapter 18.*

9. How do you create an action? *See "Creating an Action" in Chapter 19.*

10. How do you use an action? *See "Using an Action" in Chapter 19.*

Next
Chapter

▶▶

20

Creating Web Images

Because Photoshop provides some of the best tools for creating and editing images in general, it's not surprising that it offers superior options for preparing images for use in Web pages. This chapter walks you through the basic skills for preparing images for the Web, including how to:

❋ Review the Web graphic formats

❋ Understand what will happen if you choose Save As

❋ Converting an image to indexed color

❋ Create an optimized JPEG image

❋ Create an optimized GIF image

Reviewing Web Graphic Formats

The HTML Web page format spurred the growth of the Internet not only because it could present information in an attractive graphical format, but also because its files were relatively compact in size for reasonable download times. In the spirit of preserving those download times, a few different new formats for graphics files also emerged. Through special compression technology, these file formats preserve color and detail while dramatically reducing file size—sometimes eliminating megabytes in file size. The table below lists the most common Web graphic file formats and their features.

Format	Description
CompuServe GIF (.GIF)	This mode requires conversion to Indexed Color mode (which limits the image to 256 colors) and enables you to preserve transparency so that the Web page background shows through.
JPEG (.JPG or .JPEG)	This mode does not preserve transparency, but it does enable you to specify the amount of compression to use so you can control file size and quality.
PNG (.PNG)	Portable Network Graphics (PNG) mode enables you to preserve transparency and choose specific methods for reducing colors and handling dithering in the image.

Note: *Remember, when you create a new image with the File, New command, you click on the Transparent option button to set up an image with a transparent background. If you scan an image or download it from a digital camera, you cannot specify a transparent background, so it's best to copy a selection from such an image, create a new image with a transparent background, and then paste the copied selection into it.*

Using Save As

You can use the Save As command on the File menu to save an image in the common Web graphic formats. (See the section titled "Saving to Another Format" in Chapter 2 for an overview of how to use the Save As command.) When you use the Save As command and choose one of the Web file formats, you'll be prompted to make various changes depending on the selected format:

- **GIF**. The Indexed Color dialog box appears to specify color palette, transparency, and matte settings, and then the GIF Options dialog box appears to prompt you whether to choose an interlaced GIF format.

Note: *When you have Photoshop create an interlaced file, part of the image can "pre-load" on the Web page. This means that the user will see the image at low resolution until the full file downloads.*

- **JPEG**. The JPEG Options dialog box appears so you can specify image quality and matte options. Transparent areas will be filled with white when you finish the save.

- **PNG**. The PNG Options dialog box appears, so you can choose whether to add interlacing to the issue and choose a color filtering method.

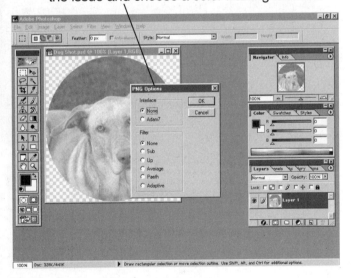

Save an Optimized Image File

To see all the settings for Web graphic file formats in a single dialog box, use the Save for Web command on the File menu. This command enables you to select a Web file format, specify settings for the format, then proceed with the save. The rest of this section shows you how to use the Save for Web command to optimize and save a file

in the two most common Web graphic formats—JPEG and GIF.

Saving a JPEG

These steps show you how to use the Save for Web command to save a JPEG file, so you can choose the optimum compression for your image.

1.   Click on **File**. The File menu will appear.

2.   Click on **Save for Web**. The Save for Web dialog box will open, with its Optimized tab selected.

3.   Click on the down arrow beside the drop-down list in the upper-left corner of the Settings box, then click on **JPEG**. The JPEG choices appear in the Settings box.

4. Choose an image quality setting, either by choosing a general setting from the drop-down list at the left or by using the Quality choice at the right. The statistics in the lower-left corner of the preview area will change to show the file size that will result from the designation quality setting.

5. Click on the down arrow beside the **Matte** drop-down list. A shortcut menu will appear.

6. Click on **Other**. The Color Picker dialog box appears so that you can use it to specify a matte for the image.

    Note: A matte color in a GIF or PNG Web graphic either helps the edges of transparent areas blend with the Web page background, or fills areas that were originally transparent in JPEG images with the specified color for blending.

7. Click on a color in the narrow band of colors near the middle of the dialog box. Photoshop will display a different range of colors in the Choose a Color box.

8. Click on a color in the Choose a color box. The color you click on will become the active matte color.

9. Click on **OK**. The Color Picker dialog box will close.

10. Click on **OK**. The Save Optimized As dialog box will appear.

11. Edit the File name text box entry as needed. The name you specify will be applied to the Web graphic file.

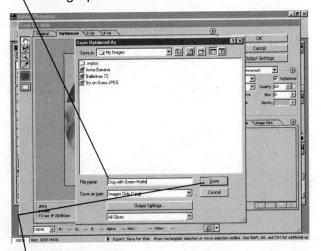

Note: You also can use the Save in drop-down list to choose another disk and folder location for the saved file, if needed.

12. Click on **Save**. The Save Optimized As and Save for Web dialog boxes will close. Only the original image will be open in Photoshop. You can find the new, optimized Web graphic file in the folder where you saved it.

Saving a GIF

Saving an optimized GIF file follows much the same process as saving an optimized JPEG file. Get started with the process now.

1. Click on **File**. The File menu will appear.

2. Click on **Save for Web**. The Save for Web dialog box will open, with its Optimized tab selected.

3. Click on the down arrow beside the drop-down list in the upper-left corner of the Settings box, then click on **GIF**. The GIF choices appear in the Settings box.

Note: You can use the drop-down list right beside the Settings label at the top of the settings dialog box to choose a pre-saved set of optimization settings, such as JPEG High or GIF 32 Dithered. Click on the Optimize menu button (the menu button with the right arrow on it just to the right of the top drop-down list) then click on Save Settings. You can then use the Save Optimization Settings dialog box that appears to save your choices on the Optimized tab of the Save for Web dialog box under one name, so you can later choose that name (and thus your saved settings) from the drop-down list beside the Settings label.

4. Choose image color settings, both by choosing a color reduction setting from the drop-down list at the left and by choosing the maximum number of colors for indexing the color using the Colors choice at the right. The statistics in the lower-left corner of the preview area will change to show the file size that will result from the designation quality setting.

5. Choose image dithering settings, both by choosing a dithering method setting from the drop-down list at the left and by choosing the amount of dithering using the Dither choice at the right. The statistics in the lower-right corner of the preview area will change to show the specified dithering method.

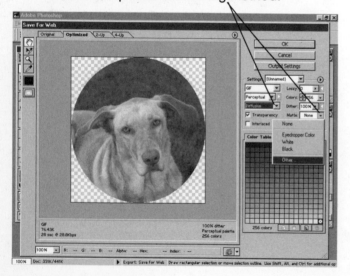

6. Leave the **Transparency** check box checked. This ensures that the transparent areas in the image will remain transparent in the final GIF file.

7. Click on the down arrow beside the **Matte** drop-down list. A shortcut menu will appear.

8. Click on **Other**. The Color Picker dialog box appears so that you can use it to specify a matte for the image.

9. Click on a color in the narrow band of colors near the middle of the dialog box. Photoshop will display a different range of colors in the Choose a color box.

10. Click on a color in the Choose a color box. The color you click on will become the active matte color.

11. Click on **OK**. The Color Picker dialog box will close.

Note: *After you specify the matte for the GIF, it won't be as obvious in the preview. That's because the matte for the GIF serves more as a blending zone between the image content and the Web page background.*

12. Click on **OK**. The Save Optimized As dialog box will appear.

13. Edit the File name text box entry as needed. The name you specify will be applied to the Web graphic file.

Note: *You also can use the Save in drop-down list to choose another disk and folder location for the saved file, if needed.*

14. Click on **Save**. The Save Optimized As and Save for Web dialog boxes will close. Only the original image will be open in Photoshop. You can find the new, optimized Web graphic file in the folder where you saved it.

Procedures

Use Save As to Save Images for the Web (Shift+Ctrl+S)

1. Click **File**.. `Alt`+`F`

2. Click **Save As**... `A`

3. Click the **Save in** arrow and navigate
   to the desired save location............... `Alt`+`I`

4. Enter a file name in the
   File name box .... `Alt`+`N`

5. Select the Web image file format
   in the **Format** drop-down list .... `Alt`+`F`

   - **CompuServe GIF (*.GIF).**
   - **JPEG (*.JPG or *.JPE).**
   - **PNG (*.PNG).**

6. In Save Options, select any applicable save
   options.

7. Click **Save** .... `Enter`

8. In the GIF/JPEG/PNG Save Options dialog
   box, make any desired settings.

9. Click **OK** .... `Enter`

Use Save for Web to Save Optimized Images for the Web (Alt+Shift+Ctrl+S)

Save JPEG:

1. Click **File**.. `Alt`+`F`

2. Click **Save for Web** .... `W`

   ✓ *The Save for Web dialog box opens with
   the Optimized tab selected.*

3. In the upper-left of the Settings area, click the
   list box drop-down arrow and select **JPEG**.

4. At the top of the Settings area, click the list
   box drop-down arrow and select the desired
   image quality.

   OR

   Click in the **Quality** box arrow and drag the
   slider to the desired setting.

OR

Type the desired percentage between 0–100
in the **Quality** box.

5. If a Matte is desired, click the Matte box
   arrow and select the desired matte from the
   drop-down list.

   ✓ *Selecting Other launches the Color Picker
   dialog box.*

   ✓ *To save custom settings, click the round
   menu arrow button ⊙ and click Save
   Settings to save the settings in the Save
   Optimization Settings dialog box.*

6. Click **OK** in the Save For Web
   dialog box... `Enter`

7. Click the **Save in** arrow and navigate
   to the desired save location................ `Alt`+`I`

8. Enter a file name in the
   File name box .... `Alt`+`N`

9. Click **Save** .... `Enter`

Save GIF:

1. Click **File** .... `Alt`+`F`

2. Click **Save for Web**................................. `W`

   ✓ *The Save for Web dialog box opens with
   the Optimized tab selected.*

3. In the upper-left of the Settings area, click the
   list box drop-down arrow and select **GIF**.

4. At the top of the Settings area, click the list
   box drop-down arrow and select the desired
   image quality.

   OR

   Create the desired Lossy, Colors, Dither,
   Matte, and Web Snap settings.

   ✓ *To save custom settings, click the round
   menu arrow button ⊙ and click Save
   Settings to save the settings in the Save
   Optimization Settings dialog box.*

5. Click **OK** in the Save For Web
   dialog box................................... `Enter`

6. Click the **Save in** arrow and navigate
   to the desired save location .... `Alt`+`I`

7. Enter a file name in the
   File name box .... `Alt`+`N`

8. Click **Save** .... `Enter`

Exercise 20

Photoshop and other tools from Adobe have become invaluable to Web site developers. The competition to create the most attractive site is hot. Sites need to have good content, fun products or features, and great graphics. This exercise leads you through the process of saving to the two most-popular formats for Web graphics: JPEG and GIF. In each case, you'll be saving an optimized file, although you can use the Save As dialog box as described early in Chapter 20 to perform a more basic save. Optimizing the file provides you with more choices, such as adding a background color or preserving transparency. Practice saving Web graphics now.

Directions

1. Start Photoshop, if needed.

2. Use the File|Open command to open the
   ⊚ **PS20** Photoshop file.

   ✓ *Notice that this image has transparent areas. Creating an image with transparency gives you the most options to prep it for the Web.*

3. Choose File|Save for Web. The Save for Web dialog box appears, with its Optimized tab selected.

4. Open the top-left drop-down list, then click on JPEG. The options on the tab will change.

5. Open the drop-down list below the one from which you selected the file type, and then click on Medium. The status information at the lower-left corner of the tab shows that the file will download in about 5 seconds after you save it.

6. Click on the color box beside the Matte choice, click Other, and then specify a new color in the Color Picker dialog box that appears.

   ✓ *In the real world, the color you'd pick would be the same color as your Web page background, or would be a complementary color.*

7. Click on OK. The Save Optimized As dialog will appear.

8. Enter **DOG1** as the File name, then click on Save to finish saving the file. The file will close, returning you to the **PS20** file in Photoshop.

9. Choose File|Save for Web. The Save for Web dialog box appears, with its Optimized tab selected.

10. Open the top-left drop-down list, then click on GIF. The options on the tab will change.

11. Change the Lossy setting to 25. The status information at the lower-left corner of the tab shows that the file will download in about 14 seconds after you save it.

    ✓ *Leave the Transparency check box checked, because you want the transparent areas of the image to also be transparent when you place them on your Web page. If you see the Matte color where the image should be transparent, clear and then recheck the Transparency check box.*

12. Click on OK. The Save Optimized As dialog will appear.

13. Enter **DOG2** as the File name, then click on Save to finish saving the file. The file will close.

14. Close the **PS20** file in Photoshop; do not save changes if prompted

15. Open the **DOG1** and **DOG2** files in Photoshop (Illustration 1) or your Web browser.

16. Close the files.

Illustration 1

21

Adding Hotspots

Web browsing hinges on the ability to navigate by following links. You can use the slice tool to identify areas for linking in an image, and then save that image as a Web (HTML) file so that image with the links can be incorporated into an overall Web site. This chapter introduces you to the basics for the slice feature, including how to:

❋ Add a slice and set its options

❋ Work with existing slices

❋ Save the sliced image in HTML format

Adding Slices or "Hotspots"

The Slice tool on the Photoshop toolbox adds slices into an image file. By then specifying the slice options, you create a link to a particular Web address called a URL (Uniform Resource Locator). After you save the image as an HTML file (as described in the final section of this chapter, called "Saving the Sliced File in HTML"), users can click on the area defined by the slice to follow the link. That's why such linked areas are called "hotspots." The steps that follow explain how to add a slice and set it up as a hotspot, once you've performed all the needed edits in Photoshop.

1. Click on the **Slice** tool in the toolbox. The Slice tool will become active.

2. Click and drag on the image to define the slice. (You don't really need to select a layer first.) When you release the mouse button, the new slice will appear.

    Note: *In addition to the slice you drew, called a user slice, Photoshop divides the rest of the image into slices called auto slices as well.*

3. Right-click on the slice number for the new slice. A shortcut menu will appear.

4. Click on **Edit Slice Options**. The Slice Options dialog box will open.

5. Specify options, as follows:

    *   **URL**. Enter the URL address for the Web page that will appear when the user clicks the hotspot. To enter an absolute address (not just a relative address on the server holding the page), be sure to include http:// at the start of your entry.

    *   **Target**. Specify the frame in which the linked page will appear. (Consult the Help system for your Web authorizing software to learn more about working with frames.)

- **Message Text**. Enter more descriptive information about the linked Web page. The description will appear in the Web browser status bar when the user hovers the mouse pointer over the hotspot.

- **Alt Tag**. Enter a description to appear in place of the image content if the ultimate page is displayed in a non-graphical Web browser.

6. Click on **OK**. The Slice Options dialog box will close and the specified settings will be applied to the slice.

Viewing and Hiding Slices

If it so happens that you do need to make further edits to the sliced image before you save it as an HTML file, you can hide the slice lines so they won't distract you. Then, redisplay the slices later, as needed.

1. Click on **View**. The View menu will appear.

2. Click on **Show**. The Show submenu will appear.

3. Click on **Slices**. Photoshop will uncheck the Slices command and hide the slices in the image file.

4. Click on **View**. The View menu will appear.

5. Click on **Show**. The Show submenu will appear.

6. Click on **Slices**. Photoshop will check the Slices command and redisplay the slices in the image file.

Note: If you need to resize a slice, right-click on the Slice tool then click on Slice Select Tool in the shortcut menu that appears. Then drag the corner of the slice area to resize it.

Saving the Sliced File in HTML

When you need to save the sliced file in HTML format, use the Save for Web command on the File menu, as demonstrated here.

1. Click on **File**. The File menu will appear.

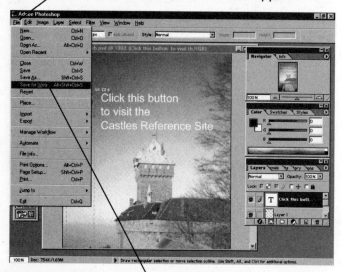

2. Click on **Save for Web**. The Save For Web dialog box will open, with its Optimized tab selected.

    Tip: *When you copy or move the Web page, be sure to copy or move the accompanying \images\ folder created by the HTML saving process. That folder holds the actual sliced image content.*

    Tip: *If you previously used the Save for Web command to save a JPEG or GIF image and specified a matte, you're going to want to be sure to remove that matte color. Click on Output Settings in the Save For Web dialog box. Open the drop-down list that has HTML selected in it by default, then click on Background. Open the Color drop-down list, click on None, then click on OK to return to the Save For Web dialog box.*

3. Click on **OK**. The Save Optimized As dialog box will appear.

4. Edit the File name text box entry as needed. The name you specify will be applied to the HTML file.

5. Click on **Save**. The Save Optimized As and Save for Web dialog boxes will close. Only the original image will be open in Photoshop. You can find the new HTML file in the folder where you saved it.

Procedures

Add Slice (Hotspot) to an Image

1. Click the **Slice tool** button 🖊 in the toolbox .... K

2. Position the mouse pointer above and to the right or left of the desired slice.

3. Drag on the image to define the slice.

4. Release the mouse button to finalize the slice area.

5. Right-click the slice number in the upper left of the slice selection area (for example, 03 ⊠) and click **Edit Slice Options**.

6. Click in the **URL** box and type the desired URL

   ✓ *Be sure to include the http:// or any other protocol (for example, an e-mail address).*

7. If desired, click in the **Target** box, enter the frame or new window in which the linked page will appear.

8. Click in the **Message Text** box and type any desired descriptive information about the linked web page.

9. Click in the **Alt Tag** box and type a description to appear in place of the image content should it be displayed in a nongraphical Web browser.

10. Click **OK** .... Enter

View a Slice in an Image

1. Click **View** .... Alt + V

2. Click **Show** .... H

3. Click **Slices** to select L

Hide a Slice in an Image

1. Click **View** .... Alt + V

2. Click **Show** .... H

3. Click **Slices** to deselect L

Save Sliced File in HTML (Alt+Shift+Ctrl+S)

1. Click **File** .... Alt + F

2. Click **Save for Web** .... W

   ✓ *The Save for Web dialog box opens with the Optimized tab selected.*

3. Click **OK** in the Save For Web dialog box .... Enter

4. Click the **Save in** arrow and navigate to the desired save location .... Alt + I

5. Enter a file name in the **File name** box .... Alt + N

6. Click **Save** .... Enter

Exercise 21

You may have come across Web page images that have various spots that you can click to go to linked Web pages. This type of spot is known as a *hotspot*. In Photoshop, you add a slice to a file to set up a hotspot, specify options for the slice, such as the HTML file (Web page) to which the hotspot links, then save the file in HTML format for inclusion on a Web page or site. This exercise enables you to practice that process.

Directions

1. Start Photoshop, if needed.

2. Use the File|Open command to open the ⊘ **PS21** Photoshop file.

3. Choose the Slice tool in the toolbox.

4. Drag around the button beside the text on the image to define the slice, as shown in Illustration 1. When you release the mouse, the new slice will appear.

    ✓   *Photoshop automatically divides the rest of the image into slices for you.*

5. Right-click on the slice number for the slice (it should be slice 03 and the slick number should be blue), then click on Edit Slice Options.

6. Enter **Castle Example** in the Name text box.

7. Enter **http://www.ddcpub.com/** in the URL text box.

8. Enter **Go to DDC instead of visiting castles** as the Message Text text box entry.

9. Click on OK to finish setting up the slice.

10. Choose View|Show|Slices to hide the slices.

11. Choose View|Show|Slices to redisplay the slices.

    ✓   *To preserve the slices in a file, you should save the Photoshop file before saving it as an HTML file for the Web.*

12. Choose File|Save for Web. The Save for Web dialog box will appear, with its Optimized tab selected.

13. Click on OK. The Save Optimized As dialog box will appear.

14. Enter **CASTLE** as the File name, then click on Save. Photoshop will save the new HTML (Web page file), create a folder named Images that holds the needed supporting graphic files, then close the HTML file, returning to the original file in Photoshop.

15. Minimize Photoshop to a button on the Taskbar, open a My Computer or Windows Explorer window, then navigate to the folder where you saved the **CASTLE** HTML file.

16. Double-click on the file to open the file in your Web browser.

17. Move the mouse over the button hotspot (slice area). As shown in Illustration 2, the Message Text text box entry appears in the status bar. The title bar displays the name of the original Photoshop file.

    ✓   *If you have a live Web connection at the system you're using, you can click on the hotspot (slice area) and then click on Connect if the Dial-Up Connection dialog box appears. Then, your Web browser should display the DDC Publishing home page.*

18. Close your Web browser.

19. Return to Photoshop.

20. Close the **PS21** file without saving changes to it, and then close Photoshop.

Illustration 1

Slice tool

Illustration 2

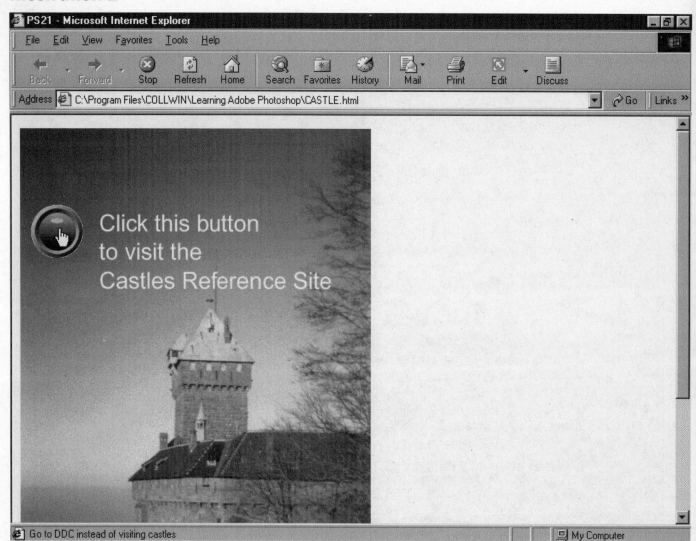

Part VI Review Questions

1. What Web graphics formats can Photoshop create? *See "Reviewing Web Graphic Formats" in Chapter 20.*

2. What happens if I use Save As to save in a Web graphic format? *See "Using Save As" in Chapter 20.*

3. How do I save an image in a Web graphic format? *See "Save an Optimized Image File" in Chapter 20.*

4. What's a matte in a Web graphic file? *See "Saving a JPEG" and "Saving a GIF" in Chapter 20.*

5. What's a hotspot and how do I create one? *See "Adding Slices or 'Hotspots'" in Chapter 21.*

6. How do I make sure a description of the link appears in the Web browser status bar? *See "Adding Slices or 'Hotspots'" in Chapter 21.*

7. The slices are in the way. Can I hide them? *See "Viewing and Hiding Slices" in Chapter 21.*

8. What do I do once I've added the slices to add the file with hotspots to my Web? *See "Saving the Sliced File in HTML" in Chapter 21.*

Appendix A

▶▶

A
Using Digital Watermark Protection

Among the many controversies regarding the Internet, protection of original material (intellectual property in legal lingo) concerns a wide variety of users—from individual graphic artists to huge record companies. To protect your work, you have to have a way to identify the digital matter you create.

Photoshop works with digital rights management company Digimarc to enable you to embed a digital watermark in your Photoshop images and read the digital watermark information in other images. Then, others who want to use your images can find your contact information via Digimarc to license the images from you.

Registering with Digimarc

To be able to add a digital watermark, you must register online with Digimarc. You can watermark up to 99 images for free. Beyond that, Digimarc charges a subscription fee based on the number of images you plan to watermark per year. The following steps detail how to register with Digimarc to obtain the PIN and Digimarc ID you need to watermark your images.

Note: *You must have an image file open before you start the following steps. Ideally, open an image to which you want to add a digital watermark.*

1. Click on **Filter**. The Filter menu will appear.

2. Click on **Digimarc**. The submenu will appear.

3. Click on **Embed Watermark**. The Embed Watermark dialog box will open.

   Note: *You have to have an image file open, as well as a layer that's not locked, to be able to display the filters. Preferably, you should open an image to which you want to add a digital watermark.*

4. Click on **Personalize**. The Personalize Creator ID dialog box will open.

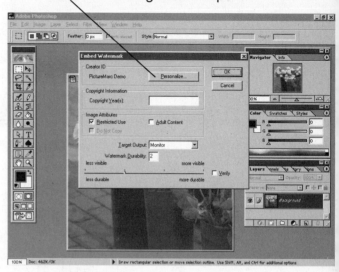

5. Click on **Register**. Your Web browser will open and the Dial-Up Connection dialog box will open to prompt you to connect to the Internet, unless you have an Internet connection that's always on, in which case you can skip to Step 7.

6. Click on **Connect**. Your system will dial its Internet connection and then will display the initial Digimarc registration page with pricing information.

7. Click on the scroll down arrow. The Web page will scroll so that you can see the registration link.

8. Click on the **Register** link. The Digimarc ID Sign-Up Web page will appear.

9. Click on the down arrow on the scroll bar. The Web page will scroll so that you can read the registration agreement.

10. Click on the **I Accept** button, then click on OK if you see a Security Alert message box. The next Digimarc ID Signup page, where you enter information, will appear.

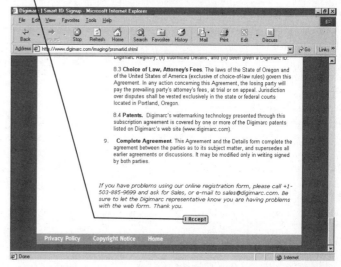

11. Click on the down arrow on the scroll bar, then make choices and fill in fields as needed to complete the registration. The Web page will scroll so that you can enter the registration information.

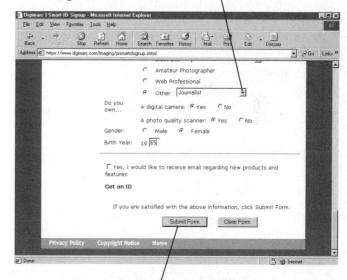

12. Click on the **Submit Form** button, then click on **Yes** if you see a Security Alert message box. After Digimarc processes your request, the Web Page indicating that your ID has been assigned appears.

13. Click on the **Print** button on the toolbar. Your Web browser will send your Digimarc PIN and ID information to the printer.

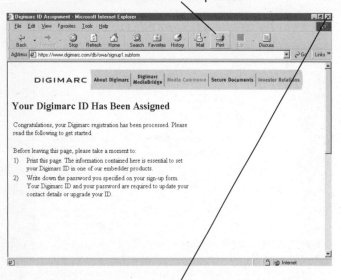

14. Click on the **Close** button (**X**), then click on **Disconnect Now** in the Auto Disconnect dialog box when it appears (if applicable). Your system disconnects from the Internet and returns to Photoshop.

15. Type your Digimarc PIN and ID in the left and right boxes of the Creator ID text box, respectively. The numbers will appear in the boxes.

16. Click on **OK**. The Personalize Creator ID dialog box will close, and the PIN and ID will be stored in the Embed Watermark dialog box.

17. Click on **OK**. The Embed Watermark dialog box will close and the digital watermark will be applied to the current image.

Embedding a Digital Watermark

Embedding a digital watermark adds your Digimarc ID to it and identifies the image as copyrighted. Digital watermarking doesn't work well on images created primarily with solid colors; in addition, the image must be adequate in size (generally 100 x 100 pixels for images to be used digitally and 750 x 750 pixels for images to be printed) to hold the watermark information. Also note that you should embed the watermark before you convert the image to a file format that will compress the image information, such as the JPEG or GIF format. Follow the process detailed next when you need to add a watermark.

Note: *For some images, you may see a prompt to flatten the image (combine its layers) or rasterize a shape or text layer (convert the layer's content to a bitmap or raster format rather than a shape or vector format). In such cases, you can click OK to proceed with flattening/rasterizing and adding the watermark. However, if you haven't finished editing the image, you may instead want to click on Cancel. You then can finish the edits, make a copy of the image file (so you have an version of the file that you can edit later), and embed the watermark in the original. In other cases, you may see a message to change the DPI of an image before adding the watermark. Again, you can do so if you wish or simply continue with the watermarking process.*

1. Open the image to which you want to add a watermark. The image appears in Photoshop.

2. Click on **Filter**. The Filter menu will appear.

3. Click on **Digimarc**. The submenu will appear.

4. Click on **Embed Watermark**. The Embed Watermark dialog box will open.

5. Type the year in the Copyright Year(s) text box. Photoshop will mark the image as copyrighted in the specified year.

6. Click on check boxes in the Image Attributes box. This will identify the image as appropriate for particular types of uses.

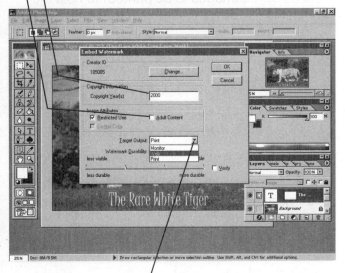

7. Click on the down arrow for the Target Output list, then click on an output type in the list. Photoshop will adjust the Watermark Durability setting to reflect the selected type of output. (You can further change those settings, if needed.)

Note: *If your image is set with 200 dpi or more and you choose Web from the Target Output drop-down list, the DPI Inconsistency dialog box appears to remind you to convert (resample) the image to less than 200 dpi. Click on OK to close the reminder dialog box. Also note that once you add the watermark using one type of target output, you can't repeat the process for another type of output. So, choose the proper Target Output type the first time.*

8. Click on **OK**. Photoshop will apply the watermark and mark the image as copyrighted. The copyright symbol will appear beside the file name in the file window title bar.

Viewing a Digital Watermark

When you open an image that you think has a digital watermark in Photoshop, you can check for the watermark and look up the identity of the image's creator.

1. Click on **Filter**. The Filter menu will appear.

2. Click on **Digimarc**. The submenu will appear.

3. Click on **Read Watermark**. The Watermark Information dialog box will open. It will identify the creator ID (Digimarc ID) for the person or organization that created the image, the copyright year, and the usage restrictions you placed on the image.

4. Click on **Web Lookup**. Your Web browser will open and the Dial-Up Connection dialog box will appear to prompt you to connect to the Internet, unless you have an always-on connection, in which case you can skip to Step 6.

5. Click on **Connect**. Your system will dial its Internet connection. Then the Web browser will display the Digimarc information for the image's creator.

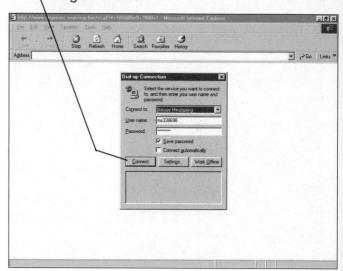

6. Click on the **Print** button on the toolbar. Your Web browser will send the image creator's name and ID information to the printer.

7. Click on the **Close** button **(X)**, then click on **Disconnect Now** in the Auto Disconnect dialog box (if needed). Your system disconnects from the Internet and returns to Photoshop.

8. Click on **OK**. The Watermark Information dialog box will close.

B

Photoshop Preferences and Settings

Photoshop offers a wide variety of preferences that you can use to adjust how it looks and operates. Use this Appendix as a reference to help you find a setting when you need it.

Using Basic Preferences

No matter which preference you need, you can use one of a few methods to find the dialog box that holds it. After you learn here how to find a set of choices in the Preferences dialog box, each subsection that follows reviews key preferences in each set of choices.

1. Click on **Edit**. The Edit menu will appear.

2. Click on **Preferences**. The Preferences submenu will appear.

3. Click on **General** or one of the seven choices in the next group on the submenu. The Preferences dialog box opens.

4. Click on the down arrow beside the list box at the top of the dialog box. The list of various preference sets will appear.

5. Click on a set in the list. The Preferences dialog box will display the selected settings.

6. Click on **Prev** or **Next**. The Preferences dialog box displays the previous or next set of choices.

Note: *Assuming Tool Tips are enabled in Photoshop, you can hover the mouse pointer over a Preferences dialog box option to see what that option does.*

General

- **Color Picker** and **Interpolation**. Control which Color Picker appears when you display the Color Picker to choose image colors and choose which Interpolation method Photoshop uses if you resample the image.

- **Redo Key**. Controls which keyboard combination you must press to redo an action you just undid.

- **History States**. Controls how many history states appear in the History palette.

- **Options**. Choose to enable various operations, such as whether Photoshop shows Tool Tips, includes Asian Text Options, beeps after an operation, or displays font names in English.

- **Reset Choices**. Resets warning dialog boxes so that they will appear in the future and resets all tools to their original options bar settings.

Saving Files

- **Image Previews**. Controls whether or not Photoshop saves small image thumbnail files for previews, or prompts you to do so.

- **File Extension**. Specifies whether Photoshop uses uppercase or lowercase characters for the file name extension when saving.

  Note: *The capitalization for the file name extension can be important if an image is for a Web page. For example, some Web sites only work if the file name extension for Web pages and graphics appears in all uppercase characters, such as .HTM.*

- **Maximize backwards compatibility in Photoshop format**. When checked, enables saved files to be used more easily with earlier Photoshop versions. (Turning off this option can make your files slightly smaller, if you have concerns about file size.)

- **Enable advanced TIFF save options**. Adds options when you save a Photoshop file in the TIFF format, such as whether the TIFF file can preserve layers and annotations or allow ZIP or JPEG compression.

- **Recent file list contains**. Controls how many files the File, Open Recent submenu lists.

Display & Cursors

- **Color Channels in Color**. When checked, the Channels palette shows each channel in color rather than grayscale.

- **Use Diffusion Dither**. When checked, Photoshop uses diffusion dithering rather than pattern dithering to eliminate the "patchy" effect that can appear when the monitor displays fewer colors (such as 256 colors, or 8-bit color) than the image file contains (such as 16.7 million colors in a 24-bit image).

- **Use Pixel Doubling**. When checked, reduces onscreen image resolution for faster previewing after some operations.

- **Painting Cursors**. Controls how the mouse pointer looks and behaves when a painting tool is active.

- **Other Cursors**. Controls how the mouse pointer looks and behaves when a tool other than a painting tool is active.

Transparency & Gamut

- **Grid Size**. Controls the size of the grid used to depict transparency in the Layers palette.

- **Grid Colors**. Controls the colors use for the grid used to depict transparency in the Layers palette.

- **Use video alpha**. When checked, tells Photoshop to use video hardware support for previewing transparency.

- **Opacity**. Controls opaque or transparent image areas.

- **Color**. Chooses the warning color to display for image areas that use a color outside the color gamut for the system.

Units & Rulers

- **Units**. Enables you to choose the default measurement units used for Rulers and Type sizes.

- **Column Size**. Enables you to choose default column Width and Gutter size used when cropping and sizing images for documents.

- **Point/Pica Size**. Controls the true sizing used for points and picas in Photoshop files.

Guides & Grid

- **Guides**. Enables you to choose the Color and Style that guides use when you display them.

- **Grid**. Enables you to choose the Color and Style for gridlines when you display them, as well as the width between major gridlines (Gridline every) and the number of minor grid sections (Subdivisions) between each pair of major gridlines.

Plug-Ins & Scratch Disks

- **Additional Plug-Ins Directory**. Check this option, then click Choose to identify another folder holding plug-ins on your system's hard disk.

- **Scratch Disks**. Enables you to specify additional hard disks as temporary storage (memory overflow) for in-progress work in Photoshop.

Memory & Image Cache

- **Cache Levels**. Controls how many levels of image detail Photoshop stores in a memory cache. Increase the number for faster screen redraw and histogram generation.

- **Use Cache for histograms**. When checked, uses the cached image information, rather than rechecking the image, for histogram information.

- **Used by Photoshop**. Controls how much system memory Photoshop can use during a work session.

Appendix C

▶▶

C

Other Online Resources

Photoshop inspires more online interaction, publishing, and software product development than many other programs due to the wealth of features and options that Photoshop offers. In addition to consulting the resources listed in this section, you can search for "Photoshop" using your favorite Web search engine to yield dozens of links to sites offering tips, help, and downloads.

Category	Resource	Description
Online Forums	www.adobe.com/support/forums/main.html	Go to this page to find links to the Photoshop Mac and Windows forums operated by Adobe. You can login as a guest, or register to be able to post messages.
Online Tutorials	www.adobe.com/products/tips/photoshop.html	Adobe's official tutorial site, with tips from leading experts.
Web Site	www.photoshopuser.com	The site for the National Association of Photoshop Professionals, providing publication reviews and training resources.
Web Site, Plug-ins	www.ultimate-photoshop.com	Find downloadable filters, plug-ins, and tips. Includes freeware, commercial, and shareware downloads.
Web Site, Plug-ins	www.desktoppublishing.com/photoshop.html	Known as the Photoshop Paradise site, provides tips and tricks, resources, and links to filters and plug-ins.
Web Site, Plug-ins	photoshop.org	A Photoshop help site providing tutorials, links to downloadable plug-ins and filters, and more.
Web Site	www.elementkjournals.com/ips/	The Inside Photoshop online magazine. Subscribe to access the greatest variety of articles.

Glossary

Action. An action is the equivalent of a macro in many other programs. You record a series of steps or commands you take in Photoshop, so that you can later play back the steps simply by running the action from the Actions palette or by pressing the shortcut key combination you assigned to the action when you created it.

Adjustment layer. Add this special type of layer when you need to display a color correction or effect, or hide it when not needed.

Alpha channel. An alpha channel is a channel you add beyond the default color channels in the image. You can use the alpha channel to store a selection or mask for the image.

Anchor point. When you create a curved path, each anchor point represents the transition between curved segments.

Animated GIF. A moving Web graphic file that you create by converting layers to frames in ImageReady (or another program capable of generating animation), specifying animation settings, and then saving the file as a GIF.

Anti-aliasing. A correction that sharpens the jagged edges of a selection, preserving as much detail as possible.

Auto Slice. See Slice.

Background erase. When you use the background eraser tool, Photoshop makes the pixels you drag over transparent on the current layer or all layers.

Background layer. When you create a new image, the first layer is a background layer that you can make white, transparent, or fill with a background color that you specify. The exception occurs when you import an image from a scanner or digital camera; in that case, the image itself becomes the background layer.

Bleed. When you create a bleed for printing, you specify that the image content should extend slightly beyond the crop boundaries of the image, so there won't be any unwanted unprinted edges once the output is trimmed to its final size.

Blur. Adding some fuzziness or decreasing the focus in selected areas of an image to soften the image appearance or camouflage a defect.

Border. A small line you specify to be printed around the edge of an image.

Brightness. A setting that controls the overall lightness of an area.

Burn. The equivalent of a traditional photo development technique, in which you increase the "apparent exposure" of an area in the image to increase the contrast and darken the specified area.

Canvas size. The size of the white page that holds your image content in the image window.

Channel. Photoshop divides the colors in a color (or grayscale) image into separate channels that you manage via the Channels palette. The default color mode, RGB color, uses four channels—one each for the red, green, and blue channels, plus a composite channel that shows the individual channels combined. Channels enable you to make color corrections for just the selected channel, without altering the other channels.

Check box. In a dialog box or on a toolbar, you click on a check box to toggle a feature on and off. The feature is on or selected when the check box is checked and off or deselected when it isn't.

Clipping path. A path you use to designate part of an image so that only that portion appears when you save the file as an .EPS, .DCS, .PDF, or .TIFF file for inclusion in another document. The areas outside the clipping path will be transparent after the save, so that you can better lay out the document text in relation to the image.

Color balance. Refers to the overall proportion of various colors in the image.

Color mode. Identifies what type of color model is being used for the image. For example, grayscale images use only shades of gray, with one grayscale color channel by default. CMYK color has been optimized for full, four-color printing, and so on.

Color separations. After an image has been converted to CMYK color, it can be used to generate color separations for professional printing. Each separation represents a film sheet that will ultimately be used to create a printing plate, with each plate representing a single ink color to be printed. Full-color printing uses a minimum of four color plates—Cyan, Magenta, Yellow, and blacK.

Command button. In a dialog box or on a toolbar, you click on a command button to choose the command the button represents. When an ellipsis (...) follows the button name, clicking on the button displays a dialog box where you can specify further options.

Context menu (shortcut menu). A specialized menu that appears when you right-click on a screen element or a toolbox tool. The menu offers commands pertaining to the current tool, image, or selection.

Contrast. A color setting that determines the overall variation between the light points and dark points in the image. In some cases, increasing contrast can help the image appear to have a bit more detail.

Direction line. When creating curved line segments, you use the direction points on direction lines emerging from the curved segment to specify the direction and depth of the curves.

Direction point. A point at the end of the direction line that you drag to specify the direction (drag horizontal to the curve segment) and depth (drag perpendicular to the curve segment) of the curve.

Dithering. When an image uses more colors than your monitor can display, Photoshop uses dithering to compensate for the color discrepancies.

Draw program. A program that creates vector objects—objects created from outlines so that you can later edit them—which often have a more compact file size and can be resized with limited quality loss.

Drop-down list box. In a dialog box or on a toolbar, a list you open by clicking on an arrow. The list presents available choices when opened, and you can click on the desired choices once the list is opened.

Droplet. An action you save as an independent program, so it can be used outside of Photoshop.

Dodge. The equivalent of a traditional photo development technique, in which you decrease the "apparent exposure" of an area in the image to decrease the contrast and lighten the specified area.

Erase. Removing the foreground pixels on a layer to reveal the background color or transparency.

Feathering. A correction that blurs the edges of a selection by adding a shift zone of a pixel width that you specify. Feathering can cause the edges of the selection to lose detail.

Gamut. The gamut represents the range of colors that your system can actually display. You can set up Photoshop to display a warning if an image includes colors outside the gamut.

Grid. Spacer lines you can display to help align objects in an image.

Halftone Screens. See Screens.

Histogram. A graph you can display to see how much of an image's content (roughly how many pixels) fall within various color intensity levels in the image.

Hotspot. See Slice.

Image resolution. See Resolution.

Image size. The dimensions of the image file, in inches, centimeters, points, picas, or pixels.

Interlaced. When you save a file and make it interlaced (an option available when you're saving an image into common Web graphic file formats), part of the image can "pre-load" on the Web page. This means that the user will see the image at low resolution until the full file downloads.

Interpolation. The method that Photoshop uses to determine how to add content (when changing to a higher resolution) or remove content (when changing to a lower resolution) when you resample the image to resize it or change its resolution.

Layer. In Photoshop, you can store different types of content on different logical "sheets" or layers in the image, so that later you can manipulate the content of each layer separately. For example, text that you add to an image with the Text tool always appears on a new layer.

Magic eraser. Use this tool to remove or change contiguous pixels of one color (or non-contiguous pixels in that color) on a layer.

Mask. A special type of select you use to hide part of a layer, so you can manipulate only the visible portions of the layer.

Glossary

Option button. In a dialog box or on a toolbar, a round button that you click on to choose or enable the option it represents. Option buttons typically appear in a group, with the members of the group being mutually exclusive. That is, when you click on one option in the group, all other options in the group will be deselected.

Options bar. When you select a toolbox tool, the options bar below the Photoshop menu bar presents choices you can use to adjust how the tool will operate.

Paint program. A program that only enables you to create the image by recoloring pixels using various tools. Paint programs typically create bitmap images, which are larger in file size and harder to edit than vector images. Resizing bitmap images to a larger size often makes them look jaggy and unattractive.

Palette. A special collection of tools or settings. Photoshop organizes its palettes on tabs in special palette windows that appear at the right side of the Photoshop window by default.

Pantone or Pantone Matching System (PMS). This color-matching system has become the standard in professional printing, design, and image processing. A PMS number identifies each unique ink color. So, for example, when you use a particular spot color (and identify it by its PMS number) in images or documents that are printed at a different time, the spot color should be identical in the print jobs.

Pixels. A variation of the phrase "picture element," each pixel is a single dot of color in the image. Higher resolution images have smaller pixels, and therefore look more detailed and smooth, and less grainy.

Plug-ins. Plug-ins are special add-in programs that you can install to extend Photoshop's functionality. Most plug-ins add new filters into Photoshop, but some offer more file formats and import/export options. You can purchase numerous plug-in collections and even download freeware and shareware plug-ins from any of dozens of Web sites.

Posterizing. This special effect reduces the number of colors used in the image, so that the image becomes composed of larger color areas, much like the way posters used to be designed and printed or like paint-by-number pictures.

ppi (pixels per inch). See Resolution.

Raster images. Also called bitmap images, these are images composed of individual colored pixels. Paint programs typically create raster images.

Rasterize. Converting vector (resizable line) objects in an image to raster (bitmap) content. In Photoshop, you sometimes must rasterize text layers (which are vector) before you can perform certain commands or add certain effects to the text layer.

Resample. Resizing an image and/or changing its resolution.

Resolution. The quantity of pixels (image dots) that print per unit of measure in the image, usually expressed as pixels per inch (ppi). The higher the image resolution value, the finer the quality of the image. For example, an image that has 300 ppi has much more color detail than an image at 72 ppi, because at the higher resolution the pixels are smaller (more pixels packed in per inch, for example). This necessitates smaller pixels of color and therefore a finer appearance.

Rollover. A special effect you create for a Web image that causes part of the image to change when the user performs a certain mouse action. For example, you might set up a glow to appear behind part of the image when the user moves the mouse pointer over that area of the image.

Screens. Used for professional printing, the screen settings specify how the image color should be broken up into printed dots.

Sepia. A variation of grayscale, where an image typically appears in ivory and brown tones rather than black and white.

Slice. An area you identify on an image for conversion to a hotspot—a clickable Web hyperlink.

Slider. In a dialog box or on a toolbar, a small thumb or bar you drag with the mouse to change the setting for an item.

Smudge. A tool you use to drag one color into another on a layer.

Spot color. A small area of color you specify to overprint other colors on an image. You set up a spot color as a separate channel. For professionally printed documents, the spot color will literally be applied by a completely separate printing plate.

Spinner buttons. Click on one of these small up and down arrow buttons beside a text box holding a value to increase (up spinner button) or decrease (down spinner button) the value held in the text box.

Text box. In a dialog box or on a toolbar, a box into which you type an entry. Text boxes that hold numeric settings often also include spinner buttons, which you can click to increase or decrease the text box entry.

Tolerance. For several tools, the tolerance setting indicates how precise Photoshop must be in matching a specified color. A higher tolerance setting means the tool typically will match more colors.

Tonal quality. The amount of highlights and shadows in an image, which can impact its overall appearance of brightness.

Toolbox. The small window or strip at the left side of Photoshop that presents its key drawing, painting, selection, and other tools.

Trapping. Specifying that blocks of (usually) solid color should overprint each other during professional printing, to compensate for possible slight shifts in the printing plates. Your print shop can tell you whether you need to add trapping for your images.

Tweening. A technique by which a program like ImageReady can improve an animation. When an application uses tweening, it extrapolates to create additional animation frames between two selected frames, so that the animation will appear more smooth and natural.

URL (Uniform Resource Locator). The unique address that identifies a Web site or page on the Internet. For example, one of Adobe's Web pages can be found at http://www.adobe.com/products/tips/photoshop.html.

User slice. See Slice.

Vector images. Images composed of editable line objects, so the objects themselves can be edited individually and the image can be resized to a great degree without quality loss.

Work area. The area that holds the image window and other tools in Photoshop.

Work path. A temporary path you create with a pen or shape tool that you can save as a path to reuse later.

Index

The Visual Reference Series

#4-2K VRB

Microsoft® Office 2000 Advanced Skills:
An Integrated Approach

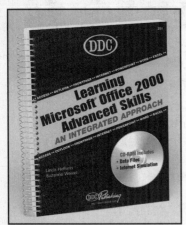

For use following Learning Office 2000, when students have mastered basic skills in each application. Each exercise incorporates more than one application. For example:

■ Embed charts and graphs in reports (Word & Excel)
■ Link tables to presentations (Word & PowerPoint)
■ Create a mail merge using a query (Access & Word)
■ Perform a merge with calculations (Excel & Access)

This book teaches students five different kinds of integration:

■ Survival Skill Integration ■ Productivity Integration ■ Power Integration
■ Web Page Integration ■ Internet Integration

These integration skills reflect the way power users work with Office in a real-world business setting using several different applications in combination to finish a complex task.

$29 *60 Exercises*
Cat. No. Z51
ISBN 1-56243-774-7
Includes CD-ROM

SUPPORT MATERIALS

Cat. No. Z51TE	Annotated Teacher Edition with Solution Files	$50
Cat. No. BTZ51	Tests in a three-ring binder	$100
Cat. No. SLZ5	Solutions on CD-ROM	$15
Cat. No. SLZ5SL	Solutions on CD-ROM Site License	$65
Cat. No. VA51	Visual Aids on Diskette (25 PowerPoint Slides)	$50
Cat. No. SLB51	Printouts of solutions in a three-ring binder	$50
Cat. No. DLZ51	Distance Learning Template CD-ROM	$150

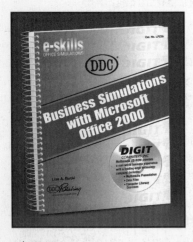

Business Simulations with Microsoft® Office 2000

Know the pressures and rewards of being a regional sales manager in

In 25 realistic business simulation projects, students use critical thinking, communications, and cross-curriculum study skills. They hone computer skills as they:

■ Interact by e-mail with boss and coworkers
■ Prepare product presentations
■ Budget finances with spreadsheets and databases
■ Make key business decisions

$29 Spiral
Cat. No. LPZ35
ISBN 1-56243-861-1
Includes CD-ROM

$15 **Solutions CD-ROM with Instructor Support Material.**
Get hints, tips, and sample solutions. Cat. No. SLLP

Preview our books online at: http://www.ddcpub.com

 DDC *Publishing*   **275 Madison Avenue, New York, NY 10016**
phone 800-528-3897 • fax 800-528-3862

#8-2KZ51&LPZ